Modern Judgements

SWIFT

MODERN JUDGEMENTS

General Editor: P. N. FURBANK

Dickens A. E. Dyson
Henry James Tony Tanner
Milton Alan Rudrum
Sean O'Casey Ronald Ayling
Pasternak Donald Davie and Angela Livingstone
Walter Scott D. D. Devlin
Racine R. C. Knight
Shelley R. B. Woodings
Swift A. Norman Jeffares
Marvell M. Wilding
Ford Madox Ford Richard A. Cassell

IN PREPARATION

Matthew Arnold P. A. W. Collins
Freud F. Cioffi
Pope Graham Martin

Swift

MODERN JUDGEMENTS

edited by

A. NORMAN JEFFARES

Aurora Publishers Incorporated
NASHVILLE/LONDON

FIRST PUBLISHED 1969 BY
MACMILLAN AND COMPANY LIMITED
LONDON, ENGLAND

COPYRIGHT © 1970 BY
AURORA PUBLISHERS INCORPORATED
NASHVILLE, TENNESSEE 37219
LIBRARY OF CONGRESS CATALOG CARD NUMBER: 72-125578
STANDARD BOOK NUMBER: 87695-092-6
MANUFACTURED IN THE UNITED STATES OF AMERICA

Contents

Acknowledgements

Professor Bonamy Dobrée, 'The Jocose Dean' (Macmillan); J. J. Hogan, 'Bicentenary of Jonathan Swift 1667–1745', from *Studies*, XXXIV (1945) (The Editor); Irvin Ehrenpreis, 'Swift on Liberty', from the *Journal of the History of Ideas*, XIII (The Editor); Louis A. Landa, 'Swift's Economic Views and Mercantilism', from the *Journal of English Literary History*, X (Dec. 1943) (The Johns Hopkins Press); J. W. Johnson, 'Swift's Historical Outlook', from the *Journal of British Studies*; F. R. Leavis, 'The Irony of Swift', from *Determinations* (Chatto & Windus Ltd); Dr. A. L. Rowse, 'Swift as Poet', from *The English Spirit*; Herbert Davis, 'Literary Satire in *A Tale of a Tub*', from *Jonathan Swift* (Oxford University Press Inc.); Virginia Woolf, 'Swift's *Journal to Stella*', from *The Second Common Reader* (Mr Leonard Woolf, The Hogarth Press Ltd, Harcourt, Brace & World Inc.; © Harcourt, Brace & World Inc. 1932, renewed by Leonard Woolf 1960); W. B. Ewald, Jr, 'M. B., Drapier', from *The Masks of Jonathan Swift* (Basil Blackwell & Mott Ltd, Harvard University Press); George Orwell, 'Politics versus Literature: An Examination of *Gulliver's Travels*', from *Shooting an Elephant and Other Essays* (Miss Sonia Brownell, Secker & Warburg Ltd, Harcourt, Brace & World Inc.; © Sonia Brownell Orwell 1950); Marjorie Nicolson and Nora M. Mohler, 'The Scientific Background of "Voyage to Laputa"' (Taylor & Francis Ltd); Kathleen M. Williams, 'Gulliver's Voyage to the Houyhnhnms', from the *Journal of English Literary History*, XVIII (1951) (The Johns Hopkins Press); 'The Houyhnhnm as Menippean Horse', from *College English* (March 1966) (Mr W. E. Yeomans and the National Council of Teachers of English).

General Editor's Preface

LITERARY criticism has only recently come of age as an academic discipline, and the intellectual activity that, a hundred years ago, went into theological discussion, now finds its most natural outlet in the critical essay. Amid a good deal that is dull or silly or pretentious, every year now produces a crop of critical essays which are brilliant and profound not only as contributions to the understanding of a particular author, but as statements of an original way of looking at literature and the world. Hence it often seems that the most useful undertaking for an academic publisher might be, not so much to commission new books of literary criticism or scholarship, as to make the best of what exists easily available. This at least is the purpose of the present series of anthologies, each of which is devoted to a single major writer.

The guiding principle of selection is to assemble the best *modern* criticism – broadly speaking, that of the last twenty or thirty years – and to include historic and classic essays, however famous, only when they are still influential and represent the best statements of their particular point of view. It will, however, be one of the functions of each editor's Introduction to sketch in the earlier history of criticism in regard to the author concerned.

Each volume will attempt to strike a balance between general essays and ones on specialised aspects, or particular works, of the writer in question. And though in many instances the bulk of the articles will come from British and American sources, certain of the volumes will draw heavily on material in other European languages – most of it being translated for the first time.

P. N. FURBANK

Introduction

THE first biographical comments on Swift's life were provided in the *Memoirs of Mrs. Laetitia Pilkington* (1748–54); chatty and anecdotal, they were succeeded by Lord Orrery's *Remarks on The Life and Writings of Dr. Jonathan Swift* (1752). Orrery was a young man when he first knew Swift, who was then sixty-three; he did not present an accurate picture of him, and obscured a good deal of his narrative with somewhat selfconscious literary moralising. The *Observations Upon Lord Orrery's Remarks On the Life and Writings of Dr. Jonathan Swift* (1754) were written by Dr Delany, a friend who had known Swift from his fiftieth year, and he corrected some of Lord Orrery's mistakes, but with too much deference and without sufficient chronological detail. A better life was produced by Deane Swift in *An Essay Upon The Life, Writings and Character of Dr. Jonathan Swift* (1755); although he made mistakes, he had known Swift and published thirty-nine letters of the *Journal to Stella*. John Hawkesworth's *Life* was prefixed to his edition of the *Works* (1755) and subsequent editions of this, and was a reasonably reliable piece of work – 'steady and uniform', as it has been described. There was an entry on Swift in the *Biographia Britannica* (1763), and Dr Johnson's *Life of Swift* was contained in the eighth volume of his *Prefaces, Biographical and Critical, to the Works of the English Poets* (I–V, 1779; V–X, 1781). Johnson wrote a casual, even at times condescending, Life, and was obviously unsympathetic to Swift – 'not a man to be loved or envied' he remarked. Yet, though he failed to realise some of Swift's subtlety as an author, he did conclude his Life with the magnanimous remark that 'perhaps no author can easily be found that has borrowed so little, or that in all his excellence and all his defects has so well maintained his claim to be considered original'. Thomas Sheridan, a godson of Swift and the son of his friend the Rev. Thomas Sheridan, corrected some of Johnson's mistakes and slights in *The Life of the Rev. Dr. Jonathan Swift* (1784), which was also printed in volume I of his edition of the *Works* (1784).

Sir Walter Scott's *Life of the Author* (which formed part of his edition of the *Works*, 1814) included a great deal of information, some of it unverified: it probably set a tone for subsequent biographies because of this inclusiveness, for, almost inevitably, it contained paradoxical material. Yet Scott had the ability to grasp Swift's greatness. He thought that Swift was original and had no models in previous writings, that he was indifferent to literary fame and that he never attempted any style of composition in which, with the exception of history, he did not reach a distinguished pitch of excellence. He regarded Swift as pre-eminent in the particular kind of poetry he wrote: he avoided the sublime and pathetic, but his satire and humour were displayed where wit was necessary; he could versify and rhyme superbly; his violent passion could create grandeur.

When Francis Jeffrey reviewed Scott's edition of Swift's *Works* in the *Edinburgh Review*, XXVII (Sept. 1816) he recorded his view that the wits of Queen Anne's time had been eclipsed by his contemporaries; he thought that the earlier writers lacked power and fancy in poetry, that they had no depth or originality in philosophy. Jeffrey regarded Swift as a political apostate and was deeply suspicious of his sexual normality. In this attitude he was not alone. Throughout the nineteenth century Swift had his detractors. His scatology, against which Dr Johnson had inveighed, upset many critics (Macaulay described his mind in a review in the *Edinburgh Review* (Jan. 1833) as stored with images from the dunghill and lazar house). His poetry did not appeal to nineteenth-century taste. Many critics viewed his relations with Stella and Vanessa with disapproval; many thought him irreligious; and many regarded him as a complete misanthropist, a libeller of human nature, especially in *Gulliver's Travels*. There were, however, some exceptions. Hazlitt, for instance, with his usual sanity, wrote well of Swift in his *Lectures on the English Poets* (1818). He was sympathetic to him, seeing that his wit (particularly in the prose works) was serious, saturnine and practical, and understanding that his trifling was a 'relaxation from the excessive earnestness of his mind. *Indignatio facit versus.*' He wrote with perception of Swift's imagination, indignation, and impatience; he thought that he viewed the infirmities of that great baby the world 'with the same scrutinizing glance and jealous irritability that a parent regards the failings of its offspring, but, as Rousseau has well observed, parents have not on this account been supposed to have more affection for other people's children than their own'.

This civilised attitude to Swift was not shared by many writers in the first three quarters of the nineteenth century. De Quincey, for instance, in a review in Tait's *Edinburgh Magazine* (Sept.–Oct. 1847) expressed dislike for Swift's attitude to religion and described his temper as vulgar. Thackeray, whose *English Humorists of the Eighteenth Century* (1853) was filled with horror at the morals of Swift's age, its manners and its criminality, failed, apparently, to appreciate Swift's irony and found him lacking in feeling, filthy, obscene. He regarded the Yahoo as Swift's view of man, an utterly wicked being. Indeed he thought the fourth book of *Gulliver's Travels* should be left unread. (In a later *Life of Swift*, prefixed to the Aldine edition of the *Poems* in 1883, the Rev. John Mitford considered the Fourth Book a work 'wide in its temper and feeling from the spirit of Christianity'.) Thackeray's views were warmly praised by George Gilfillan in *A Third Gallery of Literary Portraits* (1854); he regarded Swift as a moral monster and described him in an article in the *Scottish Review* (Jan. 1856) as a minor Satan. David Masson had suggested in an article in the *British Quarterly Review*, xx (1854) that Swift believed less in God than the Devil; he alleged that political rather than religious ambitions and belief underlay Swift's churchmanship. In the *Revue des deux mondes* (15 Aug. 1858) Taine took up the tale, describing Swift's mind as nourished on filth and folly, his soul as narrow, and his capacity for poetry as vitiated by an inability to create illusion. Lecky, who wrote of him in *The Leaders of Public Opinion in Ireland* (1861), thought his imagination was coarse and revolting.

It was time for a clearer, less emotional look to be taken, and the first balanced nineteenth-century biography to be written was John Forster's *The Life of Jonathan Swift*, vol. i (1875). Unfortunately Forster died before bringing the *Life* beyond 1711. He had discovered and worked on a large amount of unpublished material; he dispelled earlier theories that Swift was irreligious, a defamer of humanity, a slanderer of statesmen who had served him, and a destroyer of the women who had loved him. In particular he refuted the charge of political apostasy, for he realised Swift's fundamental devotion to a High Church position in religion and in politics. Though he did not convince James Russell Lowell – who, reviewing the *Life*, saw in Swift the lack of principle of his age, suggested that he thought one religion was as good as another and (elsewhere) implied Swift was a Jacobite – Forster's biography was an excellent piece of work. On it Henry Craik built *The Life of Jonathan Swift* (1882) using the wealth of manuscript material left behind by

Forster. Craik, like Forster, valued facts: he also read the text of Swift's writings intelligently and so attempted to distinguish between Swift and the invented characters who like Gulliver or the Drapier are the 'authors' of his work. In short, he distinguished between his own roles as literary critic and biographer, a task in which so many of Swift's earlier critics had failed conspicuously. As a result Craik's biography has remained a standard work of great value. Leslie Stephen's *Swift* came out in the same year (1882) in the English Men of Letters series; this well-written study took Swift to be irreligious (in *A Tale of a Tub*) yet consistent in political principle; but though Stephen avoided the kind of bias displayed by many earlier nineteenth-century writers he gave an excessively gloomy view of Swift, ignoring the gaiety which Swift possessed.

Churton Collins appeared as a fresh champion in 1893; in his *Jonathan Swift: A Biographical and Critical Study* he followed in Forster's footsteps, with the aim of further redressing the balance in favour of Swift, but his execution was not sufficiently persuasive. In the same year G. P. Moriarty, in *Dean Swift and His Writings*, objected to the modern writers who were, he thought, whitewashing Swift. Edmund Gosse's *Short History of English Literature* was full of biographical explanations. Swift, he suggested, was naturally irreligious, instinctively prone to see the shams and darknesses of life, and possessed of a brain which was out of control. In George Saintsbury's *Short History of English Literature*, however, Swift was sternly defended against charges of irreligion.

During the nineteenth century two biographical problems troubled scholars (and they have been discussed at length in this century also). One was the question of whether Swift married Stella. This was generally accepted by earlier biographers; the marriage was categorically dated 1716 by Thomas Sheridan (*Life*, p. 323, see also pp. 330 and 361) on the authority of Mrs Sican, a friend of Swift and Stella. But the idea of the marriage was treated with cool scepticism by W. Monck Mason in a history of *St. Patrick's Cathedral* published in 1820 (for details of the book see Teerink, *A Bibliography of the Writings in Prose and Verse of Jonathan Swift D.D.*, item 1383, p. 423). Scott, and later Craik, believed a marriage had taken place, whereas neither Monck Mason nor Forster was convinced, and Leslie Stephen left the question open. A sensible attitude to the problem was that of J. H. Bernard's in 'The Relations between Swift and Stella' in volume XII of the *Prose Works* ed. Temple

Scott (1897–1908). The theory of Swift's madness, perhaps caused by his allusions to 'fitts' of giddiness, was dealt with by Sir William Wilde in an article in 1847 and in *The Closing Years of Dean Swift's Life* (1849); he found no signs of madness in Swift up to 1742, His unsatisfactory work on Swift's health has, however, been completely superseded by the recent studies of Lord (then Sir Russell) Brain, 'The illness of Dean Swift' (1952), reprinted in *Some Reflections on Genius and Other Essays* (1960) and Mr T. G. Wilson's 'Swift's deafness and his last illness' in *the Irish Journal of Medical Science* (June 1939) and 'The Mental and Physical Health of Dean Swift', in *Medical History* (1958). The macabre history of how Swift's body was treated after his death can also be read in T. G. Wilson's article 'Swift's Personality and Death Masks', in *A Review of English Literature*, III (July 1962). There had been studies of *The Skull of Dean Swift, Recently Disinterred at Dublin*, in the *Phrenological Journal and Miscellany* (1834–6, and in 1847), the *London Medical Gazette* (1836), the *British Quarterly Review* (Aug.–Nov. 1846) and *Lancet* (1846 and 1847).

The last decade of the nineteenth century heralded a new development in studies of Swift, the question of establishing a canon and accurate texts. There was a great need for this work, which has continued up to the present day, for early editions of Swift's writings present many problems for bibliographers and textual critics. Some of these difficulties were caused by Swift's habit of concealing his authorship, some by the circumstances in which his work was published. *The Miscellanies in Prose and Verse* (1711) and the *Miscellaneous Works* (1720) were succeeded by Benjamin Motte's edition of *Miscellanies*, the first volume of which appeared in 1727. This was reprinted in duodecimo in 1730 and 1733. Various editions of the *Miscellanies* were printed between 1742 and 1751. An edition of the *Works and Miscellanies* appeared in 1751. The four-volume edition of the *Works* published by Faulkner in Dublin has been increasingly used by modern editors, as showing signs of Swift's revisions. The so-called Hawkesworth editions of the *Works* were published from 1754–5; they went through editions of four sizes. In 1765 Deane Swift collected and revised the text of this edition, and in 1775 John Nichols and others added another volume.

The chaos caused by the fact that the property of Swift's works had previously been vested in no fewer than five different sets of proprietors was somewhat cleared up by Thomas Sheridan's seventeen-volume edition of the *Works* (1757). A new edition of Sheridan's arrangement of the *Works*, corrected and revised by John Nichols, was published in nineteen volumes in 1801. This appeared in different editions in 1803, 1808 and 1812. Sir Walter Scott's edition of the *Works* was published in nineteen volumes in 1814 and reprinted with new material in 1824 and 1883. Textually a better edition than Sir Walter Scott's, the Temple Scott twelve-volume edition of the *Prose Works of Jonathan Swift* was published between 1897 and 1908.

G. Birkbeck Hill edited the *Unpublished letters of Dean Swift* (1899) and F. Elrington Ball, an excellent Anglo-Irish scholar, edited *The Correspondence of Jonathan Swift* in six volumes between 1910 and 1914. With *Vanessa and her Correspondence with Swift* (1921) ed. A. Martin Freeman, the *Letters of Swift to Ford* (1935) ed. D. Nichol Smith, the *Journal to Stella*, 2 vols (1948) ed. Sir Harold Williams, and the same editor's magnificent Clarendon Press five-volume edition of the *Correspondence* (1963–5), which includes the letters to Vanessa and Ford edited by Freeman and Nichol Smith, the correspondence is now available in generous measure.

Various editors have given us critically established editions based on early texts and manuscript sources. These include *A Tale of a Tub* (1920; 2nd ed. 1958) ed. A. C. Guthkelch and D. Nichol Smith; *The Drapier's Letters* (1935) ed. Herbert Davis; *The Poems*, 3 vols (1937; 2nd ed. 1958) ed. Sir Harold Williams, and the fourteen volumes of *The Prose Writings of Jonathan Swift* (1939–66) ed. Herbert Davis, who rigorously excluded material which could not be attributed to Swift with certainty. There are also many special editions of individual texts, notably Eric Partridge's edition of *Swift's Polite Conversation* (1963), and selections from the prose and verse, among which may be mentioned the late John Hayward's Nonesuch selection (1934).

Several bibliographical studies have been made. S. Lane-Poole was a pioneer in 1884; he was followed by W. S. Jackson (in volume XII of the Temple Scott edition of the *Prose Works*); a bibliography of Swift was included in *The Cambridge Bibliography of English Literature*, ed. F. W. Bateson (1940). The fifth volume of that work, ed. George Watson (1957), brings Swift studies up to 1954. H. Teerink's *A Bibliography of the Writings in Prose and Verse of Jonathan Swift D.D.* (1937) was a brave attempt to be inclusive, but the second edition, ed. Arthur H. Scouten (1963), is more reliable. Louis A. Landa and James Edward Tobin produced a useful guide in *Jonathan Swift. A List of Critical Studies from 1895 to 1945* (1945), which is supplemented by

Miss Claire Lamont's checklist of work on Swift produced since 1945, included in *Fair Liberty was all his Cry* ed. A. Norman Jeffares (1967). Donald H. Berwick's *The Reputation of Jonathan Swift, 1781–1882* (1941) provides a conspectus of Swift's standing over a hundred years, which is continued by Milton Voigt's valuable *Swift and the Twentieth Century* (1964). Catalogues of exhibitions commemorating the bicentenary of Swift's death were published in Dublin, Cambridge and Texas in 1945.

Critical, scholarly, and biographical writings on Swift in the twentieth century have been extensive, as the Landa and Tobin *List of Critical Studies* and Miss Lamont's checklist demonstrate. Many authors have been concerned with Swift's personality. Sophie Shilleto Smith attempted to rescue him from detraction in her biography *Dean Swift* (1910), and Charles Whibley's *Jonathan Swift* (1919) paid tribute to his irony, while T. S. Eliot praised the Fourth Book of *Gulliver's Travels* in an early essay in the *Dial*, xxxv (1923), but regarded the work as one of cynicism and loathing. The *Cambridge History of English Literature* (1912) contained an article on Swift by George A. Aitken. Sir Walter Firth cast light on 'The Political significance of *Gulliver's Travels*', in *Proceedings of the British Academy*, ix (1919–20), later reprinted in *Essays Historical and Literary* (1938), by referring to MS material – the Ford Letters – not then in print. His conclusions were later queried in A. E. Case's edition of 1938, and he was supported by I. Ehrenpreis in an article reprinted in *The Personality of Jonathan Swift* (1958). William A. Eddy in *Gulliver's Travels, a Critical Study* (1923) made a vast survey of possible sources for Swift's work. His assessment of the Fourth Voyage is rather reminiscent of those of the nineteenth-century critics; he liked neither the Houyhnhnms nor the Yahoos. Emile Pons took him to task in a review and suggested a biographical or psychological approach, and this appeared when Eddy edited a standard edition of *Gulliver's Travels*, *A Tale of a Tub*, *Battle of the Books*, etc., for the Oxford Standard Edition, New York, 1933. Pons's own work on Swift was careful and thorough: in his *Swift, Les années de jeunesse et le 'Conte du tonneau'* (1925) he was, however, over-much concerned to discover in *A Tale of a Tub* links with Swift's own life. Pons later explored the 'little language' of the *Journal to Stella* in 'Du nouveau sur le *Journal à Stella*', in *Etudes anglaises,* i (May 1937) and discussed the relationship between Rabelais and Swift. He edited a selection with French translations and a lively commentary (1965). Sir Herbert Read described Swift as vulgar in *The Sense of Glory* (1929) and Aldous Huxley expressed dislike for Swift's apparent opposition to life, his 'hatred of bowels', in *Do What You Will* (1929). Shane Leslie's *The Skull of Swift* (1929) was unsatisfactory, while Carl Van Doren's *Swift* (1930) oversimplified the issues and, in stressing the tragic nature of his life, neglected Swift's capacity for laughter. The factual scholarship of Sir Harold Williams in *Dean Swift's Library* (1932) comes as a relief at this point and E. A. Baker's magnificent survey, *The History of the English Novel* (1929) contained some excellent writing on Swift in volume III.

Other studies written in the 1930s were those of Virginia Woolf, who wrote perceptively of the *Journal to Stella* in the *Second Common Reader* (1932), and of Stephen Gwynn, whose *The Life and Friendships of Dean Swift* (1933) is conventional and easy to read. The less conventional views of Mario M. Rossi and J. M. Hone (1933) were contained in *Swift, or the Egotist* (1934), published in the same year as Yeats's introductory essay to his haunting play about Swift *The Words upon The Window-Pane*. In 1934 F. R. Leavis wrote his essay on 'The Irony of Swift', in *Scrutiny* II (1934), reprinted in this volume. It is time that the views expressed in this article were themselves scrutinised carefully. One of the very best brief accounts of Swift was D. Nichol Smith's admirably sane and subtle lecture, 'Jonathan Swift: some Observations', in *Essays by Divers Hands* (Trans. Royal Society of Literature, XV (1935). This develops ideas in his earlier lecture given at Liverpool and printed as *Jonathan Swift* (1930). Camille Looten's *La Pensée religieuse de Swift et ses antinomies* was published in 1935, as were two studies by German scholars, Hans Gläser's *Jonathan Swift, Gedanken und Kirche* and Max Armin Korn's *Die Weltanschauung Jonathan Swifts*, which is useful for its sane approach to the apparently contradictory elements in Swift's ideas. Shane Leslie's *The Script of Jonathan Swift and other essays* appeared in this year, in which Marjorie Nicolson also began to publish her penetrating work on the scientific background of the period. Her 'The microscope and English Imagination', in *Smith College Studies in Modern Languages*, XVI, no. 4 (1935), was followed by articles on the scientific background of the Voyage to Laputa, published in the *Annals of Science*, II (1937). Herbert Davis wrote on 'Recent Studies of Swift: a survey', in the *University of Toronto Quarterly* (Jan. 1938); this is a useful and informed comment on work written in the thirties.

Ricardo Quintana's *The Mind and Art of Jonathan Swift* (1936; 1953) is a useful handbook, thorough and modest, based on an attempt to place Swift in his historical situation as a typical thinker of his age. The same author afterwards wrote an influential article 'Situational Satire: A Commentary on the Method of Swift', in *University of Toronto Quarterly*, XVII (1948), which paved the way for the work of later scholars (and for his own rather different treatment of Swift in *Swift: An Introduction* (1955), which emphasises Swift's middle way between Dissent and Roman Catholicism. This is still one of the best introductions to Swift, though it perhaps underestimates Swift's religious belief). In 1936 Richard Foster Jones's *Ancients and Moderns. A Study of the Battle of the Books* appeared in Washington University Studies, NS, no. 6. In the same year George Sherburn's *The Early Career of Alexander Pope* (1936) added to our biographical knowledge, and an article by Mona Wilson on 'Swift's Polite Conversations' was included in *English*, I. Bertram Newman's *Jonathan Swift* (1947) was not very profound, but John Hayward's 'Jonathan Swift', in *From Anne to Victoria*, ed. B. Dobrée, was useful.

The puzzles of Swift's life have continued to exercise the ingenuity of many scholars and critics. For instance, Maxwell B. Gold in *Swift's Marriage to Stella* (1937) again argued that the ceremony took place, but Herbert Davis in his elegantly written *Stella: a Gentlewoman of the Eighteenth Century* (1942) gives us all the information available about her. Denis Johnston's 'The Mysterious Origin of Dean Swift', in *Dublin Historical Record* (1941) – attacked by Sir Harold Williams in the *Times Literary Supplement* (29 Nov. 1941) – put forward the old idea that Stella was an illegitimate daughter of Sir William Temple and asserted that Swift was the illegitimate son of Sir William's father, Sir John Temple. Johnston developed this theory in *In Search of Swift* (1959). Mrs Sybil Le Brocquy in *Cadenus: A Reassessment in the Light of New Evidence of the Relationships between Swift, Stella and Vanessa* (1962) suggests that Bryan M'Loghlin, looked after by Stella and mentioned in her will, may have been a child of Vanessa's by Swift. James Sutherland wrote a very attractive and lively but all too brief biography, 'Dr Swift in London', in *Background for Queen Anne* (1939), which deals sensibly with Swift's relationship with Stella, and conveys the author's sympathetic understanding of Swift and deep knowledge of the history of the period.

The 1930s was a period of excellent scholarship in the history of ideas, and several full-length studies and articles on various aspects of seventeenth- and eighteenth-century thought by such scholars as A. D. Lovejoy, Richard Foster Jones, R. S. Crane, Louis Bredvold and George Sherburn have contributed to the general understanding of Swift's intellectual background. In 1943 Louis A. Landa's article on 'Swift's economic views and mercantilism', in *Journal of English Literary History*, x, cleared up some misconceptions. Robert Wyse Jackson, who had earlier written *Jonathan Swift, dean and pastor* (1939) from a Church of Ireland point of view, published in 1945 *Swift and his Circle*, a book of essays dealing with Swift's friendships in a manner which is fresh and lively. J. J. Hogan argued that Swift had to be related to his times, in a forceful article in *Studies* XXXIV (1945), reprinted in this volume, and Landa's 'Jonathan Swift and Charity', in *Journal of English and Germanic Philology*, XLIV (1945), and his 'Swift, the mysteries and deism', in *Studies in English* 1944 (1945) drew fresh attention to Swift's religious beliefs and his practical application of them. Arthur E. Case's *Four Essays on Gulliver's Travels* (1945) dealt with the text, geography, satire and significance of the book. In the *Essays on the Eighteenth Century presented to D. Nichol Smith* (1945) were several graceful pieces of scholarship; 'The conciseness of Swift', by Herbert Davis; 'Deane Swift, Hawkesworth and *The Journal to Stella*', by Harold Williams; and 'Some Aspects of Eighteenth-century Prose', by James Sutherland.

From 1945 onwards the stream of criticism and biography has flowed with increasing volume and speed, and this commentary on recent critical and biographical studies must necessarily be eclectic. The sheer amount of work on Swift in the period can be judged by reference to Miss Lamont's checklist in *Fair Liberty was all his Cry* (1967). General and particular studies abound; in general terms, advances have been made in relating Swift's work to rhetoric, in evaluating and explaining particular poems, and in rehabilitating Swift as a Christian and a churchman.

While analytic scholarship has become more exact – and more exacting – in the realm of Swift Studies, there have also been new general studies. For instance, R. C. Churchill wrote a general study in *He Served Human Liberty: an Essay on the Genius of Jonathan Swift* (1946), which was followed by another somewhat similar book, *Swift* (1947) by Bernard Ackworth. Herbert Davis wrote *The Satire of Jonathan Swift* (1947): as in all his other writings on Swift this survey contained the results of careful scholarship expressed with elegant critical ease. *Hermathena*, the journal published by Trinity College, Dublin (which had in 1941 contained Provost Alton's article on College history relating to Swift and Patrick Delany), carried the late Professor H. O. White's general article on Swift's art in 1947, and other interesting contributions of this period on a smaller scale were those of Irish writers: Arland Ussher, on 'Swift and Mankind', in the *Dublin Magazine* XXII, *The Legacy of Swift*, ed. Maurice James Craig (1948), and D. A. Webb's article on 'Broadsides referring to Swift', in the *Annual Bulletin of the Friends of the Library of Trinity College, Dublin* (1946).

Ricardo Quintana's article on 'Situational Satire', in the *University of Toronto Quarterly*, XVII (1948), continued the kind of examinations made earlier by Herbert Davis, while Evelyn Hardy's *The Conjured Spirit – Swift* examined Swift in Freudian terms. Swift has occupied the attention of psychologists and psychoanalysts for some time. For instance, S. Ferenczi had earlier applied Freudian analysis in 'Gulliver-Phantasien', in *Internationale Zeitschrift für Psychoanalyse*, XIII (1927), to be followed by Cornelius Van Doorn's *An Investigation into the character of Jonathan Swift* (1931), I. F. Grant Duff's article in *Psychoanalytic Quarterly*, VI (1937), and Adolf Heidenhain's *Ueber den Henschenhass: eine pathographische Untersuchung ueber Jonathan Swift* (1934), in which Swift's 'coprophilia' is brought into prominence to explain his neuroses. Dr Karpman – in an article in *Psychoanalytic Review*, XXIX (1942) – and Dr Phyllis Greenacre have also applied modern terminology to Swift with gusto, the latter's book *Swift and Carroll: A Psychoanalytic Study of Two Lives* (1955) pushing theories to absurdity. Donald R. Roberts's article 'A Freudian View of Swift', in *Literature and Psychology*, VI (1956), attacks the inadequate bases of previous analytic interpretations, and Norman O. Browne in *Life Against Death: The Psychoanalytical Meaning of History* (1959) regards earlier interpreters of Swift in Freudian terms as having failed to appreciate Swift's own insight into 'the universal neuroses' of mankind.

Various *festschrifts* contained useful articles on Swift. They included J. C. Beckett's view of Swift as an ecclesiastical statesman, in *Essays in British and Irish History in Honour of James Eadie Todd* (1949), and articles by A. E. Case, James L. Clifford, Herbert Davies and Harold Williams in *Pope and his Contemporaries essays presented to George Sherburn* (1949). Yet more Swiftiana appeared in *The Seventeenth Century: studies in the history of English thought and literature from Bacon to Pope*, by Richard Foster Jones and others writing in his honour (1951); and other articles were reprinted in *Studies in the Literature of the Augustan Age: essays collected in honour of Arthur Elliott Case* (1952).

The problems posed by Swift's satirical attitudes have continued to fascinate critics. Miss Miriam Kosh Starkman, for instance, related *A Tale of a Tub* to the work of Swift's contemporaries in *Swift's Satire on Learning in 'A Tale of a Tub'* (1950), but she regarded Swift as a personal rather than a general satirist. Ernest Tuveson, in 'Swift: the Dean as Satirist', in *University of Toronto Quarterly*, XXII (1953), discussed the way in which *Gulliver's Travels* explores the true nature of man in society. George Orwell's well-known article, which is now somewhat dated in its language and approach, appeared in *Shooting an Elephant and other Essays* (1950); it is based on political assumptions of the 1930s and 1940s and has all of Orwell's originality – as well as distaste – informing its criticism.

The fourth book of *Gulliver's Travels* has come in for particular attention in the fifties and sixties of this century. The general view taken of the Houyhnhnms in the nineteenth century was that they were ideal creatures – a view some critics, among them A. E. Case, W. A. Eddy, J. Middleton Murry, Charles Peake, and George Sherburn, have continued to take, in various ways, in our time. Many critics, however, have seen them as portraying an ironic ideal. So much has been written (occasionally with an unnecessary pomposity which Swift would have enjoyed deflating) on the question of the Houyhnhnms and the Yahoos that some guidance is now needed through the maze of writings on the subject (see the article by W. Yeomans in this volume, pp. 258–66. Other useful articles on the subject are those by Kurt A. Zimansky, 'Gulliver, Yahoos and Critics', in *College English*, XXVII (1965–6) and William Halewood and Marvin Levich, 'Houyhnhnm Est Animal Rationale', in *Journal of the History of Ideas*, XXVI (1965). Miss Kathleen Williams has written well on the fourth book in several articles, and her book *Jonathan Swift and the Age of Compromise* (1958) argues that Swift struck a balance between extremes. R. S. Crane's contribution to *Reason and the Imagination: Studies in the History of Ideas 1600–1800*, ed. J. Mazzeo (1962) and Irvin Ehrenpreis's article in the Swift number of *A Review of English Literature* (July 1962) both develop new ideas on the subject. One of the most sensible approaches to *Gulliver's Travels* is J. K. Walton's article, in *Hermathena*, CIV (1967) 5–50, which takes a panoptic view of the whole book.

Some of the most professional of recent contributions to Swift scholarship have come from examinations of the accepted traditions and literary practices within which Swift worked. For instance, Robert C. Elliott analysed the structure of *A Tale of a Tub* in an article in *PMLA* LXVI (1957) and John M. Bullitt continued the process of close analysis in *Jonathan Swift and the Anatomy of Satire: a study of satiric technique* (1953). Martin Price's *Swift's Rhetorical Art: a study in Structure and Meaning* (1953) was followed by Charles Allen Beaumont's article 'Swift's classical Rhetoric in *A Modest Proposal*', in *Georgia Review*, XIV (1960), and his monograph on *Swift's Classical Rhetoric* in 1961. The nature of the eighteenth-century rhetorical tradition was also explored in Paul Fussell's *The Rhetorical World of Augustan Humanism: Ethics and Imagery from Swift to Burke* (1965), while Edward J. Rosenheim, Jnr, in *Swift and the Satirist's Art* (1963) went deeply into Swift's techniques.

Specialised study has followed on specialised study, and the checklist compiled by Miss Claire Lamont for *Fair Liberty was all his Cry*, ed. A. Norman Jeffares (1967), gives some idea of the quantity of highly complex work which has been undertaken on Swift between 1945 and 1965. The Irish background has been more thoroughly examined. Louis A. Landa, in *Swift and the Church of Ireland* (1954), has cleared up many points and weighed the achievements as well as the failings of the Irish Establishment. He has emphasised Swift's convictions and tenacity of purpose; he has realised that Swift's pessimism ('I have long given up all hope of Church or Christianity' he once remarked) was caused in part by his recognition that the Church of Ireland was torn by internal strife, exposed to outside attack and operating in a country where economic life was in a parlous state. In part, of course, there must have been an element of personal disappointment. The larger relationship, of Swift to Ireland, has been brilliantly explored by Oliver W. Ferguson in *Swift and Ireland* (1962) in which he traces Swift's changing attitudes to the country where he was 'dropp'd' and in which, for a long time, he did not wish to be buried. His gradual involvement in the cause of Irish liberty, his assertion of Anglo-Irish ideals, his anger that Ireland did not respond to his call, and his view that self-help was essential are all explained and carefully documented in this book. Swift's particular relationship to Irish wit and humour has been investigated by Vivian Mercier in *The Irish Comic Tradition* (1962) and some of his attitudes to his audiences are dealt with in several articles by George P. Mayhew.

Swift's links with England have been re-emphasised in Nigel

Dennis's brief study, *Swift* (1964), while Michael Foot has produced an entertaining and shrewd account of Swift's attacks on Marlborough in *The Pen and the Sword* (1957; 1966). Richard I. Cook has examined the audience for whom Swift wrote his Tory pamphlets.

The contemporary reader has been aided by specialised works such as Milton P. Foster's *A Casebook on Gulliver among the Houyhnhnms* (1961), the volume on *Gulliver's Travels*, ed. John Killham, for *Notes on English Literature* (1962) and the *Discussions of Jonathan Swift*, ed. J. Traugott (1962). Herbert Davis has edited *Jonathan Swift: Poetry and Prose* (1964), a good volume in the Clarendon English Series, and Ernest Tuveson has edited *Swift: a Collection of Critical Essays* in the Twentieth Century Views series. Some of the essays in this volume smell of the lamp, but Milton Voigt's *Swift and the Twentieth Century* (1964) is lively in its marathon and extremely valuable survey of the range and variety of Swift scholarship and criticism produced in this century.

To select the lasting, significant work on Swift from such a wealth of specialised studies is not easy, and any attempt must, almost inevitably, give an impression of cataloguing. Nonetheless the sheer multiplicity of the work must be recognised. It reveals yet again how much there is in Swift's writings which requires, and deserves to require, detailed attention and close, careful, comparative analysis. The reader approaching Swift for the first time has the benefit of being able to reinforce his pleasure by reading essays and books which, though based on detailed work, contrive to take – and give – a larger view. They include, D. W. Jefferson's 'An approach to Swift', in the *Pelican Guide to English Literature*, IV (1957), and the two excellent books by Ricardo Quintana, *The Mind and Art of Jonathan Swift* (1936; 1953) and *Swift: an Introduction* (1955). The second of these emphasises Swift's humour and explains his irony in subtle fashion. A good article on the irony, following earlier lines laid down by Professor Leavis, was that of A. E. Dyson, 'Swift and the Metamorphosis of Irony', in *Essays and Studies*, NS XI (1958). John Middleton Murry's *Jonathan Swift: a critical Biography* (1954), while inferior to Quintana's more scholarly work, is both readable and informative. Bonamy Dobrée has written with great understanding of Swift's attitudes and achievements in *English Literature in the Early Eighteenth Century 1700–1740* (vol. VII of the *Oxford History of English Literature*); his own sensitivity to the nuances of eighteenth-century life and thought gives his criticism of Swift a reassuring sense of reality which is sometimes lacking in some of the more specialised studies which can, upon occasion, isolate Swift from time and place.

In *Swift: The Man, His Works and the Age* (1962), the first volume of his life of Swift, *Mr Swift and his Contemporaries*, Professor Ehrenpreis has given us fresh details (particularly of Swift's career at Trinity College Dublin) which add to the sense of actuality produced by Professor Dobrée and by Professor Herbert Davis. The latter has written with urbanity in *Jonathan Swift: Essays on his Satire and Other Studies* (1964), a collection of his own earlier writings on Swift's satire and other aspects of his work as well as on Stella's life and writings. Professor Davis, who has edited the *Prose Works* with such distinction, is particularly interesting on Swift as a poet. His criticism is easy and simple – deceptively so, for he is much more profound than many of the authors of over-complex studies which give the impression of being aimed solely at professional scholars. There is no reason why Swift, of all writers, should be overwhelmed by the minutiæ of critical scholarship, for, as Professor Quintana has reminded us in 'A modest Appraisal: Swift scholarship and criticism 1945–1965', in *Fair Liberty was all his Cry* (1967), he is as provocative, as perplexing and hypnotic today as he has ever been: 'the judgements arrived at in our own time are as challengingly diverse as those which have delivered in the past'.

This comment admirably sums up the best of the exact historical analysis and imaginative critical appreciation of Swift which has helped to bring us closer to an understanding of the idiosyncratic art of a very great writer.

NOTE ON TEXTUAL POLICY

In these essays the notes indicate the source of quotations. Where an author has quoted, for instance, from the F. Elrington Ball edition of the *Correspondentce* (1910–1914) rather than the more recent Harold Williams edition (1963–5), or from the Temple Scott edition of the *Prose Works of Jonathan Swift* (1897–1908) rather than the Herbert Davis edition (1939–66), the quotations have been allowed to stand in the form in which they were given by the author. Any specific departure from consistency in using a particular edition as source (as, for instance, in Herbert Davis's article on literary satire) is clearly indicated.

A. N. JEFFARES

Chronology

1667	30 November, born in Dublin, his father having died some months earlier.
1673	Attends Kilkenny College.
1682	Enters Trinity College, Dublin.
1686	B.A. *speciali gratia*.
1689	Joins his mother in England; later enters Sir William Temple's household at Moor Park. There meets Stella (Hester Johnson) then a girl of eight.
1690	Returns to Ireland.
1691	Travels to England (summer); later returns to Moor Park. 'Ode to the Athenian Society'.
1692	M.A. Oxford.
1694	Ordained in Ireland, appointed to prebend of Kilroot.
1696	Returns to Moor Park.
1699	Travels to Ireland after Temple's death as domestic chaplain to the Earl of Berkeley.
1700	Vicar of Laracor, Co. Meath; prebend of St Patrick's Cathedral, Dublin.
1701	*A Discourse of the Contests and Dissentions between the Nobles and Commons in Athens and Rome etc.*
1702	D.D., Trinity College, Dublin.
1704	*A Tale of a Tub*: *The Battle of the Books*.
1707–9	In London: large circle of literary friends including Addison and Steele. (Congreve had been his junior at Kilkenny College and Trinity College, Dublin.) *Bickerstaff Papers*. Becomes friendly with Vanessa (Esther or Hester Vanhomrigh).
1709	*A Project for the Advancement of Religion*. Returns to Ireland (June).
1710	In London (September), acting on behalf of Church of Ireland to seek remission of First Fruits from Queen Anne. In

charge of the *Examiner*; friendly with Harley. *Journal to Stella* covers this period to 1713. Resumes old literary friendships, close to Prior and Arbuthnot.

1711   *Miscellanies in Prose and Verse.* Brothers' Club founded by Swift's Tory friends.

1712   *Conduct of the Allies.*

1713   Installed as Dean of St Patrick's Cathedral, Dublin (June). Scriblerus Club founded (or early in following year); membership includes Gay and Parnell. Friendship with Pope established by September. Works with Pope on *Memoirs of Martinus Scriblerus* (published in 2nd volume of Pope's *Prose Works*, 1741).

1714   Returns to Ireland after death of Queen Anne (August). Works on *The History of the Last Four Years of the Queen*, began at Windsor in 1713.

1718   Friendship with Rev. Thomas Sheridan and Rev. Patrick Delany.

1720   *A Proposal for the Universal Use of Irish Manufactures.*

1721   Works on *Gulliver's Travels.*

1722   Quarrels with Vanessa.

1723   Expects to finish *Gulliver's Travels* 'very soon' (April); Vanessa dies (June).

1724   *The Drapier's Letters.*

1725   Transcribing completed *Gulliver's Travels* (August)

1726   Travels to London, visits Pope and Arbuthnot. *Gulliver's Travels* published in London after his return to Dublin.

1727   Visits England for last time.

1728   Stella dies. Contributes to the *Intelligencer.*

1729   *A Modest Proposal.*

1731   Writes *Polite Conversation, Directions to Servants*, 'Verses on the Death of Dr. Swift', etc.

1732   Various tracts on Irish affairs and on the Test Act.

1735   *Collected Works* published in four volumes in Dublin.

1738   *Polite Conversation* published in London; fifth and sixth volumes of *Collected Works* published in Dublin.

1742   'Of unsound mind and memory.'

1745   Dies, 19 October.

BONAMY DOBRÉE

The Jocose Dean (1967)

NORMALLY, when Swift comes into our minds, we think of him as a man filled with a savage indignation that never ceased to lacerate his heart; as a man who throughout his life wrote the most withering, even bitter, satires; and to think of him dying is to think of an empire falling. Or we consider him to have lived as an unhappy being, suffering one gruelling disappointment after another and, for some reason, or reasons, inhibited in his loves. We are inclined to forget that when St John was most politically harried, nothing would refresh him more than 'to walk in the Park with the jocose Dean': that Swift could be seen to 'laugh and shake in Rab'lais' easy Chair'; and we may not remember that Ford could write to him as one of 'those who are formed for mirth and society' (8 July 1736). After all, a man cannot live wrathfully all the time; a balance is needed, and it would seem that Swift's *saeva indignatio* was offset, even perhaps sustained, by his enormous gaiety. It is this aspect that I should like to try to consider here.

Try; because, of course, it is almost, if not quite, impossible to catch the tone. How can we tell by what japes and jests, what puns and preposterous propositions he was notoriously the life and soul of any party or gathering? Why was he so indispensable at meetings of the Brothers' Club, or later with the Scriblerians? – who, incidentally, in their turn produced three classics of our literature, *The Beggar's Opera*, *The Dunciad*, and *Gulliver's Travels*, born of their conversations. So much for London. And then in Ireland, where at one time he felt that he had gone 'to die like a poisoned rat in a hole', why was he welcome for long periods at Quilca with the Sheridans, at Loughgall with the Copes, at Market Hill with the Achesons; or why were people eager for invitations to dine at the Deanery? We cannot hear the jokes, or share the gay spirit of his discourse. And are we to suppose that he was not greeted by Stella in Dublin or by Vanessa at Celbridge as much for his fun as for his tenderer communications? All we can do is to guess at this gay spirit from what he wrote, especially in his letters, for these, naturally, are the closest to conversation. We can begin with these.

We find his conversational tone, for instance, when he writes from Laracor on 17 April 1710 to Stearne, the then Dean of St Patrick's:

> ... I am this minute very busy, being to preach to-day to an audience of at least fifteen people, most of them gentle, and all simple.
>
> I can send you no news; only the employment of my parishioners may, for memory-sake, be reduced under these heads: Mr. Percival is ditching; Mrs. Percival in her kitchen; Mr. Wesley switching; Mrs. Wesley stitching; Sir Arthur Langford riching, which is a new word for heaping up riches. I know no other rhyme but bitching, and that I hope we are all past.

or when on 11 May 1711 he writes to St John, and one catches a flavour of the walks in the Park:

> Pray, Sir, find an expedient. Finding expedients is the business of Secretaries of State. I will yield to any reasonable conditions not below my dignity. I will not find fault with the victuals; I will restore the water-glass that I stole, and solicit for my Lord Keeper's salary. And, Sir, to show you I am not a person to be safely injured, if you dare refuse me justice in this point, I will appear before you in a pudding-sleeve gown, I will disparage your snuff, write a lampoon upon Nably Car,[1] dine with you upon a foreign post-day; nay, I will read verses in your presence, until you snatch them out of my hands.

Again, there is a letter he wrote to John Hill, Lady Masham's brother-in-law, on 12 August 1712 about a snuff-box he had been given by, as she then was, Mrs Hill:

> My Lord Treasurer, who is the most malicious person in the world, says, you ordered a goose to be drawn at the bottom of my box, as a reflection upon the clergy; and that I ought to resent it. But I am not angry at all, and his Lordship observes by halves; for the goose is there drawn pecking at a snail, just as I do at him, to make him mend his pace in relation to the public although it be hitherto in vain. And besides, Dr. Arbuthnot, who is a scholar, says you meant it as a compliment for us both: that I am the goose who saved the Capitol by my cackling, and that his Lordship is represented by the snail, because he preserves his country by delays.

One senses there something of the bantering spirit Swift would indulge in when conversing with his friends; and there is, too, a touch of satire on Harley's dilatoriness, or, as we, free from Swift's impatience, might see it, his wise holding back from precipitate action.

One can tell something of the sort of interchange in jesting between Swift and his friends from some of the letters they wrote to him. Thus on 8 December 1713 Pope writes from Binfield:

> Not to trouble you at present with a recital of all my obligations to you, I shall mention only two things, which I take particularly kind of you – your desire that I should write to you, and your proposal of giving me twenty guineas to change my religion, which last you must give me leave to make the subject of this letter.
>
> Sure no clergyman ever offered so much out of his own purse for the sake of any religion. . . .

Pope develops the subject entertainingly, arguing that far more money is needed for that sort of transaction. Especially when you come to consider prayers for the dead (a matter that Pope is reluctant to give up), since masses are expensive:

> Old Dryden, though a Roman Catholic, was a poet; and it is revealed in the visions of some ancient saints, that no poet was ever saved under some hundreds of masses. I cannot set his delivery from purgatory at less than fifty pounds sterling.

He goes on to say that there is one person especially whom he would wish the Ministry concerned with these matters to see to:

> The person I mean is Dr. Swift, a dignified clergyman, but one who, by his own confession, has composed more libels than sermons. If it be true, what I have heard often affirmed by innocent people, that too much wit is dangerous to salvation, this unfortunate gentleman must certainly be damned to all eternity.

Swift will have chuckled over the neat way of turning a compliment, and still more perhaps at the way Pope goes on with a little joke about their important political friends: 'But I hope his long experience in the world, and frequent conversation with great men, will cause him, as it has some others, to have less and less wit every day.' Bolingbroke, of course, was recognised as a stimulating intellectual, while Harley, now Lord Oxford, known among the group as 'the Dragon', was a by no means dull or unperforming member of the Brothers' Club. In private conversation, Swift told Archbishop King, Harley was 'wholly disengaged and very facetious'.

On 25 July 1714 Swift writes to another Brother, namely John Arbuthnot, who had offered him a loan:

> The mischief is, I never borrow money of a friend. You are mightily mistaken; all your honour, generosity, good nature, good sense, wit, and every other quality, will never make me think one jot the better of you. That time is now some years past, and you will never mend in my opinion. But really, Brother, you have a sort of shuffle in your gait; and now I have the worst that your most mortal enemy could say of you with truth.

As good a jocose way as could be imagined of paying a handsome tribute to an affectionate friend.

He tends always to be amusing in his private letters, and Bolingbroke could write to him (12 August 1714): 'I swear I did not imagine, that you could have held out through two pages, even of small paper, in so grave a style.' The 'style', needless to say, varies enormously. The letters to Stella abound with gaiety; they are jocular in the sense that they are full of affectionate raillery, what one might call teasing, with puns and jingles and April-fooling, these being in a way extensions of the 'little language'. In the *Journal to Stella* we hear too of what he was doing by way of conversational amusement: thus in October 1710: 'Then I visited Lord Pembroke, who is just come to town, and we were very merry talking of old things, and I hit him with one pun.' And in November 1711: 'I designed a jaunt into the city to-day to be merry, but was disappointed.' Among letters too might be placed *A Decree for Concluding the Treaty between Dr. Swift and Mrs. Long*, a kind of epistle to Vanessa, heightening what was evidently a joke in the Vanhomrigh circle.

His letters immediately after his departure into 'exile' are not so lively; but he gradually overcame his depression, being able to write to Archdeacon Walls on 16 December 1716: 'I'm sorry you disturbed yourself so early this morning as four o'clock. I doubt you were ready to sleep at your own sermon.' On 29 May 1718 Prior writes to him: 'I have nothing more to tell you, but that you are the happiest man in the world; and if you are once got into *la bagatelle*, you may despise the world.' On 28 September 1721 Swift writes to Archbishop King:

> I have a receipt [against melancholy] to which you are a stranger; my Lord Oxford and Mr. Prior used to join with me in taking it, to whom I often said, when we were two hours diverting ourselves with trifles, *vive la bagatelle*.

He really recovered himself completely after the success of *The Drapier's Letters*, which brought him so much fame in Ireland and the love of the Dublin populace. But we do not find him joking much with his English friends, though he writes happily, and to Pope occasionally mentions *vive la bagatelle*. With Gay also he can be a little jesting, as when the latter's *Wife of Bath*, originally a failure, was being successfully revived: he writes on 20 November 1729:

> I have heard of the Wife of Bath; I think Shakespeare. If you wrote one it is out of my head, I had not the cant word damned in my head; but if it were acted and damned and printed, I should not now be your counsellor to new lick it.

His 'mistake' is obviously intentional: he knew his Chaucer. But on the whole he talks more seriously to those in far-away England.

To make up for this, he gives rein to all his jocoseness with his Irish acquaintance, especially Thomas Sheridan, largely in the matter of word play. In June 1735 he has a long letter devoted to chat, and the suffix -ling:

> I suppose you are now angle ling with your tack ling in a purr ling stream, or pad ling and say ling in a boat, or sad ling your stum ling horse with a sap ling in your hands, and snare ling at your groom, or set ling your affairs, or tick ling your cat, or tat ling with your neighbour Price; not always toy ling with your school. . . .
>
> A lady whose understanding was sing ling me out as a wit ling or rather a suck ling, as if she were tick ling my fancy, tang ling me with question, tell ling me many stories, her tongue toe ling like a clapper; says she, an old man's dar ling is better than a young man's war ling.

It is as though in his old age, feeling his general wit no longer as active as it used to be, he is finding refuge in word games with Sheridan, as when he plays with their *Latino-Anglicus*, for instance in a letter of 30 September 1735:

> . . . I shall describe a certain female of your acquaintance whose name shall be Dorothy; it is in the following manner: Dollies astraper, astra mel, a sus, a quoque et, atra pes, an id lar, alas i bo nes, a præ ter, at at lar, avi si ter, age ipsi, astro lar . . .

meaning 'Doll is a strapper, a trammel, a souse, a coquette, a trapes, an idler, a lazy-bones, a prater, a tattler, a visitor, a gipsy, a stroller . . .' He concludes the first of two long paragraphs:

Sir, I entreat you will please to observe, since I must speak in the vulgar language, that in the above forty-three denominations for females, many of them end with the domestic deity Lar, to show that women were chiefly created for family affairs; and yet I cannot hear that any other author hath made the same remark.

It all seems rather desperate, though the last sentence is a release into slightly acid wit from the drudgery, as it must to some extent have been, of composing a letter in *Latino-Anglicus*, or the separate *Consultation of Four Physicians* in the same manner.

But we get a more bantering tone when he and Sheridan together write to Mrs Whiteway, Swift's housekeeper at the Deanery. Swift had been ailing, and gone away to recuperate at Cavan with Sheridan. Swift begins with a more or less normal letter about practical matters, the document being taken over by Sheridan, who goes on:

I can assure you, dear Madam, with pleasure, that the Dean begins to look healthier and plumper already; and I hope will mend every day. But, to deal plainly with you, I am a little afraid of his good stomach, though victuals are cheap, because it improves every day, and I do not know how far this may increase my family expenses. He pays me but two crowns a week for his ordinary, and I own, that I am a little too modest to grumble at it; but if you would give him a hint about wear and tear of goods, I make no doubt but his own discretion would make him raise his price. I am, to you and yours, as much yours as the Dean aforesaid.

Then Swift:

I desire you will hint to the Doctor that he would please to abate four shillings a week from the ten, which he most exorbitantly makes me pay him; but tell him you got this hint from another hand, and that all Dublin cries shame at him for it.

As a final example from the correspondence I would give a letter he wrote to Mrs Whiteway on 30 October 1738, after having been given a box of soap and a shaving brush by Deane Swift:

Mr. Swift's gimcracks of cups and balls, in order to my convenient shaving with ease and dispatch, together with the prescription on half a sheet of paper, was exactly followed, but some inconveniences attended; for I cut my face once or twice, was just twice as long in the performance, and left twice as much hair behind as I have done this twelvemonth past. I return him therefore all his implements, and my own compliments, with

abundance of thanks, because he has fixed me during life in my old hum-
drum way.

Something of the old jocosity is still there. But is there also just a touch
of irritation? Why can't they leave me alone!

We can also gather what he was like in company from occasional
lines in a poem, as, for instance, in 'My Lady's Lamentation and
Complaint against the Dean', supposedly written by Lady Acheson,
whom he called 'Skinny' and 'Snipe', and who complains that he is
always chipping her habits, her appearance and so on; and then:

> He's all the day saunt'ring,
> With labourers bant'ring,
> Among his colleagues,
> A parcel of Teagues
> (Whom he brings in among us
> And bribes with mundungus).

And then in another poem 'written' by Lady Acheson, 'A Panegyrick
on the Dean', she says at one point:

> Now, as a Jester, I accost you;
> Which never yet one Friend has lost you.
> You judge so nicely to a Hair.
> How far to go, and when to spare:
> By long Experience grown so wise,
> Of ev'ry Taste to know the Size;
> There's none so ignorant or weak
> To take Offence at what you speak.

Or he writes to Sheridan in answer to a poem by the latter, who next
refers to Swift's 'Billingsgate Muse' –

> Hum – excellent good – your anger was stirr'd:
> Well, punners and rhymers must have the last word . . .

– the whole going on in the jocose manner Swift usually employs with
Sheridan, as in the epistle dated 14 December 1719, *at Night*, about the
muddle Sheridan seems to have made about bottling the wine he has
sent. And again we have the riddles in verse he concocted for Sheridan,
or the 'circular' letters, that is, verse written in circles. This appears
to be something other than jocoseness; it would involve too great and
sustained an effort; it is not impulsive, and would seem to be done as a

relief from more troublesome thoughts. Certainly much of all this – including the George Nim-Dan-Dean letters, and those pretended to be written by somebody else, Delany or others – strikes us as very boring.

We can get some idea, then, of why everybody found Swift such good comany, some notion of his response to others and the effusion of high spirits that seemed always to accompany him. Yet there is one very strange aspect of his personality in company. Edward Young told Spence that 'Swift had a mixture of insolence in his conversation', an insolence which, however, must have been largely humorous, as we gather from the Lady Acheson poems. Yet Pope told Spence, 'Dr. Swift has an odd blunt way, that is mistaken, by strangers, for ill-nature. – 'Tis so odd that there's no describing it but by facts.' And he goes on:

> One evening Gay and I went to see him: you know how intimately we were all acquainted. On our coming in: 'Hey-day, gentlemen,' says the Doctor, 'what's the meaning of this visit? How come you to leave all the great lords, that you are so fond of, to come hither to see a poor Dean?' – Because we would rather see you than any of them. – 'Ay, any one that did not know you so well as I do, might believe you. But since you are come, I must get some supper for you, I suppose?' – No, Doctor, we have supped already. – 'Supped already! that's impossible: why, 'tis not eight o'clock yet.' – Indeed we have. – 'That's very strange: but if you had not supped, I must have got something for you. – Let me see, what should I have had? a couple of lobsters? ay, that would have done very well; two shillings: tarts; a shilling. But you will drink a glass of wine with me, though you supped before your time, only to spare my pocket?' – No, we had rather talk with you than drink with you. – 'But if you had supped with me, as in all reason you ought to have done, you must have drank with me. – A bottle of wine; two shillings. – Two and two is four; and one is five: just two and sixpence a piece. There, Pope, there's half a crown for you; and there's another for you, sir: for I won't save anything by you I am determined.' This was all said and done with his usual seriousness on such occasions: and in spite of every thing we could say to the contrary, he actually obliged us to take the money.[2]

It is all rather puzzling. How far was it a joke? How far behind it all was there a feeling of unease, a sense of insult, even? Had they indeed supped before their time on purpose to save his pocket? Was he aware that some people thought him over-careful, mean even, in casual expenditure, and he suspected that they were taking this rather ungenerous view of him? And again, 'his usual seriousness *on such occasions*'. One feels that very often Swift's humour was deliberate, rather than a spontaneous bubbling-up of mirth.

With a few notable exceptions, especially 'Cadenus and Vanessa' and the verses on Stella's birthdays, Swift's poetry, after the dismal pindarics, is for the most part laughter-provoking. Dryden was well inspired when he said: 'Cousin Swift, turn your thoughts another way [that is, express yourself differently, choose other subjects], for nature never intended you for a Pindaric poet'. Nearly always, however, an element of satire intrudes, even though it is light-heartedly humorous as in 'Helter-Skelter':

> Now the active young Attornies
> Briskly travel on their Journies,
> Looking big as any Gyants,
> On the horses of their Clients;

and there are, notoriously, the bitingly satiric ones, such as the rather vicious 'The Salamander', or the virulent 'The Legion Club', compared with which 'Sid Hamet's Rod' is genial. It is as though he felt that, generally speaking, satire in itself, if too heavily taken, was something rather ridiculous. Ordinary humour, rather than jocoseness, pervades such a masterpiece as 'Verses on the Death of Dr. Swift', to which I shall return. One senses about so many of Swift's autobiographical verses that he is saying, 'You may sometimes think me a dreadful bore with my moralisings, but all the same I'm rather fun!' Then again it may be the other way round: fun might change to seriousness; there would be too much point in the drollery of 'A Dialogue between an Eminent Lawyer and Dr. Swift Dean of St. Patrick's, being an allusion to the first Satire of the second book of Horace':

> ... there are persons who complain
> There's too much satire in my vein,
> That I am often found exceeding
> The rules of raillery and breeding ...

for Swift's mind appears to have been exceptionally unified in its complexity; he could bind together a medley of emotions. Suddenly, in the middle of a light conversation, he would break out, making Lady Acheson expostulate:

> DEUCE is in you, Mr. DEAN;
> What can all this Passion mean?
> Mention Courts, you'll ne'er be quiet;
> On Corruptions running Riot.

He had been generously given the gift to see himself as others saw him, perhaps too generously, as might be suggested by the odd encounter with Pope and Gay referred to above. But at least detachment went with the gift, permitting him to be humorous about himself.

There is some difficulty in distinguishing between jocoseness and humour, the former being of a more vigorous social sort, perhaps deliberately provoking a retort in kind. Quiet humour is apparent in Swift's verse from the moment that he turned his thoughts another way, and produced 'The Lady's Ivory Table-Book', which, however, turns to mild satire at the end. Where we meet humour, especially, is in the fairly early 'Mrs. Harris's Petition' and the much later 'Mary the Cook-Maid's Letter', from each of which a little may be quoted. 'The Humble Petition of Frances Harris' humbly sheweth:

> That I went to warm my self in Lady *Betty's* Chamber, because I was cold,
> And I had in a Purse, seven Pound, four Shillings and six Pence, besides Farthings, in Money, and Gold;
> So because I had been buying things for my *Lady* last Night,
> I was resolved to tell my Money, to see if it was right;
> Now you must know, because my Trunk has a very bad Lock,
> Therefore all the Money, I have, which, *God* knows, is a very small Stock,
> I keep in a Pocket ty'd about my Middle, next my Smock . . .

That is a story, told simply as such, Swift jokingly, but with some sympathy, putting himself into Mrs Harris's self: in 'Mary the Cook-Maid's Letter to Dr. Sheridan' Swift carries on a humorous rally of name-calling with his friend:

> Well; if I ever saw such another Man since my Mother bound my Head,
> You a Gentleman! marry come up, I wonder where you were bred?
> I am sure such Words does not become a Man of your Cloth,
> I would not give such Language to a Dog, faith and troth.
> Yes; you call'd my Master a Knave: Fie Mr. *Sheridan*, 'tis a Shame
> For a Parson, who shou'd know better Things, to come out with such a Name.

Knave in your Teeth, Mr. *Sheridan*, 'tis both a Shame and a Sin,
And the Dean my Master is an honester Man than you and all your kin:
He has more Goodness in his little Finger, than you have in your whole
    Body,
My Master is a parsonable Man, not a spindle-shank'd hoddy doddy.
And now whereby I find you would fain make an Excuse,
Because my Master one Day in anger call'd you Goose. . . .

   You say you will eat Grass on his Grave: a Christian eat Grass!
Whereby you now confess your self to be a Goose or an Ass . . .

Here we get a glimpse of the sort of conversation, if that kind of
schoolboy interchange can be called such, carried on in the intervals of
more serious talk, from which Swift possibly sought the easing of mirth.
We find him achieving the same species of relief in his more deeply
felt autobiographical verses, as in those 'On the Death of Dr. Swift'.
For that poem is not by any means altogether joking. Here and there it
has touches of light humour, but it seems characterised for the most
part by a humour that is slightly sardonic – unless this be the wise
detachment of a man sixty-four years old. He worked over this poem
tremendously hard, telling Gay on 1 December 1731:

> I have been several months writing near five hundred lines on a pleasant
> subject, only to tell what my friends and enemies will say on me after I am
> dead. I shall finish it soon, for I add two lines every week, and blot out four
> and alter eight.

He repudiated having composed what has been considered as a draft of
the poem, namely 'The Life and Character of Dean Swift', but it seems
likely that it was really his. The final complex 'Verses on the Death of
Dr. Swift' reads in some parts as a mollifying, rather touching, affectionate tribute to his friends, especially when we remember that for
several days he was to leave unopened a letter from Pope, having a
premonition that it contained the news of Gay having died. But one
passage at least has a certain jocoseness, as though he were digging his
friends in the ribs, while at the same time paying them his tribute:

> Why must I be outdone by Gay,
> In my own hum'rous biting Way?
>   ARBUTHNOT is no more my Friend,
> Who dares to Irony pretend;
> Which I was born to introduce,
> Refin'd it first, and shew'd its Use.

a tone repeated with sad overtones, the result of experience reflected upon in:

> Poor Pope will grieve a Month; and GAY
> A Week; and ARBUTHNOT a Day.
> St. JOHN himself will scarce forbear
> To bite his Pen, and drop a Tear.

And here the tone changes to one of detachment:

> The rest will give a Shrug and cry
> I'm sorry; but we all must dye . . .

A common remark, which we may have made ourselves about people whom we have scarcely met or only heard of: 'Oh, well. We've all got to die some time.' Earlier we have read – and this is mirth overcoming the justifiable annoyance about the matter to which it refers:

> Kind Lady *Suffolk* in the Spleen,
> Runs laughing up to tell the Queen.
> The Queen, so Gracious, Mild, and Good,
> Cries, 'Is he gone? 'tis time he shou'd. . . .'

But we get a more central view of him as the genial companion at the end of the poem, where the generality of people say:

> 'He knew an hundred pleasant Stories,
> With all the Turns of *Whigs* and *Tories*:
> Was chearful to his dying Day,
> And Friends would let him have his Way.'

There is no need to pursue Swift's jocoseness in the poems, most of them being intentionally humorous or light. It is more revealing to see how it would keep breaking in even with the serious – often deadly serious – prose pieces. This, too, from the very beginning. There is no doubt that he felt he had something important to say in *A Tale of a Tub*, and also that to write a dull theological treatise would be quite ineffectual. Ordinary satire, again, would be too blunt; and besides, to write a fable, an absurdly exaggerated story, would be such enormous fun! And with him the sense of fun was almost irrepressible. As he says in 'The Author upon Himself':

> S—— had the Sin of Wit no venial Crime;
> Nay, 'twas affirm'd, he sometimes dealt in Rhime:
> Humour, and Mirth, had Place in all he writ:
> He reconcil'd Divinity and Wit.

Nevertheless we may be allowed to think that this, his first book, is rather fumbling; it is, in a way, too full: 'What a genius I had when I writ that book.' Yes; but it is the genius of overfulness, of too great exuberance. But how amusing it must have been to write, near the end of the Preface:

> But I forget that I am expatiating on a Subject, wherein I have no concern, having neither a Talent nor an Inclination for Satyr; On the other side, I am so entirely satisfied with the whole present Procedure of Human Things, that I have been for some Years preparing a *Panegyric upon the World* . . . but finding my Common-Place-Book fill much slower than I had reason to expect, I have chosen to defer them to another Occasion.

And, as a contrast to this bland 'satyr', in section XI he describes how Jack (the Dissenters) treats the Will, that is, the New Testament:

> He had a Way of working it into any Shape he pleased; so that it served him for a Night-cap when he went to Bed, and for an Umbrello in rainy Weather. He would lap a Piece of it about a sore Toe, or when he had Fits, burn two Inches under his Nose; or if any Thing lay heavy on his Stomach, scrape off and swallow as much of the Powder as would lie on a silvery Penny, they were all infallible Remedies.

And so on. This, surely, is not satire, so much as sheer inventive, though pointedly critical, fun.

And, obviously, it was ingenious sense of fun that made him write *A Meditation upon a Broom-Stick*, to be solemnly read to the Countess of Berkeley as one of Robert Boyle's pietistic effusions. There was double amusement in this; that of taking off Boyle, and that of taking in Lady Berkeley, who, at first gulled into believing it authentic, took it in good part when the truth was told her. Swift must have enormously relished the doing of it, quite apart from the reading of it:

> This single Stick, which you now behold ingloriously lying in that neglected Corner, I once knew in a flourishing State in a Forest. It was full of Sap, full of Leaves, and full of Boughs: But now, in vain does the busy Art of Man pretend to vie with Nature by tying that withered Bundle of Twigs to its sapless Trunk. . . . When I beheld this, I sighed, and said within my self, SURELY MORTAL MAN IS A BROOMSTICK. . . .
> But a Broom-stick, perhaps you will say, is an Emblem of a Tree standing on its Head; and pray what is Man but a topsy-turvy Creature?

In the same vein, though unlike it, is *A Tritical Essay upon the Faculties of the Mind*, in which Swift gathered together all the trite sayings that occurred to him, and aped a serious essay, not, it must be confessed, very brilliantly.

A great deal must be left out in an article on a subject that it would take a book to deal with adequately; but one cannot omit the essay against the abolition of Christianity. The full title is wonderful, and one can imagine it arising out of a conversation in which Pope, perhaps, or Gay, or Arbuthnot said: 'Mightn't it be rather inconvenient if Christianity were to be abolished?' And then Swift, immensely entertained by the mild epithet, devising the heading: *An Argument to prove, That the Abolishing of CHRISTIANITY IN ENGLAND, May, as Things now Stand, be attended with some Inconveniences, and, perhaps, not produce those many good Effects proposed thereby.* And how he must have chuckled to himself as he discovered certain things to say which, otherwise phrased, would be directly satirical or devastatingly withering. After all, Swift was profoundly serious in this matter. So we read:

> I hope, no Reader imagines me so weak to stand up in the Defence of *real* Christianity; such as used in primitive Times (if we may believe the Authors of those Ages) to have an Influence upon Mens Belief and Actions: To offer at the Restoring of that, would indeed be a wild Project; it would be to dig up Foundations; to destroy at one Blow *all* the Wit and *half* the Learning of the Kingdom; to break the entire Frame and Constitution of Things; to ruin Trade, extinguish Arts and Sciences with the Professors of them; in short, to turn our Courts, Exchanges and Shops into Desarts: . . .

How too he must have enjoyed his beautiful double-shafted joke: 'Nor do I think it wholly groundless, or my Fear altogether imaginary: that the Abolishing of Christianity may perhaps bring the Church in Danger; or at least put the Senate to the trouble of another Securing Vote.' Swift, of course, was passionately for the Church; but what effect would it have to answer the attackers of Christianity, the Tolands and Asgills, in their own dull language?

> My method of Reforming
> Is by Laughing, not by Storming,

not only because it was more telling – 'ridicule is the test of truth' – but because it was infinitely more enlivening to oneself.

A proportion of what he wrote is obviously fun, as in the *Bickerstaff Papers*, especially in making play with the astrologer Partridge. Here, besides the obvious need to explode silly nonsense, there was his desire to reduce Partridge as a man who favoured the abolition of the Test Act. The churchman, as well as the common-sense man, came into play once more. But suppose that Bickerstaff were to foretell the death of Partridge, then declare that he had died on the predicted day, and then scoff at him when he declared that he most certainly was alive! If Partridge had had only a tithe of Swift's sense of humour, how entertaining he might have found it to write from the grave!

To make a jump, take *The Drapier's Letters*, in which Swift was fighting hard against what he regarded as an intolerable imposition on the people of Ireland. Certainly, indignation was behind it all, but it is as though he were always, not searching for, but overtaken by the ridiculous through the sheer make-up of his nature. Here, for instance, is one of the passages in which he supposes that Wood's half-pence have been imposed upon Ireland:

> They say that Squire Connolly has Sixteen Thousand Pounds a Year; now if he sends for his *Rent* to Town, *as it is likely he does*, he must have *Two Hundred and Fifty Horses* to bring up his *Half Year's Rent*, and two or three great *Cellars* in his House for Stowage . . .

That sort of thing was amusing enough; but what probably tickled him most was the finding of terms in which to describe the unfortunate Wood: we get in Letter I: 'Mr. Wood, *a mean ordinary Man, a Hard-Ware Dealer*', and almost immediately '*an ordinary Fellow*', to be followed soon by '*this sorry Fellow*, Wood': and in the next, 'this Honest Liberal Hard-Ware-Man Wood'; and soon after, 'this little impudent *Hard-Ware-Man*' at the beginning of a paragraph which ends with 'one single, diminutive, insignificant Mechanick'. He revels through Letter III in variations on the theme: 'one *Single, Rapacious, Obscure, Ignominious* PROJECTOR', or 'a *poor private obscure Mechanick*', or 'one obscure *Ironmonger*'. Not very dignified, nor perhaps very honest; but what good popular pamphleteering! And what opportunities for entertaining oneself in devising such variants!

Gulliver's Travels does not, on the whole, offer much scope for adventitious fooling. The first two books and the last embody too serious a philosophical pondering on the nature of man to permit of much jocularity, though there is plenty of humour throughout. Occasionally, however, there is the more light-hearted note, as when he describes the handwriting of the Lilliputians, in the spirit, one imagines, that characterised his converse with his friends:

. . . their Manner of writing is very peculiar; being neither from the Left to the Right, like the *Europeans*; nor from the Right to the Left, like the *Arabians*; nor from up to down, like the *Chinese*; nor from down to up like the *Cascagians*; but aslant from one Corner of the Paper to the other, like Ladies in *England*.

It is, rather, in the interpolated third book that he gives a loose to his sense of the ridiculous, especially in a favourite amusement of driving ideas to their logical conclusion. So taking Sprat's dictum in the *History of the Royal Society* that the ideal of prose was to deliver 'so many "Things", almost in an equal number of "Words" ', Swift propels this to:

. . . a Scheme for entirely abolishing all Words whatsoever: And this was urged as a great Advantage in Point of Health as well as Brevity. For, it is plain, that every Word we speak is in some Degree a Diminution of our Lungs by Corrosion; and consequently contributes to the shortning of our Lives. An Expedient was therefore offered, that since Words are only Names for *Things*, it would be more convenient for all Men to carry about them, such *Things* as were necessary to express the particular Business they are to discourse on . . .

The objections being that women and the vulgar and illiterate were determined to be allowed to speak with their tongues, after the manner of their forefathers; and that it would be impossible for the learned and wise to carry about with them as many objects as they wished to talk about.

It is easy to guess that as Swift lost contact with his friends in England, or they died, he found most of the society in which he had to pass his time in Dublin more than tiresome; and perforce subjected to the sort of talk current in drawing-rooms, he got his amusement – and his revenge – out of it by composing *A Complete Collection of Genteel and Ingenious Conversation*, etc., appropriately written by Simon Wagstaff (he seems to have made early jottings in 1704), with a beautifully mocking Introduction, from which a passage, totally irrelevant, may be taken. He has been talking about fame, and how, after all that he, Simon Wagstaff, has accomplished, he would consider himself most inhumanly treated, and 'would resent it as the highest indignity, to be put upon the Level, in Point of Fame, in after Ages, with *Charles* XII late King of *Sweden*'. He goes on:

And yet, so incurable is the Love of Detraction, perhaps, beyond what the charitable Reader will easily believe, that I have been assured by more than one credible Person, how some of my Enemies have industriously whispered about, that one *Isaac Newton*, an Instrument-Maker, formerly living near *Leicester* Fields, and afterwards a Workman in the Mint, at the Tower, might possibly pretend to vye with me for Fame in future Times. The Man, it seems, was knighted for making Sun-Dyals better than others of his Trade, and was thought to be a Conjurer, because he knew how to draw Lines and Circles upon a Slate, which no Body could understand. But, adieu to all noble Attempts for endless Renown, if the Ghost of an obscure Mechanick [he seems to have been fond of that phrase], shall be raised up, to enter into Competition with me, only for skill in making Pothooks and Hangers, with a Pencil; which many thousand accomplished Gentlemen and Ladies can perform as well, with a Pen and Ink, upon a Piece of Paper, and in a Manner as little intelligible as those of Sir *Isaac*.

It were to be wished that the three dialogues of genteel conversation were a tithe so amusing. It is a little depressing to think that all these repartees, rejoinders, and so on, he had 'with infinite Labour and close Application, during the Space of thirty six Years been collecting'. The labour may not have been infinite, nor the application very close, but even so the result seems incommensurate with the care and time the writing must have taken. Yet it is well to remind ourselves that it was all part of a serious campaign for preserving the language, including the foundation of an English Academy, on the lines of the French one, as set out in *A Proposal for Correcting . . . the English Tongue*, and *Hints towards an Essay on Conversation* of many years earlier. But no doubt Swift derived a good deal of amusement from noting the idiocies of small-talk.

Naturally an element of satire enters into such things, just as most satire implies a certain amount of fun, as we find in the more clearly satirical *Directions to Servants*, which evidences a good deal of irritation. This piece again he may have been making jottings for as early as 1704, to return to it in 1731, and tinker with until 1739. It is better reading than 'Genteel Conversation', and, as he said, might prove 'very useful as well as humorous'. It certainly shows that he was well aware of what went on below stairs, whether he is considering the footman, the coachman, the waiting-maid, or any of the others. The cook may provide us with a brief group of directions:

Scrape the Bottoms of your Pots and Kettles with a Silver Spoon, for fear of giving them a Taste of Copper.

When you send up Butter for Sauce, be so thrifty as to let it be half Water; which is also much wholesomer.

Never make use of a Spoon in any thing that you can do with your Hands, for fear of wearing out your Master's Plate.

Some is jocose, but much evidences disgust:

You are to look upon your Kitchen as your Dressing-room; but, you are not to wash your Hands till you have gone to the Necessary-house, and spitted your Meat, trussed your Pullets, pickt your Sallad, nor indeed till after you have sent up the second Course; for your Hands will be ten times fouled with the many Things you are forced to handle; but when your Work is over, one Washing will serve for all.

All that, we may think, is gruff humour rather than exuberant amusement.

But what really, we begin to ask ourselves, was the basis of Swift's jocoseness, which persisted to almost the end of his life? Was it an attempt to throw off the savage indignation which never ceased to lacerate his heart? – an evident over-statement. It would seem that in his early days it was what one would call exuberance, given, of course, that he had a natural sense of humour. There is no indignation in *A Tale of a Tub*, only a sharp critical spirit making its point in this way. *A Meditation upon a Broom-Stick*, and its use, is a sheer lark. Later, it might be conjectured, his passionate rebellion against the folly, meanness, injustice and dishonesty of mankind often relieved itself by an overwhelming sense of the ridiculous, or a more coolly directed sense of what would tell. The bitter jokes in *A Modest Proposal* cannot be classed as jocose. As to jesting, much of this, as already suggested, especially as regards the Sheridan 'exercises', as one may call them, must have been an attempt to break the tedium of his Dublin existence, the boredom of genteel conversation, finding something to do – especially after the deaths of Vanessa and Stella. As he aged, feeling some of his old superabundant energy, physical as well as mental, beginning to fail, he indulged more and more in horse exercise, and took to walking faster than anyone else, so that those who walked with him panted behind. Even while expiring 'a driv'ller and a show', he satisfied his need both for exercise and for convincing himself that he needed it, by walking endlessly up and down stairs. So what was there left for him in the intellectual sphere but to force himself to fantastic humour? Laughter is the release that men such as Swift are granted for combating the evils of existence.

NOTES

1. Probably Billy Carr, apparently a sort of hanger on, who in September 1714 was appointed a Groom of the Bedchamber to George I.

2. Joseph Spence, *Anecdotes, Observations, and Characters of Books and Men* (1820) pp. 19–20.

J. J. HOGAN

Bicentenary of Jonathan Swift 1667–1745 (1945)

THE common touch is one of the most obvious things about Swift. He had a full and practical knowledge of the ordinary world. He knew how to cut a hedge, drain a ditch, manage a bog, sail a boat – and swim if anything went wrong. He could make and do all sorts of things, and he detested the lack of plain sense which makes many people so incapable – the pedantry, pretence and folly of the bungler. The job of literature, to him, was something straightforward and no mystery; it was just putting proper words in proper places. Good manners he holds to mean no more than being at our ease and putting others at theirs; the formalities are needless and useless, except in so far as reason dictates them. He loved to teach such a lesson practically. When a lady, awed by the occasion of having the Dean to dinner, made a great preliminary fuss about the inadequacy of her table, he took her at her word: 'Nay, ma'am, since you have made no better preparation, I'll e'en go home and eat a herring.' Swift could be as downright in common sense as Johnson. When Sheridan, who had learnedly annotated Persius, left an obscure word unexplained, Swift's remark was: 'Where you are ignorant, you should confess you are ignorant.' But he certainly knew more about everyday things than Johnson, who was acute, but whose senses were dull; Swift would never have defined the pastern of a horse incorrectly.

Swift's grasp of the common world is seen in *Gulliver*, where it enables him, under enormous handicaps, to rival Defoe's narrative plausibility. It is in all he wrote, and no books are so stuffed with facts and things, unenhanced by poetry but alive. His common touch helped him to be the idol of the mob. He did useful jobs for them; lent them money on a business basis; controlled the weights and measures in the Liberties; devised a system of badges for beggars. The plain people could

even read his books; for, as Johnson says (with an intention of disparage-
ment) the reader of Swift needs little previous knowledge; 'it will be
sufficient if he is acquainted with common words and common things'.
Swift addressed the people as rational and political beings, making them
in a sense his equals. In the *Drapier* he wrote their very language, rough
and shrewd, and when he composed rhyming cries for the fishwives and
apple-women. This zest for common life must have helped Swift in his
later years; and the memory of him walking through the Liberties, not
merely known to all but almost knowing all, is one of the great Dublin
memories. He knew Ireland too, much of it, and the country people.
His burlesques of O'Rourke's Feast, Dermot and Sheelah, etc., have ugly
colours but some true drawing; they set others observing, and pointed
forward to Maria Edgeworth and the Anglo-Irish novel of country
manners.

It is a short step from Swift's realism and common sense to his
philosophy of life, based on 'nature and reason'. And when we say his
philosophy of life, we mean at the same time his politics. For in his view
all high-flying speculation, all 'originality', was folly; therefore the
mind must be applied to reality and literature must be a criticism of life
in a very immediate sense. All the writing of the age was social; but
while a quieter temper might be satisfied with commenting apart,
Swift's energy and ambition impelled him to leadership and government. That zest for common life contributed its urge. Nearly all Swift's
works are in some way political. Some are aimed at an immediate
practical effect. In others, frustrated of direct influence on affairs, he
devises fictitious commonwealths to embody the ideal and satirize the
actual.

It was an age of reason, and men thought that intelligence could solve
and order all things. Politics to Swift seemed no mystery, for 'God hath
given the bulk of mankind a capacity to understand reason where it is
fairly offered; and by reason they would easily be governed, if left to
their choice'. Society's leaders should be those possessing most of this
enlightenment. Late in life Swift wrote to Pope: 'I have often endeavoured to establish a friendship among all men of genius, and would
fain have it done; they are seldom above three or four contemporaries,
and if they would be united, would drive the world before them. I
think it was so among the poets in the time of Augustus.' Pope, too,
believed in reason and persuasion as the forces that ought to govern
society. The golden moment when they should at last do so seemed to

have arrived in the later years of Queen Anne. For four years Swift, by his counsel in the cabinet and his ceaseless, masterly 'propaganda' outside, was the great support of the Tory administration. His *Conduct of the Allies* was one of the most effective of all political pamphlets. But things went wrong; and Swift, having, by right of his abilities as it seemed, gone straight to the peak of power in England, never again had any real influence in that country. At first it must have appeared that his exclusion could not last. Political journalism had shown its immense power. Surely that meant that henceforth the wits were indispensable to the parties. And could not the wits exact their price, in compelling the parties to submit to intelligence? But in truth the parties soon discovered that quantity in journalism was more important than quality; or perhaps rather that the wits provided better literary than political quality, for with the exception of Swift they were but amateur politicians. When next, at the end of the century, great literature came to sway politics, it no longer spoke with the voice of reason; it was Burke declaring that 'politics ought to be adapted, not to human reason, but to human nature, of which reason is but a part, and that by no means the greatest part'.

This looks like a sharp contradiction. Burke decried reason in politics; Swift believed in reason absolutely. But it was a long time from Anne and Louis XIV to George III and Louis XVI, and the sense of that word *reason* underwent a change. Burke attacks the reason of the *philosophes* and Jacobins because it is irresponsible, rapacious, a tool of the individual and his selfishness, destructive of all order; it is reason out of hand and perverted. But Swift stood with the scholastic and humanist tradition, though near the end of it – a tradition which held reason to be, except for revelation, the highest thing in the world. Burke associated reason with the 'sophisters, economists, and calculators'; and, as we shall see, Swift agreed with him in so far as he detested their predecessors. He did not know that such people would take his weapon of reason and turn it against all it should defend – though perhaps he did more than a little to produce that result.

Reason governs in the Utopia of the Houyhnhnms, a Utopia which has striking resemblances to More's own. (We remember that Swift spoke of More as 'the person of the greatest virtue this kingdom ever produced'.) 'Their grand maxim is to cultivate reason and to be wholly governed by it.' Reason, for all its kinship to common sense is a thing, great enough to include virtue, and Gulliver's master tells him 'That our institutions of government and law were plainly owing to our gross defects in reason, and by consequence in virtue.' The passions, in Swift's view of life, are to be repressed, because they cloud reason and deform it into that curse of society, opinion. Friendship therefore takes the place of love in Houyhnhnm land, the sexes are equal, and marriage and parenthood simply eugenic. These are no fanciful speculations; they hardly go beyond Swift's social doctrine. He saw the sovereign reason beset by another rebel scarcely less dangerous than passion, and it was intellect. This must not be licensed to range beyond the natural and the normal; even if it lighted on nothing dangerous, as it might do, frivolity disgraces a rational creature. Swift's chief satire upon intellectualism is in the Third Book of *Gulliver*, with its academy of Lagado. There also applied science is mercilessly flayed. Two centuries have scoffed at Swift's attitude to science, but perhaps today we can forgive his attempt to strangle in its cradle what he apprehended might grow to be a monster – intellectualism interfering with nature. There was a further complication and danger; science might ally itself with interest. That experiment of extracting concentrated sunshine from cucumbers would cease to be innocuously crazy if somebody became a millionaire out of it. Such a person already had his name, he was a 'projector'. Swift hated him. He hated too the new capitalist, getting rich upon credit, and the expanding science or trade of banking. Also he hated the war-monger, and saw pretty clearly how he fitted into the whole scheme of 'progress'. Worst of all was that offspring of passion and disordered intellect which Swift would call zeal or 'enthusiasm'. None did he dislike more than the man who thought himself exempted from reason by some private and direct insight. He saw this chiefly in sectarian terms, as dissent, but he saw it in party divisions also, if not in its remoter shape of nationalisms.

Swift's position in regard to religion and the Church can now be fairly well understood. Christianity has shown its excellence by its fruits. It is rational to accept what is good without comprehension when plainly we are unfitted to comprehend. Apart from its mysteries Christianity is nature and reason at their best. Swift was therefore a great churchman, and always held a high idea of *clergy* as a social fact working for reason and morality. Perhaps his stand on the Church is the chief positive affirmation of his doctrine of reason in society, which otherwise we have seen to be chiefly negative, a clearing of the ground. But other positive proposals he did make. He had a good deal to say about education. He wanted annual parliaments, so that the landed interest might be truly represented and there might be no corruption. He entertained ideas of what would now be called social security, and there is a sort of Beveridge plan in operation among the Lilliputians. But he is ready to trust reason; if that has its way, there will be no need for schemes and projects.

Mistakes are often made about Swift's work in Ireland. It was not exile in a provincial town. Swift was Irish enough, and a Dubliner; *Hibernus es et in Hiberniam reverteris* one of his college friends wrote to him when he seemed to be establishing himself in the greater kingdom. Dublin, though it had yet scarcely one of the eighteenth-century buildings that were to be its glory, was easily the second city in the English-speaking world. Incidentally, it certainly was not, as has been said by one writer after another, 'Protestant from the street-hawkers up to the bishops'. Swift's intervention in Irish politics, again, was no mere Tory *fronde*, to make trouble for the Whigs in England. He wrote far too sincerely for that; and the mere volume of his Irish work in pamphlets, poems, and monitory letters is enormous.

When Swift sought freedom for Irish trade, he was necessarily seeking to improve the lot of the Catholics who were the bulk of the population. When he attacked oppressive landlords and admonished or advised others according to the degree of their exactions, he was working directly for Catholics. But he spoke no word for Catholic emancipation or an alleviation of the Penal Laws. He would not compromise his rigid attitude to dissent; and it seems that he believed Catholicism would really disappear and leave only a social and political problem.

Swift could thus attack the complex Irish problem with a fierce simplicity. He had no sentimental patriotism, any more than he had sentimental attachments to anything else. Here as elsewhere he saw stupidity and selfishness opposed to reason and justice, but in an extremer opposition. Ireland must recognize herself and be recognized by others as a nation. A nation must be a kingdom, and there were no half-ways; there could be no such thing as a 'depending kingdom'. The Anglo-Irish upper class must change their hearts; they must drop some of their 'loyalty', their attachment to another country, and discover more 'public spirit' – more attachment to their own. As a nation Ireland must have ranks and orders, but cannot endure a system of ascendancy, of privilege and exclusion. Swift was no colonial patriot, if by that is meant the patriot of a class; he had no notion of erecting an Anglo-Irish freedom upon native helotry. He wished, on the contrary, that all unnatural distinctions should disappear. 'It would be a noble enterprise to abolish the Irish language in this kingdom' – for Irish was a badge of the conquered, an obstacle to the civilization he desired to share. Again, when many Protestants did not, he wanted to have all Irishmen in the Established Church. There could be no nation without a national Church; he wished it to be his own, though in his Will he contemplates another possibility. In sum, no narrowness of prejudice in Swift could lessen the force and universality of his principles. Certain great sentences from the Fourth *Drapier's Letter* were to change the destinies of Ireland – and of other countries as well. 'By the laws of God, of Nature, of Nations, and of your Country, you are and ought to be as free a people as your brethren in England.' 'All government without the consent of the governed is the very definition of slavery.'

Fundamental in Swift was a tremendous energy. He would row like a waterman, ride like a postboy; he was the greatest walker in London or Dublin. In early life he read feverishly; later on he despatched endless business; and his pen was never idle. The gift of repose was rarely his. He fed that hungry spirit of activity, as we have seen, upon political action and speculation. But we have to examine its other diet and to witness what might be called its cannibalism.

One of Swift's great outlets, of course, was invention. His mind was 'a conjured spirit, which would do mischief if he did not give it employment'. Perhaps it sometimes did mischief *when* he gave it employment, but often it delighted himself and others. This is the Swift who 'laughed and shook in Rabelais' easy-chair', the wit, humourist, satirist; though I fancy him rather sitting to his table with intent and silent satisfaction. His invention is as quick and fertile as any poet's, but it is not poetry, for there is not the poetic aura, the vagueness and suggestiveness, but all is sharp and defined. Swift does not body forth the shapes of things unknown, he conjures known things into unexpected shapes.

His range is from pure fun to the strongest sarcasm. So much has been said of the profound meaning of *Gulliver*, and of its pessimism, that we almost forget it is a very entertaining book – though of course we knew that when we were children. There is many an unbarbed arrow, such as this account of writing in Lilliput: 'Their manner of writing is very peculiar, being neither from the left to the right, like the Europeans; nor from the right to the left, like the Arabians; nor from up to down, like the Chinese; but aslant from one corner of the paper to the other, like ladies in England.' Many men have amused in single jests, or struck single cuts of satire; Swift is unique in his persistence, his tireless humorous and satirical logic. One way he has, which it would take too much space to illustrate, is to make metaphor start out of metaphor, analogy out of analogy, until all things under the sun seem to be linked in the chain of his perverse but unbreakable argument. Another of his ways is to turn the eye of pure reason upon things, so that they squirm and contort into caricatures of themselves. It is a single eye, not the double one of common vision, and so it deprives the object of all solidity and relation to its surroundings. You can't deny that it *is* the thing, for all your protest against the trick you know is being played. Dealing with an abuse, he will refuse to admit its real causes, its mitigations and excuses, while ostentatiously protecting it with mere shadows of these. An excellent example is when Gulliver tries to do the King of Brobding-nag a good turn by putting him in possession of powder and guns. Swift goes on as if our civilization had produced nothing better than gun-powder and as if wars were waged simply for the sake of destruction, and he keeps Gulliver smugly assured that nothing European can be wrong. The passage is not without topical interest:

I told him . . . that we often put this powder into large hollow balls of iron, and discharged them by an engine into some city we were besieging, which would rip up the pavements, tear the houses to pieces, burst and throw splinters on every side, dashing out the brains of all who came near. That I knew the ingredients very well, which were cheap and common; I understood the manner of compounding them, and could direct his work-men how to make those tubes, of a size proportionable to all other things in his majesty's kingdom; . . . twenty or thirty of which tubes . . . would batter down the walls of the strongest town in his dominions in a few hours, or destroy the whole metropolis, if ever it should pretend to dispute his absolute commands. This I humbly offered to his majesty, as a small tribute of acknowledgement, in return of so many marks that I had received of his royal favour and protection.

The king was struck with horror at the description I had given of those terrible engines, and the proposal I had made. He was amazed how so impotent and grovelling an insect as I (these were his expressions) could entertain such inhuman ideas, and in so familiar a manner as to appear wholly unmoved at all the scenes of blood and desolation which I had painted as the common effects of those destructive machines; whereof, he said, some evil genius, enemy to mankind, must have been the first contriver. As for himself, he protested that although few things delighted him so much as new discoveries in art or in nature, yet he would rather lose half his kingdom than be privy to such a secret; which he commanded me, as I valued my life, never to mention any more.

A strange effect of narrow principles and views! That a prince possessed of every quality which procures veneration, love, and esteem; of strong parts, great wisdom, and profound learning, endowed with admirable talents, and almost adored by his subjects, should, from a nice unnecessary scruple, whereof in Europe we can have no conception, let slip an opportunity put into his hands that would have made him absolute master of the lives, the liberties, and the fortunes of his people. Neither do I say this with the least intention to detract from the many virtues of that excellent king, whose character, I am sensible, will on this account be much lessened in the opinion of an English reader; but I take this defect among them to have risen from their ignorance, by not having hitherto reduced politics into a science, as the more acute wits of Europe have done. For I remember very well, in a discourse with the king, when I happened to say there were several thousand books among us written upon the art of government, it gave him (directly contrary to my intention) a very mean opinion of our understandings. He professed to abominate and despise all mystery, refinement, and intrigue, either in a prince or a minister. He confined the art of governing within very narrow bounds, to common sense and reason, to the speedy determination of civil and criminal causes, with some other obvious topics which are not worth considering. And he gave it for his opinion that whoever could make two ears of corn or two blades of grass to grow upon a spot of ground where only one grew before, would deserve better of mankind, and do more essential service to his country, than the whole race of politicians put together.

The learning of this people is very defective, etc.

When we pass to the pessimistic and misanthropic Swift, we are on difficult ground. The critics who have persisted in clearing away all difficulties have discovered either all misanthropy or none; they have simplified Swift into a monster or a decent, ordinary fellow – neither of which can be right. To take an instance, are we to call the *Modest Proposal* ghastly or delightful?

Whoever could find out a cheap, fair, and easy method of making these children sound useful members of the commonwealth, would deserve so well of the public as to have his statue set up for a preserver of the nation. . . .
I have been assured, by a very knowing American of my acquaintance in London, that a young healthy child, well nursed, is at a year old a most delicious, nourishing, and wholesome food, whether stewed, roasted,

baked, or boiled; and I make no doubt it will equally serve in a fricassee
or a ragout. . . .

Those who are more thrifty (as I must confess the times require), may
flay the carcase; the skin of which, artificially dressed, will make admirable
gloves for ladies and summer boots for fine gentlemen. . . .

As to our city of Dublin, shambles may be appointed for this purpose in
the most convenient parts of it, and butchers we may be assured will not
be wanting; although I rather recommend buying the children alive, then
dressing them hot from the knife, as we do roasting-pigs.

How much here is beneficent purpose, to cure the Irish landlord of
his cruel stupidity by pushing it to a fantastic extreme? How much is
pessimism, a sense that man, whether he be the oppressor or the sordid
victim, is bestial, and perverse delight in convincing others that it is so?
And if we think the latter is the stronger motive, how far is the harm
taken out of it by the katharsis of wit?

Nor would all agree with Thackeray about the last Book of *Gulliver*:
'As for the moral, I think it horrible, shameful, unmanly, blasphemous;
and giant and great as this Dean is, I say we should shoot him.' It may
be replied that the Yahoos are true; if reason and virtue be the distinction
of man and he shows them not, what is he but a beast? Lear saw pretty
nearly what Gulliver saw. And again it may be answered that the book
still maintains a positive ideal, though it is embodied in other creatures
and not in the animal man. But the Houyhnhnm life is no life at all,
comes the objection; to be countered by saying that no Utopia from
Plato down has seemed livable. Swift himself may be allowed to decide
the question. He regarded the thing as a document in misanthropy, an
outpouring of his physical disgust and intellectual scorn – though his
verdict still concedes something to the other side: 'O, if the world had
but a dozen Arbuthnots in it, I'd burn my *Travels*.'

There is a sombre eloquence of pessimism in many a phrase of the
Journal and the letters. 'I am able to hold up my sorry head no longer.'
'Life is a tragedy, wherein we sit as spectators awhile, and then att
our own part in it.' Or again, another metaphor from the drama to
express the meaninglessness, the indignity of life: 'It is not a farce, it is a
ridiculous tragedy, which is the worst species of composition.' 'Your
proposal will come to nothing; there is not virtue enough left in mankind.' 'I never wake without finding life a more insignificant thing than
it was the day before.' 'I am sure my days will be few; few and
miserable they must be.' Lastly, speaking of a lady, a deeply valued

friend, who died young: 'I hate life, when I think it exposed to such accidents; and to see so many thousand wretches burdening the earth while such as her die, makes me think God did never intend life for a blessing.'

Pessimism was in the man's orginal nature. 'I remember,' he says, 'when I was a little boy I felt a great fish at the end of my line, which I drew up almost on the ground, but it dropped in, and the disappointment vexes me to this day, and I believe it was the type of all my future disappointments.' Swift's boyhood and youth were not happy. He was an orphan; he was slow to find his abilities and make his way. Even when he had become prominent, he was still unprovided for and insecure. In London he was a great man by day perhaps, but rather a small one when he went back to his cheap lodging and wrote home those tender, often self-pitying pages to Stella. 'The ministry all use me perfectly well, and all that know them say they love me. Yet I can count upon nothing, nor will, but upon MD's love and kindness. They think me useful; they pretended they were afraid of none but me.' Then came the great disappointment and fall.

Swift, we have noted, distrusted the intellect. But he could not curb his own. Keen in the criticism of all things, it joined with his original temper and his ill-adjustment and disappointments to make him unhappy. It enlarged folly and evil into universal principles. When that conjured spirit once got going, there was no stopping it, and its pitiless analysis would cut away every reason for living. In the *Tale of a Tub* he set out with a limited scope, to help his own church by satirizing Rome and Geneva, but the attack developed into one upon Christianity itself. Swift was a good clergyman. The prayers he wrote in Stella's last illness show him attracted by piety and seeking its aid. He was certainly nothing so simple as a secret disbeliever. But the corrosive working of his intellect must have left him very little consolation in religion.

What of Swift's anger, the *saeva indignatio*? Biographers have filled their pages with such phrases as 'fierce impatience', 'savagely irritable', 'imperiousness', 'moments of towering egotism', 'intolerable arrogance', 'coarse and capricious violence', 'savage recklessness in sarcasm', 'terrible hatred'. Perhaps these are flung too wildly. Swift was never feared by contemporaries as Pope was feared. He was a good friend, an exceedingly charitable man, and not unkind. A certain rudeness and pride came from his uncertainty of himself and his position in the earlier days. But even then, and certainly later on, he wore eccentricity as a mannerism; he knew and liked himself as a rough humourist, a 'character'. The worst indictment against him is his alleged harshness to Vanessa and to Stella; but the famous 'scenes' between them probably never took place at all. Scott speaks well of the 'stern, haughty, and dauntless turn of his mind'. One may believe that it was upon the public affairs of Ireland, more than any other subject, that Swift was deeply angered, and for that there was justification. Certain letters paint Dantean landscapes, with Dantean anger, of famine and desolation. 'Only one thing I know, that the cruel oppressions of this kingdom by England are not to be borne.' That is, his indignation arose from what he himself ascribes it to in his epitaph, the cause of liberty. He would fling out too in short angry protests against his own share in this oppression, crying that his bones must be carried to Holyhead, for they could not rest in a country of slaves.

The misanthropic and the angry Swift are exaggerated in what may be called the Romantic account of him, which is still widely accepted. A later age saw in him elements of its own Rousseau and Byron, and completed the half-likeness out of its imagination. The result is not a true portrait. Where, in his writings, is the romantic Swift? Chiefly in the Journal. There he shows much tenderness, some self-pity, and there are frequent notes of nostalgia; he longs to be 'back to his willows in Ireland'. 'I do not say I am unhappy at all, but that everything is tasteless to me for want of being where I would be.' And there is something romantic in his later attitude of the lonely giant, the Lear or Timon who stands above the world by his bitter knowledge of its evil and folly. But it is an attitude he never keeps up for very long. The romantic Swift, in truth, is chiefly the Swift of legend, as Scott gathered and perfected it. The legend is very largely untrue. The secret marriage, the various pathetic and terrible 'scenes' with Vanessa and Stella, are not authentic biography.

Swift fought against the Romantic in himself – on the whole successfully. In *Cadenus and Vanessa* we see that 'romance' dissolved into reason, wit and humour. Vanessa's fate was most tragic, but it is not proved that Swift could have prevented it or was very greatly to blame. Upon Stella's death he wrote her *Character* with the deepest affection and sense of loss, but the feeling is perfectly controlled: 'I knew her from six years old, and had some share in her education, by directing what books she should read and perpetually instructing her in the principles of honour and virtue; from which she never swerved in any one action or moment of her life. She was sickly from her childhood until about the age of fifteen, but then grew into perfect health, and was looked upon as one of the most beautiful, graceful, and agreeable young women in London, only a little too fat. Her hair was blacker than a raven, and every feature of her face in perfection.' A romantic might take his cue from *hair blacker than a raven*; but he could make no use of *a little too fat*.

Here we see why the pessimistic, angry, romantic Swift is only the smaller part of the real man. He was rational – sometimes cheerfully, sometimes sternly – with himself, and he kept self-control. We see here too what was one of the means of his success, as well as the proof of it – friendship. His many friendships, of which that with Esther Johnson was the greatest, evinced the truth of his rational humanism. His deepest misanthropy was after all not bottomless, for the true account of it was this: 'I hate the animal called man, but I love John, Peter, Thomas, and so forth.' His friendships ranged from the highest to the lowest; for though he said he liked no titles but those on books, he made exceptions for more than one lord and lady; and he had humble friends at Quilca and in the Liberties. But he preferred those of middling rank – and, later on, of middling understanding too, for he did not feel equal to making close acquaintance with another generation of wits; his own brilliant contemporaries of Queen Anne's London were enough. In those days of power he helped every deserving man but himself; he could say that he had placed fifty, and not one of them a relation. He kept Steele in office, though he got no thanks for it. He did his best to preserve Addison's friendship in the midst of the political feud. With the wits of those great days – Pope, Gay, Arbuthnot, Bolingbroke – he kept up a continuous correspondence as long as they all lived. His letters, written rapidly and without thought of publication, fill many volumes. They are as interesting almost as anything he wrote.

IRVIN EHRENPREIS

Swift on Liberty (1952)

I

SWIFT shared none of Johnson's disdain for political liberty. So far from being an amusement to 'keep off the *taedium vitae*', it was the theme of his epitaph. His resentment at servility or tyranny in others appears in the unbridled expression of his letters after 1727. 'Enslaved', 'slavish', 'slaves' are repeated to monotony among the comments on Ireland. The bitterness increased until he called for an English burial to rescue his corpse from a land of slaves. The great shortcoming of a Dublin residence, he said, was the frustration of his zeal for freedom – making him melancholy, sick, and ill-tempered. His political activities were inspired by a frantic emotion.

What this ideal of liberty meant has always been obscure. Swift assumed that normal people agree on the ethics of behavior when they are not upset by passions or misled by propagandists. He had a Houyhnhnm's contempt for any fine-spun probing of social issues. The consequent lack of self-analysis has made for continual ambiguities, and the term needs definition: 'freedom' or 'liberty' as opposed to slavery, tyranny, and oppression.

II

Swift, like Burke, discouraged aimless, 'Laputan' speculations about the meaning of liberty or any matter with no practical immediacy. Recognizing, however, the semantic difficulties of so elusive a concept, he did try to limit it. For him it had no body apart from his general political theory and was inseparable from an understanding of the whole constitution. By 'liberty' Swift meant only a condition of the citizens of a parliamentary monarchy. They were free when ruled by laws made with their own consent. 'Government without the consent of the governed, is the very definition of slavery' (*Works*, VI 115).[1]

This Lockian eloquence received immediately an un-Lockian

qualification: since power follows property, only the consent of the substantial landowners – or a majority of them – need be counted. 'The possessors of the soil are the best judges of what is for the advantage of the kingdom.'[2] Even their part in lawmaking was mainly the election of M.P.s who, in co-operation with king and peers ruled the country. For all citizens who then adhered to the established constitution (of State *and* Church), liberty involved the usual civil rights and the benefits of common and statute law.

The sovereignty of a free country resided in this legislative body, to whose decrees *every* person owed unqualified obedience. 'The freedom of a nation consists in an absolute unlimited legislative power, wherein the whole body of the people are fairly represented, and in an executive duly limited' (*Works*, III 74). In this axiom, although Swift followed Locke practically *literatim*, he stopped carefully short of the other's insistence that the legislative is a fiduciary power which the people should resist when misused. E. D. Holst marks this difference between the two men as fundamental.[3] Swift recognized no limitation on the united legislature, but divided it into three sections, which had to agree for their authority to be effective: a chief executive, the King; an aristocracy, the House of Lords; and the people, or the House of Commons. Each element of the government must live up to its responsibilities, but none might overstep its limitations. 'In all free states, the evil to be avoided is tyranny, that is to say, the *summa imperii*, or unlimited power solely in the hands of the One, the Few, or the Many' (*Works*, I 262). Out of the delicate tensions of these freedoms and strengths – 'the nobility often contending for power, the people for liberty, and the King for absolute dominion'[4] – arose the most reliable form of political liberty.

So elastic a concept needed clarification. This Swift gave not by a statement of measurable distinctions, but through examples. Henry VIII had been overweening toward his parliament and people; so his rule was tyrannical. During the Civil Wars, a mad minority had overcome the king, the legislature, and the citizens; Charles I had died on a scaffold rather than betray the liberties of his people. Under the Marlborough-Godolphin coalition the Whigs had exceeded their bounds and outrageously restricted royal prerogative, or liberty. Other illustrations, from Greek, Roman, and British history, fill *A Discourse of the Contests and Dissensions* and *An Introduction to the History of England*. Swift traced the balance from its low point at the Norman Conquest to its height in the middle of Elizabeth's reign, then through an erratic decline.

From reason, nature, and common sense, he drew the principle that a mixed government provided the most freedom; he also acknowledged that the form dated back to antiquity. However, he usually took it to be an institution typical of the Goths, whom he associated with freedom. To them Swift also attributed the frequent parliaments which he thought were a guarantee of liberty, although Burke feared them as mischievous. In 1735 Swift cursed Walpole for crushing the last stronghold of 'the Gothic system of limited monarchy' and with it English liberty.

Such a breakdown followed the triumph of the party principle. Swift loathed parties as much as Burke respected them. In *Gulliver* he proposed that the brains of rival leaders be interchanged. Burke's remark that 'whatever their merits may be, they have always existed, and always will', would have seemed to him the coolest cynicism. Swift believed that the ambitions of leading men drove them to organize groups of supporters who in return for trivial satisfactions joined to ruin national liberty. Being pro-Tory, yet against all parties, he insisted that the Tories were the natural majority and spoke for the country. Like Johnson he defined 'Whig' as the 'name of a faction', an inconsiderable minority, selfishly clutching at power and operating against the interests of the nation. To account for the success of such a clique, he argued that

> there cannot, properly speaking, be above two parties in such a government as ours; and one side will find themselves obliged to take in all the subaltern denominations of those who dislike the present establishment, in order to make themselves a balance against the other; and such a party, composed of mixed bodies, although they differ widely in the several fundamentals of religion and government, and all of them from the true public interest; yet, whenever their leaders are taken into power, under an ignorant, unactive, or ill-designing prince, will probably, by the assistance of time or force become the majority, unless they be prevented by a steadiness, which there is little reason to hope, or by some revolution, which there is much more reason to fear. (*Works*, v 475)

Through this rationalization he arrived at the conviction that Whig supremacy meant party rule and therefore tyranny, while any Tory advance meant government above party and therefore freedom.

Passive obedience to the throne, divine right, and absolute monarchy seemed dangers rather than ideals to Swift. Only the combined legislative body could demand complete obedience; but that demand was legitimate and without restriction. Coleridge's sneers at the political idea of absolute sovereignty would not have amused Swift. Divine right, however, was dismissed as absurd; Swift attributed the stability of an inherited throne (as Sir William Temple did) to the veneration inspired by a long and unbroken succession. His case for monarchy, like Burke's, was 'historical and practical, rather than sentimental and romantic'. Swift always condemned absolutism, regarding with horror what he considered the approach of it in England. To prevent it he opposed a standing army and believed that frequent parliaments were indispensable.

Without relaxing his confidence in monarchical government, Swift liked to describe the king as servant of the nation. Burke, while wary of this phrase, was at one with him in assuming (like most eighteenth-century publicists) that government should be for the sake of the governed, and not the governors. Swift insisted on a reciprocity between prince and subjects, the one deserving his place to the degree that he fulfilled his responsibilities, the others owing allegiance so long as their rights were respected. He even granted the theory of a contract obliging the king to govern by law and the people to obey and serve. However, he admitted that a tyrannical monarch, who set himself above the laws and took to himself the powers of the whole legislature, was to be resisted.

Intermediary between the prince and commons stood the lords. A slavish dependence of the king upon his people was a sign of arbitrary power in the latter, a symptom that national liberty had failed. The great purpose of the peerage was to assert royal prerogative against popular encroachments, freedom against dictatorship. Admitting that the lower house was more representative than the upper, Swift defended the lords mainly as a counter-weight necessary to maintain free government. This is the argument of the *Contests and Dissensions*: from an impeachment of the five Whig lords in 1701 could issue only a tyranny of the Many over the One and the Few. As Burke would have said, 'The tyranny of a multitude is but a multiplied tyranny.'[5]

Swift defended the peerage creations of December 1711, which forced a peace treaty through the upper house. In this reversal of the impeachment crisis he put forward the same argument: without a balance government was halted; the people and the court agreed on peace; a negligible minority, corrupted by republican principles, blocked it. Yielding to the Whig lords would be yielding to tyranny. It was time for the queen to restore the equilibrium that meant freedom.

So long as the restoration could be amicably effected, there was no justification for revolt. But if one branch resisted the others to the point of violence, it was time – provided the cause was adequate – for rebellion. The rarity of a situation like that impressed him, as it did Burke, more than anything else. Only the most extreme mistreatment should induce a nation to stray from peace and obedience. When, however, the benefits of a revolution outweighed its innumerable evils, the people might indeed fight.

Ordinarily, though, obedience to the law was the soundest expression of a subject's liberty. In Montesquieu's words, 'Liberty is a right of doing whatever the laws permit.'[6] If Locke thought the end of law was 'to preserve and enlarge freedom', Swift believed freedom was preserved and enlarged only in law. Let the legislature modify it as they would, every citizen must acquiesce in the changes. Unless even the king was required to obey its laws – an echo of James I and of Locke – no country could pretend to freedom. For Lilliput he imagined a special set of privileges to reward whoever was strictly law-abiding for more than six years. When he himself ignored certain English laws, Swift argued that these had no application in Ireland.

In order to be practically effective, laws must, as Locke had shown, command the assent of a majority, not indeed of all people, but of the landowners. While it was everyone's duty to submit to the laws, it was the proprietor's responsibility to direct them – a doctrine close to Burke's 'trusteeship' of the aristocracy. Without going so far as Johnson who would have turned out (if he had any) those tenants who refused to vote for his own candidate, Swift did deliver it as a maxim that 'Law, in a free country, is, or ought to be, the determination of the majority of those who have property in land' (*Works,* I 279, also VI 195). From this electorate he, like Burke, carefully distinguished the 'lower sort', whom he sometimes called the 'people'. The liberties of manual and skilled laborers, small merchants, and farmers, granted them no active part in the government. He exhorted them to accept legislative decrees without question. As Walton had said, '*Laws are not made for private men to dispute, but to Obey.*'[7] Only with this understanding did either Swift or Burke claim that liberty was every man's birthright.

In defending Ireland, attacking Walpole, and defeating Wood's halfpence, Swift used 'freedom' and similar words with helpful concreteness. His proof that the descendants of English settlers in Ireland were enslaved, gathered in many of his characteristic arguments and was the precedent for Burke's and Johnson's still broader attitudes. Like all human beings – he began, agreeing with Locke's disciple, Molyneux[8] – the Anglo-Irish had a natural right to be free. They were the unconquered children of English citizens. Nevertheless they wanted every mark of liberty: freemen in London, or even Edinburgh, they were slaves in Dublin. They were denied freedom of trade and expression, and the typical powers of a free country. Their liberty of conscience was continually threatened, and they were delivered up to the whims of a political machine. They were deprived of the major public offices, which went to carpetbaggers from across the Irish Sea. The appearance of a triply-balanced constitutional monarchy approved by the nation, was a fraud: it was government by dictatorship. What Swift did for Ireland 'was from perfect hatred at tyranny and oppression'.[9] In 1710 he accused England of trying to enslave his compatriots, and he never discarded that conviction.

III

On two rights now taken to be necessary elements of a theory of liberty, Swift had no self-contained or systematic view. These were freedom of the press and freedom of conscience. He interpreted both only as aspects of larger issues. Speaking for his party, he never attacked the free press, or for that matter defined it. Swift thought all publications should be tolerated which did not threaten the constitution of England (as he understood that). But in 1708, commenting venomously on Tindal's *Rights of the Christian Church*, he suggested 'Why not restrain [i.e. deny] the press to those who would confound religion, as in civil matters?' (*Works*, III 124). And during the Harley–St John campaign for peace, he begged the secretary to 'make examples' of the opposition pamphleteers. Like the King of Brobdingnag, Swift 'knew no reason, why those who entertain opinions prejudicial to the public should not be obliged to conceal them . . . for a man may be allowed to keep poisons in his closets, but not to vend them about for cordials.'[10]

He certainly approved when fourteen booksellers and printers were arrested in the fall of 1711. Yet until that time he made capital in the

Examiner of the freedom which the Tories, after their success, had left temporarily to the fallen Whigs. Boastfully, he contrasted the new policy with the old restrictions: 'When the Whigs were in power, they took special care to keep their adversaries silent . . . though by a sort of indulgence which they were strangers to, we allow them equal liberty of the press with ourselves' (*Works*, v 35). Since liberty, of all sorts, was a warcry of the Whigs, he must have enjoyed seething them in their own milk.

Naturally Swift did not hesitate to change sides under Walpole, puff 'the old Whiggish principle . . . of standing up for the liberty of the press' (*Works*, vii 380), and condemn Walpole for following the course he himself had recommended to St John. One recalls Johnson's sceptical insight, 'The liberty of the press is a blessing when we are inclined to write against others, and a calamity when we find ourselves overborne.'[11] Swift would have argued that his stand had not shifted. When a Whig faction tried to monopolize Parliament and restrict the liberties of queen and people, their voices must be silenced. When Tory patriots were struggling to re-establish the constitution, however, it was outrageous for a tyrant to smother them. In his own light Swift was not inconsistent – the others were.

Concerning religious toleration his opinion was clear and straight-forward. The Established Church was as necessary a part of the constitution as the king; to reject either was to reject the whole. While he was willing to tolerate sects (only so much as the law allowed), he thought even 'the greatest advocates for general liberty of conscience' would admit that the growth of dissent ought to be curtailed (*Works*, iii 55). Swift granted the sects a full freedom of religion in the narrowest sense: the privilege of thinking as they liked or of practising their faith in private. He insisted, however, that they be restrained from voicing their conviction, persuading others to believe it, or putting it into effect. Johnson's summary of this issue is only a slight rephrasal of Swift's sentiments:

> People confound liberty of thinking with liberty of talking; nay, with liberty of preaching. Every man has a physical right to think as he pleases; for it cannot be discovered how he thinks. . . . But, Sir, no member of a society has a right to *teach* any doctrine contrary to what the society holds to be true.[12]

Further removed from the sectarian intensities of the Restoration,

Burke could match Swift's devotion to the Establishment without
sharing his narrowness.

Swift would have refused office or vote to the dissenters on two
grounds. First, they were themselves evangelical and intolerant; their
natural drive would be to corrupt the Church of England. Secondly,
their faith meant republicanism; granted authority, they would over-
throw the monarchy: 'a government cannot give them too much ease,
nor trust them with too little power' (*Works*, III 62). The Roman
Catholics, being no danger to the state, Swift did not fear. As a crushed
minority, they would be the first to suffer from a political fight. It was
the dissenters whose power was growing steadily and whose ancestry
sprang from the Civil War. Keeping these contrasts in mind, Swift
minimized those perils of Popery with which the Whigs beat their
dead opposition, while he unfailingly defended the sacramental test and
the penal acts. In these anxieties he anticipated Burke, whose otherwise
aggressive support of religious toleration seems well ahead of his time.
The privileges which Swift would not give dissenters, Burke denied to
atheists. The Tory saw Civil War in Presbyterianism; the Whig saw
Revolution in Free Thought. Neither feared the beaten Papacy.

IV

When Swift appealed in the *Drapier's Letters* to radical Whiggist
precedents, he named no author whose work had been done after 1700.
For these doctrines were not novel. They were neither original with
Swift nor consistent among themselves, and they passed only very
gradually from one political side to the other. As for party affiliations,
it would be less accurate to say that Swift became converted to the
Tories than that by 1710 the Tory leadership had been converted to
Swift's principles. According to pre-1685 standards he would have
seemed sharply anti-Tory.

In 1683 the convocation of Oxford University, triumphantly Stuart,
condemned twenty-seven propositions as damnable and destructive of
all human society. The first five were crucial, and of these Swift was
an exponent from the date of his earliest political tract: all civil authority
is derived originally from the people; there is a mutual compact, tacit
or expressed, between a prince and his subjects, and they are discharged
from their duties if he fails to perform his; if lawful governors turn
tyrants, they forfeit their right to the government; the sovereignty of

England is in the three estates – king, lords, and commons – and the king may be overruled by the other two; birthright and proximity of blood give no title to rule, and it is lawful to preclude the next heir from his succession to the crown. The twenty-two other propositions contained little that was distasteful to him.

During the revolution crisis, such theses took on a moderate complexion. At the trial of the seven bishops in the summer of 1688, Finch, Somers, and Pollexfen used several of 'Swift's' ideas for the defense: tripartite mixed government, the supremacy of law over the king, the sovereignty of the legislature. 'The whole legislative power', said Finch, 'is in the king, Lords, and Commons.'[13] The trial was a token that these conceptions were becoming acceptable not only to the Whigs but also to the more reasonable of their opponents. Although Somers and Pollexfen were lifelong Whig representatives, Finch sided with Sacheverell throughout his trial and was a leader of non-Jacobite Tories until the ministry of Harley and St John.

At the convention parliament the following year, the consensus of the speakers, including that wing of Tories led by Danby and Compton, tended to the existence of an original contract between king and subjects. Sir Robert Howard, a Whig, upheld the right of the people to take back power from a king who was not willing to rule by law. A member of strong Whiggish leanings, Sir George Treby, expounded the doctrines that government must be directed by a landowning minority and obeyed by all, that a king who broke his country's laws should be dethroned, and that true laws were made with the people's consent. Serjeant Maynard, also anti-Tory, called the English government a mixed one, 'not monarchical and tyrannous', located its beginning in the people, and put a limit beyond which a king might not transgress without rightful resistance from his subjects. Gilbert Dolben, a middle-of-the-roader, argued that the interest of the nation was the standard of good government. The Tory Sir Robert Sawyer reserved to the estates represented in the convention parliament the 'superiority of determination' of the government but granted the people themselves a power of consent.

Half a year earlier a letter to Princess Mary from Clarendon, the fading old Tory, had stated the religious views which were to guide the settlement and which were always Swift's:

> I can with a very good conscience give all liberty and ease to tender consciences, for in truth it is against all conscience to hinder men from

worshipping God their own way; but I cannot in conscience give those men leave (as far as lies in me to prevent it) to come into employments in the State, who, by their mistaken consciences, are bound to destroy the religion I profess, and, as they call it, the Northern Heresy. . . .[14]

Finally, the Declaration of Right, under which William accepted the throne, not only made the law superior to the king but included two of Swift's pet safeguards of liberty, the discontinuance of a standing army and the demand for short parliaments. All this congeries Swift eventually labeled 'old Whiggish', an expression with which the high Tory Charles Davenant had attacked the 'modern Whigs' of William's closing years.[15]

From 1690 to the accession of Anne, Robert Harley was piecing together his moderate Tory platform – a compound of the formulae just surveyed – and grouping his forces about the 'spirit which will maintain the ancient government of England in Church and State.'[16] In the Tory defense of Sacheverell, 1709–10, Harley's program became identified with the dominant party trend. 'The supreme power in this kingdom is the legislative power; and the Revolution took effect by the Lords and Commons concurring and assisting in it', said Sacheverell's first counsel, Harcourt; 'it is utterly unlawful to resist the supreme power.'[17] The second counsel, Samuel Dodd, heartily agreed with the Commons that 'the law of the land is the measure of the prince's authority'.[18] Of course all the managers pressed Clarendon's and Swift's interpretation of liberty of conscience. In a peroration to his defense, Sacheverell outlined that harmony and unity of a free country under one faith which was Swift's ideal:

So far was I from intending to persuade her majesty's subjects to keep up a distinction of parties and factions . . . that my aim was to persuade them to lay aside all distinctions, to unite in one well-compacted body, to be obedient to their governors, and to support the present establishment.[19]

By the time of Walpole's ascendancy it was true that Swift and other leading Tories, like Bolingbroke and Wyndham, stood for the 'Old Whig' principles, 'upon which Harley had consistently acted, and which Bolingbroke in the two sanest periods of his life professed'.[20] Feiling's report of an enlightened Tory of that time, Archibald Hutchison, might serve as a fragmentary account of Swift's ideology.

[He] repudiated any notion of divine right, arguing that a government's title came from the happiness of its subjects. He based his opposition on fact and law. The Septennial Act was a breach of trust with the constituencies, triennial parliaments were a gift of 'the late happy Revolution,' and there were natural rights which no House of Commons could take away. Long-lived parliaments meant long-lived pensions, and corrupt interests battening on the National Debt. A standing army inflamed Jacobite passion; martial law threatened our old liberty . . . he asked for a tightening-up of the property qualification for members, to fill the Commons again with 'gentlemen of free and independent fortunes.'[21]

The political philosophy of Swift's later career was no violation of his Queen Anne period. For him one may repeat B. H. Bronson's judgment of Johnson's character: 'the last two decades [are] marked by a resistance to dominant forces which is little different, at bottom, from that of the young iconoclast'. In either man the change of tone 'which he appears to have undergone is in reality rather outside him than within.[22]

Burke, whose devotion to 'manly liberty' was as vociferous as Swift's, went through an opposite course for parallel reasons.

> In his earlier career he saw authority and royal influence usurping our popular institutions, and so he withstood the influence of the Crown in the name of liberty. . . . The scene changed, and when the French Revolution had come, he saw in Radical ideals and popular movements a menace to the constitution from another side; and so he withstood them too.[23]

In Swift the rationalism of Locke and the ratiocination of Bolingbroke were still vital; in Burke they were deadwood, to be pushed aside by a mystical empiricism. Both men, however, reverenced the equipoise, the living unity of the constitution; both 'changed front without changing ground'.[24]

V

Far beyond party lines, the pedigree of these doctrines was lengthily respectable. For centuries, classical authors, especially Polybius, had been the acknowledged source of the idea of mixed monarchy; during the Civil War period it appeared chiefly as a royalist argument, the first important statement of it in political controversy being Charles I's reply to the Nineteen Propositions of 1642. Introduced by Jean Bodin's *République* (1576), the problem of sovereignty was made familiar to seventeenth-century England by Hobbes and Pufendorf. The merging of both ideas in the supreme authority of king-commons-nobles had, according to Holdsworth, been anticipated in 1610 by

James Whitelock[25] and in 1628 by Sir Edward Coke.[26] For them in turn precedents went back to Henry VIII. Soon after 1650 in England, mixed government and freedom began to be linked with Gothic institutions. Sir William Temple made the connection in his essay 'Of Heroic Virtue'.

The *salus populi* tradition is too common to bear pinning down. One of its forms was the proposition that rule by consent must be truly representative. This was joined in James Harrington's *Oceana* (1656) with the novel thesis that sovereignty derives from ownership of land.[27] For Harrington, 'Gothic' meant the decay of liberty; and he aspired to a commonwealth, not at all to a mixed monarchy. But his maxim, in becoming a commonplace, came to imply different conclusions from those which it had been formulated to support. It did not remain an argument against further concentration of landed property. Instead, it turned into a prop for the belief, a favorite of Swift and of the old country party, that landowners ought to control the government.

The idea of a landed qualification for members of parliament was of the Tories' stock-in-trade from the April, 1696, debate on it to the 1711 session when it was finally carried. Burke's qualms about the 'monied interest' were less radical than Swift's, but he did not veil his mistrust. In the 'warfare between the noble ancient landed interest, and the new monied interest',[28] both writers displayed the same loyalties.

Practically every one of Swift's tenets can in this manner be followed to an immediate source in some publicist famous during the later Stuarts' reigns: government above party, to Halifax; national religious conformity, to Hobbes; the identification of liberty with government by consent, to Sidney. Ultimately one whole aspect of Swift's 'freedom' went still further back, into the Middle Ages, while another leaned toward the French Revolution.

His ideal was a community in which political authority was combined with the control of land. He envisioned a people wholly under the power of laws that expressed their own customs and consent. Instead of concentrating this sovereignty, he distributed it over a legislative body with divided authority but harmonious aims. He desired a nation united under a single Church and prince, undisturbed by partisan rivalries. With these materials Swift built freedom into the very shape of the state; the citizen had a natural right to be free when he enjoyed the freedoms allowed him by a natural government. If he demanded more, he was making himself a tyrant.

But this was the medieval community, in which the 'combination of political authority with the control of land tended to destroy any clear distinction between public and private relations'.[29] A. J. Carlyle has shown that the peculiar marks of medieval polity were, first, the lack of an absolute human authority, the place of which was filled by the supremacy of customary law; and, second, the derivation of political power immediately from the people. As the head of the body politick, the medieval king was 'every inch a man', with no 'divine' right to his office.[30] When he ruled illegally, he deserved to be opposed. Resistance to an unjust authority, St Thomas taught, was not sedition.

Swift's affection for 'Gothick' institutions was thus a sign of his inner sympathies. Two massive expressions of social purpose were available to him – the first, 'an internal harmony among the parts of society'; the second, 'an equilibrium of conflicting interests'.[31] Of these he preferred the old to the new. Refusing to adapt himself to the clash of dissenter against Anglican, financier against proprietor, or Whig against Tory, as more than a passing malady, Swift remained negatively oriented to the social forces of his time. His rapport was with medieval political theory, which 'emphasizes the harmony between the individual and organized society . . . [and] sees political organization not as merely restrictive but as positively necessary to the fulfilment of human nature'.[32]

Yet he had to allow for the reality. When he dwelt upon the balance of powers characteristic of a free mixed monarchy and thereby settled the location of national sovereignty, he was admitting that the new age involved essentially conflicting interests within society, a fact inconsistent with his dislike of factions. In so resolving the sovereignty, however, he revealed again a medieval incomprehension of it. Swift was open to the same objection which under the early Stuarts any royalist might fairly have made to the embryonic theory that *potestas suprema* lay in the 'king in Parliament': 'in effect, it left the state with no sovereign at all, unless king and Parliament were in agreement'.[33] A distributed authority cannot be absolute and recalls the medieval disregard for the whole issue of sovereignty.

By promoting the doctrine of ministerial responsibility, Swift meant to defend monarchy. Actually he was in this way reducing the king to a symbol, replacing the triple by a duple balance, granting the impossibility of reconciling the rising with the declining powers, and accepting the supremacy of parliament alone.

Through his defense of Ireland he voiced a nationalism which would characterize Europe a hundred years after his death but which, once more, militated against his all-inclusive and harmonious community of the nation. Again the valid rights of one section were opposed to rights presumed equally valid by the remainder.

Now in neither his 'medieval' nor his 'modern' approach did Swift treat liberty as a philosophical entity. From the one point of view the problem did not exist at all, the individual having the same ends as the state. From the other, Swift begged the question by identifying freedom with the very structure of the state. When he expressed these incompatibilities in the misleading language of Locke, and used that language both ironically and hyperbolically, he invited the misunderstandings which this paper has been an attempt to correct.

Like Harley and Burke, Swift accepted the order of 1689 as finality. He worked to conserve the values of the society in which he had grown up. His belief in mixed government, his opposing of the old, well-born, country families to the *nouveau-riche* moneylenders and tradesmen, his resentment of the rabble, and his loathing for oppression were all typical of the late seventeenth century. Under these he exhibits those neo-classical traits made familiar by A. O. Lovejoy as uniformitarianism, rationalistic anti-intellectualism, and a negative philosophy of history.[34] The result is plain. Seeming to evolve politically, Swift was almost running in place. His loyalty to the declining landed aristocracy and his rejection of the middle-class merchants and financiers – who as Whig oligarchs were the new governors of Britain – precluded the success he desired in public life. Not 'an old redhair'd, murd'ring Hag, a crazy Prelate, and a royal Prude',[35] but a vision turned early, firmly, nobly, and mistakenly to the past, ruined his career.

NOTES

1. *The Prose Works of Jonathan Swift*, ed. Temple Scott (1897–1908). This edition is referred to in the text as *Works*.
2. *The Correspondence of Jonathan Swift*, ed. F. E. Ball (1910–14) III 21.
3. 'Swift's Politics' (unpublished Ph.D. dissertation, University of Wisconsin, 1941) fo. 29.
4. *Gulliver's Travels*, ed. A. E. Case (New York, 1938) p. 142.
5. *Correspondence of the Right Honourable Edmund Burke*, ed. Earl Fitzwilliam and Sir Richard Bourke (1844) III 147.
6. *The Spirit of the Laws*, trans. T. Nugent, rev. J. V. Prichard (1878) I 161.

7. *The Life of Mr. Richard Hooker* (Oxford World's Classics ed.: 1927) p. 207.

8. See William Molyneux, *The Case of Ireland's Being Bound* . . . (Dublin, 1698) p. 3 and *passim*.

9. Swift's *Correspondence*, V 64.

10. *Gulliver*, p. 134.

11. Quoted by J. W. Krutch, *Samuel Johnson* (New York, 1944) p. 73.

12. James Boswell, *The Life of Samuel Johnson*, ed. G. B. Hill, rev. L. F. Powell (Oxford, 1934) II 249.

13. Howell's *State Trials* (1816) XII 367; quoted by K. G. Feiling, *History of the Tory Party* (Oxford, 1924) p. 222.

14. *HMC Buccleuch*, II 31; quoted in Feiling, op. cit. p. 223.

15. See [Charles Davenant], *The True Picture of the Modern Whig* . . . (1701).

16. *HMC Portland*, III 634.

17. Howell's *State Trials*, XV 196–7.

18. Ibid. p. 214.

19. Ibid. pp. 374–5.

20. Feiling, *History of the Tory Party*, p. 480.

21. K. G. Feiling, *The Second Tory Party* (1938) pp. 25–6.

22. B. H. Bronson, *Johnson Agonistes* (Cambridge, 1946) p. 44.

23. John McCunn, *The Political Philosophy of Burke* (1913) p. 25.

24. John, Viscount Morley, *Burke* (1923) p. 245 (paraphrased).

25. W. S. Holdsworth, *A History of English Law* (1903–38) VI 84–5.

26. Sir Edward Coke, *Institutes* (1797) IV 1–3.

27. See Hugh F. R. Smith, *Harrington and His Oceana* (Cambridge, 1914) pp. 23–4 and *passim*.

28. *Reflections on the French Revolution*, ed. H. P. Adams, 2nd ed. (1927) p. 114; Burke's *Correspondence*, IV 352.

29. George H. Sabine, 'State', in *Encyclopaedia of the Social Sciences*, XIV 329–30.

30. F. W. Maitland, 'The Crown as Corporation', in *Law Quarterly Review*, XVII (April 1901) 132.

31. Paul K. Crosser, *Ideologies and American Labor* (New York, 1941) p. xiv.

32. Ewart Lewis, 'Organic Tendencies in Medieval Political Thought', in *American Political Science Review*, XXXII (Oct. 1938) 876.

33. Holdsworth, *English Law*, VI 85–6.

34. A. O. Lovejoy, ' "Nature" as Aesthetic Norm', in *Modern Language Notes*, XLII (1927) 446–7; *The Great Chain of Being* (Cambridge, Mass., 1936) p. 201; 'Optimism and Romanticism', in *PMLA* XLII (1927) 921–45.

35. Swift, 'The Author upon Himself', in *Poems*, ed. Harold Williams (Oxford, 1937) pp. 192–3.

LOUIS A. LANDA

Swift's Economic Views and Mercantilism (1943)

I

COMMENTATORS on Swift have traditionally, and quite properly, called attention to his preference for the landed interest of Great Britain, an attitude, it is usually pointed out, that stems from his Toryism. This view of Swift was, of course, current in his own day. Witness the words of one of his contemporaries, the anonymous author of *Torism and Trade Can Never Agree* (*c.* 1713), who attacked the *Examiner* – i.e. Swift – as a 'Daemon of Torism' who 'never fail'd to maul' the trading interest or eulogize the landed interest.

> Can we imagine that Persons who have two such Interests on their side, as a *Church Interest* and a *Land Interest* will be mindful of so Paltry an interest as Trade. The *Examiner*, who was possess'd more than any Man with the *Daemon* of *Torism*, was always launching out in his Panegyricks on the *Land Interest* and *Church Interest*, and tho he had not quite Front enough to stand by what his old Friend Castlemain said, that we should have no *Trade at all*, yet he never fail'd to maul it when ever it fell in his way.[1]

The purely partisan intention in this pamphlet – it is a violent attack on the French trade and the Tory sponsored commercial treaty with France at the Treaty of Utrecht – discredits the author's words; yet the equations set up, in which Toryism and land or Whiggism and trade become interchangeable terms, have often been accepted in modern scholarship, to the obscuration of the many individual differences that prevailed in the eighteenth century. Tories who defended the primacy of trade were not by any means as numerous as Whigs, but they did exist – for example, Sir Dudley North, Sir Josiah Child, and Charles Davenant, to mention three obvious instances. There is no reason to believe that these staunch Tories assumed in the eyes of their contemporaries a particularly anomalous or heterodox position, such as would logically be imposed on them by the oversimplified distinctions and formulae of scholars who are tempted to accept at face value the Whiggish insistence of our anonymous author, that 'the *Tories* will, upon all Occasions, be Enemies to Trade'.[2]

Swift, too, has suffered from the obscuration of individual differences. By insisting that he was a Tory in Church and a Whig in politics,[3] he himself protested against being enclosed within the confines of a term, a formula, a single group, although no one was more culpable in utilizing this device against opponents, as witness his persistent identification of Whigs with dissenters and Presbyterians with antimonarchists. In any case, the traditional view of Swift as a supporter of the Tory landed interest, true as it is and deserving of emphasis, need not preclude some emphasis on the importance with which he viewed trade. Indeed, Swift has not been given sufficient credit for his very strong realization of the importance of trade in the economy of a nation. This realization, it is true, came only belatedly out of his residence in Ireland after 1714; still he was no less wholehearted in his acceptance of certain principles of trade as necessary to Ireland or England's welfare than the most ardent Whig. These principles and the assumptions underlying them are constantly iterated in his Irish tracts; and on their application to Ireland's economy, as well as on the utilization of the land, Swift believed the welfare of the country depended. It will serve as a corrective to the conception of Swift as wholly of the landed Tory interest to examine his major ideas about trade, so often casual and unelaborated, and to relate them to the dominant economic theory of his day, that complex of ideas which Adam Smith attacked under the name of the commercial or mercantile system.[4]

II

Swift viewed problems of trade from the vantage of a small country lacking freedom of action and occupying, more or less, the status of a colony subject to restrictive colonial measures. It was this fact that stimulated him to concern himself with economic problems at all and to seek a sound economic solution consistent with the harsh realities of Ireland's dependency; and from this fact is, of course, derived the emotional tone of his tracts on trade. From 1720, when the first of these tracts appeared, to the end of his active writing career, he tirelessly, though rather hopelessly, protested England's restrictions on Ireland's trade. A passage from *A Short View of the State of Ireland* (1728) is typical:

> Ireland is the only Kingdom I ever heard or read of, either in ancient or modern story, which was denied the liberty of exporting their native commodities and manufactures wherever they pleased, except to countries at war with their own Prince or State, yet this by the superiority of mere power is refused us in the most momentous parts of commerce, besides an Act of Navigation to which we never consented, pinned down upon us, and rigorously executed, and a thousand other unexampled circumstances as grievous as they are invidious to mention. (*Works*, VII 85–6)[5]

These protests were not limited to works intended for publication. They appear in his private correspondence,[6] and he even issued them from the pulpit. One of his few sermons to come down to us, *On the Causes of the Wretched Condition of Ireland*, is devoted to an analysis of Ireland's economic difficulties, in which he complains bitterly that 'The first cause of our misery is the intolerable hardships we lie under in every branch of trade, by which we are become as hewers of wood, and drawers of water, to our rigorous neighbours' (*Works*, IV 212).

The discriminatory acts against which Swift wrote began after the Restoration and were part of the vigorous protectionist policy for home industries. Ireland was simply one of many victims. The Navigation Acts to which he often refers dated from 1663.[7] They constituted a series of enactments designed to make more difficult and expensive the importation into Ireland of commodities from the colonies and exportation from Ireland to the colonies. The Cattle Acts of the same period reduced drastically a thriving trade between England and Ireland in cattle and animal products, to the detriment of Irish raisers of cattle, sheep, and swine.[8] At the end of the seventeenth century came the restriction which Swift terms 'this fatal act', 10 & 11 Wm. III, c. 10, designed to prevent the Irish woollen industry from competing with English growers and manufacturers by prohibiting the exportation of woollen goods from Ireland to any country except England. These discriminatory acts, which seemed so unjust to Swift and other Irishmen, were viewed in a different light by the English, who merely had been putting into effect the prevailing mercantilist principle that a colony or dependent nation is intended to serve the national economic interest of the mother country.

The colonial relationship between England and Ireland by which

English mercantilists justified their treatment of Ireland was expounded at length at the end of the seventeenth century by John Cary, famous merchant of Bristol and a correspondent of John Locke:

> We come now to speak of *Ireland*; which of all the Plantations setled by the *English* hath proved most injurious to the Trade of this Kingdom, and so far from answering the ends of a Colony, that it doth wholly violate them; for if People be the Wealth of a Nation, then 'tis certain that a bare parting with any of them cannot be its Advantage, unless accompanied with Circumstances whereby they may be rendered more useful both to themselves, and also to those they left behind them, else so far as you deprive it of such who should consume its Product and improve its Manufactures you lessen its true Interest, especially when that Colony sets up as Separate, and not only provides sufficient of both for its self, but by the Overplus supplys other Markets, and thereby lessens its Sales abroad. . . .
>
> Nor is there any reason to be offered why *Ireland* should have greater Liberty than *our other Plantations* [italics mine], the inhabitants whereof have an equal Desire to a free Trade, forgetting that the first design of their Settlement was to advance the Interest of England, against whom no Arguments can be used which will not equally hold good against *Ireland*.
>
> 1. As it was settled by Colonies spared from *England*.
> 2. As it hath been still supported and defended at the Charge of *England*.
> 3. As it hath received equal Advantages with the other Plantations from the Expence *England* hath been at in carrying on Wars Abroad and Revolutions at Home . . . so that 'twould be a piece of great Ingratitude for the Free-holders of *Ireland* unwillingly to submit to any thing whereby the Interest of England may be advanced. . . .[9]

Cary's words are echoed by Charles Davenant, who maintained that Ireland is England's colony 'by the Interpretation both of Law and Reason' and that 'it seems the Right of *England*, and as well for the Benefit of *Ireland* its best and noblest Colony, that the Legislative Authority here should . . . make such Regulations and Restrictions, relating to Trade especially, as shall be thought for the Weal-Publick of both Countries'.[10]

These are merely statements of the old colonial policy as it was also being applied to the American colonies, and thus the English had accepted economic dogma as their support when they restricted or abolished those branches of Irish trade and industry which operated to the disadvantage of English trade and industry. Even those who were moved by a genuine consideration for the ills of Ireland did not question the rightness of this principle, for example, Swift's patron, Sir

William Temple, whose *Essay upon the Advancement of Trade in Ireland*
appeared in 1673:

> one Thing must be taken notice of as peculiar to this Country [Ireland],
> which is, That as it is the Nature of its Government, so in the very improve-
> ment of its Trade and Riches, it ought to be considered not only in its own
> proper Interest, but likewise in its Relation to *England*, to which it is
> subordinate, and upon whose Weal in the main that of this Kingdom
> depends, and therefore a Regard must be had of those Points wherein the
> Trade of *Ireland* comes to interfere with any main Branches of the Trade
> of *England*; in which Cases the Encouragement of such Trade ought to
> be either declined or moderated, and so give way to the Interest of Trade
> in *England*, upon the Health and Vigour whereof the Strength, Riches and
> Glory of his Majesty's Crown seems chiefly to depend.[11]

After the turn of the century the same view was set forth by Sir Francis
Brewster, who argued for a union between Ireland and England, yet
insisted in the same breath that even from union Ireland could not
expect equality in matters economic: 'I do not mean, nor would insinuate, that all the Priviledges and Immunities *England* hath in Trade
and Manufactures, should be allow'd to *Ireland*; but only encouraged
in such a way as will advance *England* in theirs.'[12] Among the Irish
expounders of mercantilism in Swift's day was Arthur Dobbs, who
pleaded for the removal of restrictive measures not so much on the
grounds that such action would be right but that it would be more
profitable: the people of Ireland 'in the Possession of their Properties,
Rights, and Privileges, *consistent with the good of its Mother Country*
[italics mine] . . . will be of the greatest Moment to them, in contributing to support the Honour and Dignity of the Crown, and the
Power, Wealth, and Naval Strength of Britain'.[13]

Swift does not challenge the rightness of the mercantilist attitude
toward a dependent kingdom or the justice of restricting a dependency
in the interests of the mother country. To have done so, as he must
have realized, would have been to run counter to widely accepted
views. Instead he bases his arguments on another level – a constitutional
one. Whatever his real interpretation of the constitutional relation
between England and Ireland or his views of the respective rights of
native Irish and Anglo-Irish,[14] he saw the necessity and persuasiveness
of arguing from the premise that the people of Ireland are in no way
distinct from the people of England, that they are fellow subjects,
citizens entitled to the same rights. His reliance upon this position is

presented most elaborately in *The Drapier's Letters*, for example in his comment on the Report of the Committee of the Privy Council at that point where the Report refers to the 'liberty or privilege of the King's subjects of Ireland'. Swift challenges the implication that the liberty or privilege of the Irish subject is different from the liberty or privilege of the English subject:

> in specifying the word *Ireland*, instead of saying 'His Majesty's subjects,' it would seem to insinuate that we are not upon the same foot with our fellow-subjects in *England*; which, however, the practice may have been, I hope will never be directly asserted, for I do not understand that Poining's act deprived us of our liberty, but only changed the manner of passing laws here ... by leaving the negative to the two Houses of Parliament. But, waiving all controversies relating to the legislature, no person, I believe was ever yet so bold as to affirm that the people of Ireland have not the same title to the benefits of the common law, with the rest of His Majesty's subjects, and therefore whatever liberties or privileges the people of England enjoy by common law, we of Ireland have the same; so that in my humble opinion, the word *Ireland* standing in that proposition, was, in the mildest interpretation, *a lapse of the pen*. (*Works*, VI 77–8)

In another of the *Drapier's Letters* he protests against ignorant and weak people who refer to Ireland as a ' "depending kingdom," as if they would seem, by this phrase, to intend that the people of Ireland is in some state of slavery or dependence different from those of England' (*Works*, VI 113). There is no statute, Swift insists, that 'makes Ireland depend upon England, any more than England does upon Ireland'. All that can be said is that the two have the same king: 'We have indeed obliged our-selves to have the same king with them, and consequently they are obliged to have the same king with us' (*Works*, VI 113).[15]

It was doubtless Swift's intention that these passages should be read as a challenge to the recent act of the English parliament which had affirmed in no uncertain terms the political dependency of Ireland.[16] If he had accepted this subordinate status for Ireland, he could not have made, given the prevalent mercantilist view that a dependency has only inferior economic rights, as strong a case against England's treatment of Ireland. The restrictive measures under such a relationship were both legal and conformable to economic dogma. Swift prefers, therefore, to blacken England by showing, not merely that the restrictive policies are short-sighted and unprofitable, but that they are constitutionally invalid because they are based upon force and upon an illegal denial of

Irish rights as fellow-subjects. Thus we find him complaining, as a prelude to his analysis of Ireland's economic difficulties in his sermon *On the Causes of the Wretched Condition of Ireland*, that these difficulties 'are not to be remedied, until God shall put it in the hearts of those who are stronger to allow us the common rights and privileges of brethren, fellow-subjects, and even of mankind' (*Works*, IV 212).[17] In *A Short View of the State of Ireland* he writes that Ireland is prevented from exporting freely 'by the superiority of mere power', and he adds: 'It is too well known that we are forced to obey some laws we never consented to', a point he repeats in *The Story of an Injured Lady*.[18] It was necessary to exercise caution in presenting this theme, as Swift well knew from the fate of the Drapier's *Fourth Letter*[19] and his first pamphlet on Irish economic matters, *A Proposal for the Universal Use of Irish Manufacture*,[20] both of which had been charged with sedition. Possibly here is the reason that Swift used the idea of independence with restraint; but he left little doubt that he believed, as he wrote to the Earl of Peterborough after an interview with Sir Robert Walpole in 1726, that Irishmen were being denied 'a natural right of enjoying the privileges of subjects'.[21]

III

Much of Swift's comment on Ireland's economic condition is predicated on his belief that Ireland is potentially a great trading nation. In *The Drapier's Letters* he wrote that 'we are denied the benefits which God and Nature intended to us; as manifestly appears by our happy situation for commerce, and the great number of our excellent ports' (*Works*, VI 202). In a later Irish tract he remarked on 'the conveniency of ports and havens which Nature bestowed us so liberally', with the complaint that they are 'of no more use to us, than a beautiful prospect to a man shut up in a dungeon' (*Works*, VII 85). Thus the onus is on England for not permitting the utilization of these natural resources. He also affirmed that Ireland possessed another requisite of a great trading nation, potential richness in native products. Ireland 'is capable of producing all things necessary . . . sufficient for the support of four times the number of its inhabitants' (*Works*, IV 211). At another point he wrote: 'As to the first cause of a Nation's riches, being the fertility of its soil, as well as the temperature of climate, we have no reason to complain' (*Works*, VII 85). And again: 'Thus Ireland is the poorest of all civilized countries in Europe, with every natural advantage to make it one of the richest' (*Works*, VII 148). In the expression of these views he was echoing sentiments expressed by such English observers as Sir William Temple, Sir William Petty, Sir Frances Brewster, as well as many Irishmen, among whom were John Browne and Bishop Berkeley.[22] One passage from the *Dublin Society's Weekly Observations* may be taken as representative:

> The natural soil of this Island, and the number and Ingenuity of its Inhabitants, would under proper management, make it as remarkable for Wealth as it now is for Poverty. There is no Country in the Northern Parts of *Europe* which it does not equal in Fertility, and most of them it remarkably excels. . . . No Kind of Growth, that can be rear'd under a Northern Sun, has miscarried in this Climate.[23]

Although mercantilists stressed the primacy of manufactures and foreign trade, they had a definite realization of the importance of the land. There was due recognition that land, linked with labor, constituted a significant factor in the wealth of a nation. As one writer on trade expressed it at the end of the seventeenth century: 'Land is the Foundation, and regular Labour is the greatest Raiser of Riches.'[24] The concern of the mercantilist for the land and its products was expounded at length by Charles Davenant, who prefaced his remarks with the statement: '*That Gold and Silver are indeed the Measure of Trade, but that the Spring and Original of it, in all Nations, is the Natural or Artificial Product of the Country; that is to say, what their Land, or what their Labour and Industry produces.*'[25] The fertility of soil was important, among other reasons, because a country could thereby provide for its inhabitants and at the same time have a surplus to be exported, particularly in manufactured form. Thus John Bellers declared: 'Without we increase our Husbandry (by improving our land) we cannot increase our Manufactures, by which we should increase our Trade.'[26] The great emphasis in mercantilist literature is on exportations; natural resources are viewed mainly with an eye to what they will contribute to foreign trade. That Swift could think and write like his mercantilist contemporaries is evident from a list of rules he set forth as 'the true causes of any country's flourishing and growing rich'. The first of these rules is relevant at this point: 'The first cause of a Kingdom's thriving is the fruitfulness of the soil, to produce the necessaries and conveniences of life, not only sufficient for the inhabitants, but for exportation into other countries' (*Works*, VII 83).

It is particularly in his attitude toward exports and imports that Swift manifests his acceptance of prevalent English mercantilist theory. To a great extent his solutions for Ireland's economic problems are based on a fundamental mercantilist assumption, that importations are, economically speaking, an evil, that an excess of exports over imports – a favorable balance of trade – is the means by which a nation may be enriched. The expressions of this principle in the seventeenth and eighteenth centuries are numerous. 'The ordinary means', wrote Thomas Mun in *England's Treasure by Forraign Trade* (1664), 'to increase our wealth and treasure is by *Forraign trade*, wherein wee must ever observe this rule; to sell more to strangers yearly than we consume of theirs in value.'[27] By the turn of the century the principle had been so widely enunciated that Sir Francis Brewster could write: 'The Maxim is thread bare, *that no place can be Rich, where their Imports exceed their Exports*.'[28] In Ireland Bishop Berkeley posed the question: 'Whether that trade should not be accounted most pernicious wherein the Balance is most against us?'[29] The emphasis on exports and a favorable balance of trade is obvious; and the reasoning back of these general statements was as follows: if the imports from a foreign country to England exceed in value the exports to that country, an overbalance is created against England and in favor of that country, a situation which results in a flow of treasure into that country and the impoverishment of England; if, however, England's exports to that country exceed the imports, the balance is favorable and treasure flows in to enrich England. The concern of the mercantilist was in 'the balance of payments' in the sense that one nation in its commercial relation with another incurs a net balance of indebtedness, an obligation to pay in specie. This flow of specie from one nation to another was significant because of the importance attached to the national stock of money. Obviously the favorable balance of trade was a means of increasing that stock. A succinct statement of this fundamental mercantilist attitude was set forth in *The British Merchant*, a repository of orthodox mercantilism, under the heading of 'Propositions':

1. That the Prosperity and Happiness of this Kingdom depend very much upon our foreign Trade.

. . .

3. That we gain Gold and Silver from those Countries which do not sell us so great a value of Manufactures as they take from us; for in this case the Balance must be paid in Money.

4. That we must pay a Balance in Money to such Countries as sell more Manufactures than they take from us; and that the capital Stock of Bullion is diminished by such a Commerce, unless the Goods we import from an over-balancing Country shall be re-exported.

5. That we are most enriched by those Countries which pay us the greatest Sums upon the Balance; and most impoverish'd by those which carry off the greatest Balance from us.[30]

This reasoning Swift accepted. It is to be found both implicit and explicit in his Irish tracts, not elaborated, of course, because he has no desire to theorize – and no need to justify theory that so widely prevailed. He could merely apply the balance of trade theory to a particular situation and expect his reader to see its logic, as did the anonymous author of a tract sometimes attributed to Swift, *The Present Miserable State of Ireland*, who wrote: 'Our exportations to England are very much overbalanced by our importations; so that the course of exchange is generally too high, and people choose rather to make their remittance in specie, than by a bill, and our nation is perpetually drained of its little running cash' (*Works*, VII 162). In the *Answer to the Craftsman* Swift proposed ironically that Irish trade be operated for the benefit of England because the English 'have a just claim to the balance of trade on their side with the whole world' (*Works*, VII 223). And at various other points Ireland's trade with England is commented on with reference to its unfavorable balance (e.g. *Works*, VII 112, 140). The trade with France, on the contrary, received his approval, though hardly an enthusiastic one. 'If an original extract of the exports and imports be true, we have been gainers, upon the balance, by our trade with France, for several years past; and, although our gain amounts to no great sum, we ought to be satisfied, since we are no losers' (*Works*, VII 197). In *A Proposal for the Universal Use of Irish Manufacture* he credited the woollen trade with France with bringing in 'the little money we have to pay our rents and go to market'; but he was disturbed, obviously thinking of Ireland's depleted stock of money, that the country was paying for French wines in specie (*Works*, VII 18; cf. p. 88). Once again the anonymous *The Present Miserable State of Ireland* explicitly states Swift's position: he disapproved of Ireland's trade with 'the northern nations' because with them the Irish are 'obliged, instead of carrying woollen goods to their markets, and bringing home money, to purchase their commodities', whereas he approved the trades with France, Spain, and Portugal since they bring to Ireland 'moydores, pistoles, and louis-dores'. Like many of the mercantile writers of the seventeenth and early eighteenth centuries, Swift appeared to accept the view that profit or loss to a nation engaged in foreign trade should be judged by particular balances resulting from trade with separate countries rather than by the general balance accruing to the nation. Thus he judges the trade with England bad, with France good, and so on, though it is not altogether evident that he thought seriously about the matter. The validity of judging by particular or general balance was being vigorously debated in his day, the proponents of the East India Company defending the Indian trade, despite its unfavorable balance, on the ground that it contributed in the long run to a favorable general balance for the nation at large.[31]

Swift accepts without qualification the prevalent mercantilist distinction between importations of manufactured and of raw materials. Although importations of any kind were ordinarily looked at askance as being economically disadvantageous, there were degrees of badness. Importation of manufactured articles was worse than importation of raw materials. Raw material at least provided employment for the native worker, thereby circulating money and increasing internal trade, whereas the importation of the finished product tended to draw bullion from the nation, thus decreasing its wealth. Particularly bad were those imported manufactured articles which competed with the domestic product. Thus John Cary wrote: "tis a certain Rule, that so far as any Nation furnishes us with things already manufactured . . . so much less is our Advantage by the Trade we drive with them; especially if those Manufactures interfere with our own, and are purchased with Bullion.'[32] He applies this rule specifically to England's trade with Spain, Turkey, and Portugal, which 'are very advantagious, as they vend great Quantities of our Manufactures, and furnish us with Materials to be wrought up here' and to the African and West Indian trades, which are 'most profitable to the Nation, as they imploy more of our People at Home'.[33] In the widely circulated British Merchant, among the 'general Maxims in Trade which are assented to by everybody', appeared the following:

> Foreign Materials, wrought up here into such Goods as would otherwise be imported ready manufactured, is a means of saving Money to the Nation; and if saving is getting, that Trade which procures such Materials ought to be look'd upon as profitable. . . .
> That Trade is eminently bad, which supplies the same Goods as we

manufacture our selves, especially if we can make enough for our Consumption.[34]

In *The British Merchant* stress was laid on what was later called 'the balance of employment'. The argument was that those foreign countries which imported goods manufactured in England bought not merely these goods but also the labor engaged in making them. These foreign consumers thus contributed to the 'Employment and Subsistence of our People'. On the other hand, when the English imported manufactured goods, England paid for the labor in the country which produced and manufactured these goods.

> If his [the laborer's or manufacturer's] whole Time is taken up in working for the Consumption of the *Portuguese*; for instance, if his whole Wages are paid him by that Nation, he gains from *Portugal* the whole Value of his yearly Labour. And the same thing must be said of the *Portuguese* Manufacturer that works for the Consumption of the *English* Nation; he clears his whole Wages from this Kingdom.

Thus, the writer argues, 'It is certain, that all the Consumption of *Portugal* pays to the English Labourers, more than is paid by the Consumption of *England* to the Labourers of *Portugal*, is clear Gain to England, and so much Loss to *Portugal*.'

Among the contemporary Irishmen who advanced these views was John Browne, whom Swift attacked violently in *The Drapier's Letters* and later forgave and praised for his public spirit.[35] As a preliminary to his discussion of Ireland's trade Browne laid down certain general maxims, among which were the following:

> That Trade is the least beneficial, which takes of the primums of Manufactures, and not the Manufactures themselves, because it deprives the People of matter to work upon, and gives it to Strangers, *et Vice Versa*, that Trade is more advantagious which takes off our Manufactures, than that which takes primum only, because it pays not only for the Produce of our Lands, but for the Art and Labour of our People also.
>
> It is better to buy the primums of Manufactures from abroad, than the Manufacture itself, because in the first Case, Value issues only for the Materials, but in the last, we must not only pay for the Materials, but for the Labour and Art also which brought them to perfection.[36]

The viewpoints expressed by these writers find unqualified acceptance in Swift. His most direct statement of the important distinction between manufactured and raw materials is presented in *A Short View of the*

State of Ireland, where he lays down a set of maxims much in the manner of economic writers of the day. These are the 'rules generally known, and never contradicted . . . of any country's flourishing and growing rich', three of which have an application to the point under discussion:

> The second, is the industry of the people in working up all their native commodities to the last degree of manufacture.
> The third, is the conveniency of safe ports and havens, to carry out their own goods, as much manufactured, and bring in those of others, as little manufactured as the nature of mutual commerce will allow.
>
> .   .   .
>
> The fourteenth, is a disposition of the people of a country to wear their own manufactures, and import as few incitements to luxury, either in clothes, furniture, food or drink as they possibly can live conveniently without. (*Works*, VII 83, 84)

The same principles are pervasive in the Irish tracts, applied particularly to manufactured goods shipped in from England. With the Irish parliament powerless, where England was concerned, to impose duties or prohibit importations, Swift realized that appeals had to be made to the Irish people. Accordingly, with the publication of *A Proposal for the Universal Use of Irish Manufacture* in 1720, he began a campaign to persuade the Irish that their economic welfare depended upon a drastic reduction in their use of foreign commodities. He made shrewd use of patriotic feelings and resentment against England's restrictive policies to enforce his economic plea. In this first tract is also evident an appeal to readers who recognize the validity of the common mercantilist view that importation of manufactured articles hinders home industry whereas the substitution of a native product encourages domestic manufacturers, increases employment, stimulates internal trade, and reduces the flow of money abroad. Thus he pleaded with the Irish to wear only cloths of Irish growth and manufacture. The women are told that they will look as handsome in Irish 'stuffs' as in imported brocades. The wearers of silks, velvets, calicoes – all imported and finished materials – ought to be considered enemies of the nation. Here, too, is the first of several appeals to the Irish clergy to utilize only native cloths in their habits. The economic disadvantage of sending out raw materials to be manufactured and then imported in the finished product is clearly implied in his ironic treatment of the grievances that 'poor England suffers by impositions from Ireland'. One project on foot to relieve the distress of England is the shipment of Ireland's 'best wheaten straw' to Dunstable, to be made up into straw hats which the Irish will be obliged by law to import (*Works*, VII 23).

The mercantilist bias was persistent thereafter. In the Drapier's seventh Letter Swift complained that the importation of 'Indian stuffs, and calicoes' has been profitable to England and 'an unconceivable loss to us; forcing the weavers to beg in our streets' (*Works*, VI 189), an obvious bias against importations on the ground that they do not provide employment for home laborers. The same principle is involved in his remark on wool: 'Our own wool returned upon us, in English manufactures, to our infinite shame and damage; and the great advantage of England (*Works*, VI 189). He was particularly urgent in 1728 and 1729, when a succession of bad harvests aggravated Ireland's difficulties, that the 'ruinous importation of foreign luxury and vanity' be stopped and that the Irish 'utterly discard all importations which are not absolutely necessary for health or life' (*Works*, VII 138, 124). In *A Proposal That All Ladies Should Appear in Irish Manufactures* he stressed the economic evil of imported manufactured products in which foreign labor is embodied. He computed that Ireland imports annually 'ninety thousand pounds worth of silk, whereof the greater part is manufactured'. 'I allow', he added, 'that the thrown and raw silk is less pernicious, because we have some share in the manufacture' (*Works*, VII 199). The principle is given ironic statement in the *Answer to the Craftsman*, where he wrote that England 'may very reasonably demand the benefit of all our commodities in their natural growth, to be manufactured by their people, and a sufficient quantity of them for our use to be returned hither fully manufactured' (*Works*, VII 223; cf. p. 222).

In mercantilist literature the economic prejudice against importations in general is intensified in the case of importations of luxuries. Although there was some dissent or qualification, it was commonly believed that imported luxuries were economically indefensible. Sir Josiah Child wrote that '*Luxury* and *Prodigality* are as well prejudicial to *Kingdoms* as to Private *Families*; and that the expense of Foreign Commodities . . . is the worst expence a Nation can be inclinable to'.[37] Much criticism of England's trade with France was based on the supposedly harmful economic effects of importing luxuries. Thus John Cary wrote: 'the *French* Trade is certainly our Loss, *France* being like a Tavern, with whom we spend what we get by other Nations and 'tis strange, we should be so bewitcht to that People, as to take off their

Growth, which consists chiefly of things for Luxury, and receive a Value only for the Esteem we put on them'.[38] Both Sir Theodore Janssen and William Wood assented to the general maxim, 'That the importing *Commodities* of *mere Luxury*, is so much *real Loss* to the Nation as they amount to.'[39] To these writers and others, luxuries were economic evils because they were usually manufactured products and thus embodied foreign labor. Similar attacks appeared in Irish journals and tracts. 'The next thing I shall mention, highly prejudicial to Trade,' wrote Arthur Dobbs, 'is, our Luxury and Extravagance in Food, Dress, Furniture and Equipage.' 'What is spent in Luxury', he adds, 'is just so much lost to the Nation in the way of Trade: For if it be in foreign commodities, it increases our imports; and if in the things of our own Country . . . it lessens our Exports.'[40] The author of *An Inquiry into Some of the Causes of the Ill Situation of Ireland* (1732) complained bitterly that the Irish send to foreign markets 'the Necessaries of Life, and bring home Trifles; for Instance we send to *France Butter* and *Beef*. . . . In Return of these Necessaries what do we import from *France*, of any Value, but *Vanities for our Backs, Diseases for our Bodies, and Poverty and Idleness for our Manufacturers and Husbandmen?*' (p. 52). In Bishop Berkeley's *The Querist*, the attack on imported luxuries is a persistent note. Two queries may be taken as representative. 'Whether an Irish lady, set out with French silks and Flanders lace, may not be said to consume more beef and butter than a hundred of our laboring peasants?' 'Whether it be possible for this country to grow rich, so long as what is made by domestic industry is spent in foreign luxury?'[41]

To these voices Swift added his. Among the rules he laid down to make a country rich is the 'disposition of the people . . . to wear their own manufactures, and import as few incitements to luxury, either in clothes, furniture, food or drink as they possibly can live conveniently without' (*Works*, VII, 84). In his sermon on Ireland's economic condition he referred to the importation of luxuries as 'another cause of our low condition' (*Works*, IV, 213), and he wrote with animus, in the *Letter to the Archbishop of Dublin Concerning the Weavers*, against the 'vanity and luxury' of Irish women who deplete the nation's stock of money by their purchases of such importations as tea, coffee, chocolate, laces, silks and calicoes – all 'unwholesome drugs, and unnecessary finery' (*Works*, VII 140). In another tract he catalogued and computed the value of the 'ruinous importations of foreign luxury and vanity' (*Works*, VII 199), but pleaded for the continued importation of wine without duties on the ground that the people of no other nation are 'more in want of some cordial to keep up their spirits, than in this of ours' (*Works*, VII 197). Swift did not elaborate his objection to the importations of luxuries as distinct from other importations. Actually he tended to identify all importations as luxuries since Ireland could afford none; with the case against importations of any kind so strong, the case against imported luxuries was too obvious to need elaborated argument. It is of interest that Swift kept his argument against luxuries wholly on the economic level. Moral considerations did not enter the discussion.[42] He called for frugality and consumption of native products in the interests of native industries, without emphasizing that prodigality and high living were, as many mercantilists believed, in some special way corrupting and thus conducive to national weakness. Yet he did not align himself with those writers on trade who maintained that "'tis no wrong to the Commonwealth, if men of estates drink, drab, live profusely, and dye beggars, as long as every penny comes to the natives. . . . The mischief only is, when forraigners are the better for this disorder, for that does insensibly ruine the Commonwealth.'[43]

In the Drapier's seventh Letter Swift listed among the 'wishes of the nation' that the Irish parliament would declare 'by some unanimous and hearty votes, against wearing any silk or woollen manufactures, imported from abroad' (*Works*, IV 199). He expressed the same hope in the first of the Irish economic tracts and at least twice in tracts written in 1729 (*Works*, VII 19, 143, 199). As a matter of fact, the Irish parliament had passed resolutions against importation in 1703, 1705, and 1707, the wording of the first of which gives the impression that Swift had taken it as the theme of his *Proposal for the Universal Use of Irish Manufacture*:

> *Resolved, Nemine Contradicente.* That by Reason of the Great Decay of Trade and Discouragement of Exportation of the Manufactures of this Kingdom, many poor Tradesmen are reduced to extream Want and Beggary. Resolved, Nemine Contradicente, That it will greatly conduce to the Relief of said Poor, and to the Good of the Kingdom, that the Inhabitants thereof should use more of the Manufactures of this Kingdom in their Apparel, and the Furniture of their Homes.[44]

What effect these resolutions had may easily be inferred. Swift may or may not have known of them; in any case it is difficult to believe that he had any faith in the efficacy of such resolutions. His was, of course, anything but a lone voice pleading for wider use of native products and for decreased importations, as an examination of the pages of the *Dublin Journal* and the *Tribune* and of the tracts of such public-spirited Irishmen as Berkeley and Madden will reveal.[45]

In his pleas for reduced importations Swift used, in support of his arguments, an analogy from personal finance. This analogy, of long standing in mercantilist theory, assumed the resemblance between the income of an individual and that of a nation. Just as an individual spending in excess of his income threatens himself with debt, poverty, and eventual ruin, so does a nation whose importations exceed exportations tend toward the same condition by virtue of the decrease in its treasure. The analogy was widely used, and in Swift's own library it was to be found in the economic writings of Sir William Temple and John Locke.[46] The statement of it by John Pollexfen, one of the Commissioners of Trade and Plantations, is representative:

> It is with Nations as with Families: Those Masters that are careful and good Husbands themselves, and keep their Servants to their Labour, and frugal in their Expences, generally thrive most; so with Nations, those that have the most Industrious People, and are most Parsimonious, will be the Richest. . . .
>
> A Gentleman that hath but 500 *l per Annum*, that is Industrious with his Servants in Husbandry, and content with his own, for Food and Apparel, and careful tó avoid unnecessary Outgoings and Expences, may bring Money into his House and keep it too; but a Gentleman that hath 1000 *l per Annum*, that keeps Idle Servants, despises his own Food and Cloathing, and instead thereof takes in Silks, Wines, and dear bought Commodities from Abroad in the room of them, at the end of the Year either cannot bring Money into his House, or not keep it long because of his Debts: The same with Nations that . . . despise their own Commodities, and are fond of those that are far fetcht, and dear bought. That undeniable Maxim, *That the way to be Rich is to be careful in Saving, as well as industrious in Getting*, hath the same reference to Nations as to particular Persons, or Families.[47]

Swift uses the analogy several times. In the *Letter to the Archbishop of Dublin Concerning the Weavers* he wrote:

> If a private gentelman's income be sunk irretrievably for ever from a hundred pounds to fifty, and that he hath no other method to supply the deficiency, I desire to know . . . whether such a person hath any other course to take than to sink half his expenses in every article of economy, to

save himself from ruin and the gaol. Is not this more than doubly the case of Ireland . . . ? Therefore instead of dreams and projects for the advancing of trade, we have nothing left but to find out some expedient whereby we may reduce our expenses to our incomes. (*Works*, VII 139; cf. pp. 124-5, 195)

Even on occasion where he does not make overt use of the analogy, Swift appears to think of the economy of a nation as being that of a family or individual writ large.

From the assembled evidence it is reasonable to conclude that Swift was fully aware of the importance of both the trading and the landed interests in the economy of a nation. His awareness of their relationship is evident throughout the Irish tracts, where he frequently mingles proposals for both. There is a sense of urgency in his discussion of the problems of trade, significantly not less strong than in his discussions of the problems of agriculture. Of the extent of his reading in economic literature and of his knowledge, there is not much to be said. His library, with only a few works in the field,[48] suggests that his reading was in no way extended, though we need not assume that his reading was limited to books he owned or preserved. It would be utter folly to make serious claims for Swift as an economic thinker. He utilized the same pleas and arguments to be found in such Irish contemporaries as Berkeley, Prior, Dobbs, Browne, and in the Irish journals. The atmosphere was thick with the assumptions of mercantilism, and these he accepted without criticism, applying them to Ireland. It was not part of his purpose to be either systematic or independent; he was simply adapting the commonly accepted principles of the day to an instance of special pleading using invective, irony, cajolery – all the arts of attack and persuasion so manifest in his political and religious writings – to mitigate Ireland's plight.

The reader of the Irish tracts is likely to suffer from the delusion – perhaps intentionally created by Swift – that Ireland's case was unique, that Ireland was an isolated instance, a country singled out by England for oppression and restrictive measures. It is important to correct this impression by viewing the economic legislation as part of the trend toward protectionism which became increasingly a dominant aspect of mercantilism in the last part of the seventeenth century. 'All the Nations of *Europe* . . . concur in this *Maxim*,' wrote an author in *The British Merchant*, 'That the less they consume of foreign Commodities, the better it is for them' (I, 14). The logic of this position necessitated the discouragement of imports, and England applied this logic to India, to France, to its colonies in America, as well as to Ireland, 'its best and noblest Colony', to use the words of Charles Davenant. The English woollen industry that acted as a pressure group to force the Act against Ireland in 1699 is not to be distinguished from the woollen industry that fought violently against the East India trade and achieved the protection for home industries enacted in 1700. The conceptions of national self-interest and self-sufficiency rooted deeply in mercantilist thought dictated a policy towards Ireland's competitive industries not to be distinguished from the policies toward the competitive industries of Turkey or Spain. Religious and political issues cut athwart English economic policies in the treatment of Ireland; but the fundamental fact is that the English, in their desire to secure the national welfare by vigorous protection of home industries, looked upon Ireland as a dependency which must not be permitted to become a trade rival. It was the situation created by this attitude that gives meaning to almost everything Swift wrote concerning the trade of Ireland.

In the last analysis Swift, it may be freely admitted, was an ardent defender of the landed interest. 'I ever abominated', he wrote to Pope in 1722, 'that scheme of politics . . . of setting up a moneyed interest in opposition to the landed: for I conceived, there could not be a truer maxim in our government than this, that the possessors of the soil are the best judges of what is for the advantage of the kingdom.'[49] These words echo what he had written a decade earlier in his reference to an 'acknowledged maxim' of the Whig party 'as dangerous to the constitution as any I have mentioned: I mean, that of preferring, on all occasions, the moneyed interest before the landed' (*Works*, IX 231). Nor can the reader of the Irish tracts ignore the persistent emphasis embodied in the statement that 'There is not an older or more uncontroverted maxim in the politics of all wise nations, than that of encouraging agriculture' (*Works*, VII 134). What must be guarded against, in the interest of a better balanced conception of Swift, is permitting these statements to obscure the fact that he recognized the importance of trade, particularly after 1714. The Swift of the *Examiner* who 'never fail'd to maul' trade was transformed into a person who realized that great benefits would accrue to Ireland if she were permitted liberty of trade.

NOTES

1. p. 16. 'Trade' is used in this pamphlet – and throughout this article – in one of the usual eighteenth-century acceptations: foreign trade. Although I have been unable to trace the remark of Swift's 'Old Friend Castlemain', the allusion must be to the husband of the mistress of Charles II. Roger Palmer, Earl of Castlemain (1634–1705), an ardent apologist for Catholicism and a member of a secret council to James II, was tried for complicity in the Popish Plot. By linking Swift with him (there is not, so far as I am aware, any evidence that the two were acquainted), the author of the pamphlet was making the usual implication that Tories and Papists are one and the same.

2. *Torism and Trade Can Never Agree* (n. d.) p. 1. Cf. Swift's attributing to the Whigs a maxim 'dangerous to the constitution': '. . . that of preferring, on all occasions, the moneyed interest before the landed' (*The Prose Works of Jonathan Swift, D. D.*, ed. Temple Scott, 12 vols (1897–1908) IX 231, hereafter referred to as *Works*).

3. *Works*, III 214; V 65. Cf. also *The Correspondence of Jonathan Swift, D. D.*, ed. F. Elrington Ball (1910–14) II 279, 354.

4. There has been little attempt by scholars to relate Swift's economic views to contemporary economic theories. In 'A Modest Proposal and Populousness', in *Modern Philology*, XL (1942) 161–70, the present writer has related *A Modest Proposal* to prevailing theories of population.

5. For similar complaints see also *Works*, VI 201; VII 66, 100, 138, 157 ff, 195, 198, 220.

6. For example, *Correspondence*, III 311.

7. The chief Navigation Acts which crippled the Irish trade were 15 Charles II, c. 7; 22 & 23 Charles II, c. 26; 7 & 8 William III, c. 22.

8. The Cattle Acts were 15 Charles II, c. 8; 18 Charles II, c. 23; 20 Charles II, c. 7; 22 & 23 Charles II, c. 2; 32 Charles II, c. 2. See A. E. Murray, *A History of the Commercial and Financial Relations between England and Ireland from the Restoration* (1903) pp. 23 ff.

9. *An Essay on the State of England in Relation to Its Trade, Its Poor, and Its Taxes* (Bristol, 1695) pp. 89, 105–6. In *The Case of Ireland's Being Bound by Acts of Parliament in England, Stated* (1698), William Molyneux, whose arguments for Ireland's independence impressed Swift, denied that Ireland 'is to be look'd upon only as a *Colony* from *England*' – a view without the 'least *Foundation* or *Colour* from *Reason* or *Record*' (1720 ed. p. 125). Cary answered Molyneux on this point in *A Vindication of the Parliament of England, in Answer to a Book, Written by William Molyneux of Dublin, Esq.* (1698) pp. 123–4; see also *An Answer to Mr. Molyneux* (1698) pp. 140 ff, a work credited to Cary.

10. *An Essay upon the Probable Methods of Making a People Gainers in the Ballance of Trade* (1699) pp. 106. 120.

11. *The Works of Sir William Temple* (1731) I 112–13.

12. *New Essays on Trade* (1702) pp. 75–6; cf. also p. 71.

13. *An Essay on the Trade and Improvement of Ireland* (Dublin, 1729) p. 66. See also *Works*, VI 188, where Swift uses a similar argument: 'I conceive this poor unhappy island to have a title to some indulgence from England; not only upon the score of Christianity, natural equity, and the general rights of mankind; but chiefly on account of that immense profit they receive from us; without which, that kingdom would make a very different figure in Europe, from what it doth at present.'

14. In *Intelligencer*, no. 19, he wrote: 'what is lawful for a subject of Ireland, I profess I cannot determine' (*Works*, IX 327). Cf. also *The Drapier's Letters*: 'Then I desire, for the satisfaction of the public, that you will please to inform me why this country is treated in so very different a manner, in a point of such high importance; whether it be on account of Poining's act; of subordination; dependence; or any other term of art; which I shall not contest, but am too dull to understand' (*Works*, VI 149). On the problem of Swift's

attitude toward the native Irish and the Anglo-Irish, see Daniel Corkery, 'Ourselves and Dean Swift', in *Studies*, XXIII (1934) 203–18. It is not altogether clear whether Swift wanted independence (that is, independence of action) for the 'Whole People of Ireland' or merely for the English in Ireland.

15. See also p. 126 and *The Answer to the Injured Lady*, where Swift writes: 'That your family and tenants [Ireland] have no dependence upon the said gentleman [England], further than by the old agreement, which obligeth you to have the same steward, and to regulate your household by such methods as you should both agree to' (*Works*, VII 105).

16. The Act was 6 George I, c. 5. Its language affirming the dependency of *Ireland* is unequivocal: 'That the said kingdom of Ireland hath been, is, and of right, ought to be subordinate unto and dependent upon the imperial crown of *Great Britain*, as being inseparably united and annexed thereunto; and that the King's majesty, by and with the advice and consent of the lords spiritual and temporal and commons of *Great Britain* in parliament assembled, had, hath, and of right ought to have full power and authority to make laws and statutes of sufficient force and validity, to bind the kingdom and people of Ireland' *Statutes at Large* (Cambridge, 1765) XIV 205.

17. Swift adopts some of the language of William Molyneux who, had argued that Ireland's being bound '*by Acts of Parliament made in England, is against Reason, and the Common Rights of all Mankind*' (op. cit. p. 127).

18. *Works*, VII 86; cf. also pp. 84, 103; *Correspondence*, III 311. Molyneux discusses 'consent' at length (op. cit. pp. 127–30).

19. Cf. *The Drapier's Letters*, ed. Herbert Davis (Oxford, 1935) pp. xli ff.

20. Cf. Swift's letter to Pope, 10 Jan. 1721–2, in *Correspondence*, III 113–16.

21. Ibid. p. 309.

22. See *The Works of Sir William Temple* (1731) II 111; Sir William Petty, *Political Arithmetic*, in *Later Stuart Tracts*, ed. G. A. Aitken (Westminster, 1903) p. 30; John Browne, *An Essay on Trade in General; and, on That of Ireland in Particular* (Dublin, 1728) pp. 38–9; George Berkeley, *The Querist* (1735) ed. J. M. Hone (Dublin and Cork, n. d.) part 1, nos. 130–33; part 2, nos. 2–3; part 3, no. 2.

23. (Dublin, 1739) I, 10–15.

24. John Bellers, *Essays about the Poor, Manufactures, Trade, Plantations, and Immorality* (1699) Preface.

25. Davenant, *Ballance of Trade*, p. 12.

26. Bellers, *Essays*, p. 9.

27. Reprinted in *A Select Collection of Early English Tracts on Commerce* ed. J. R. McCulloch (1856) p. 125.

28. Brewster, *New Essays*, p. 40.

29. Berkeley, *The Querist*, part 1, no. 167.

30. [Charles King], *The British Merchant* (1713; 3rd ed., 1748) I 18.

31. See P. J. Thomas, *Mercantilism and the East India Trade* (1926) pp. 8 ff.

32. *Discourse on Trade, and Other Matters Relative to It* (1745) p. 78. This is a rewriting of a work published in 1695.

33. Ibid. pp. 78–9.

34. These and the following quotations were first printed in the 1721 edition of *The British Merchant* (I 2, 4, 18, 19). They were originally published in Sir Theodore Janssen's *General Maxims of Trade* (1713) pp. 6, 8. These are essentially the rules of trade set forth by William Wood in his *Survey of Trade* (1718) pp. 224 ff. It is pleasant to observe that Swift and the man he attacked so violently in *The Drapier's Letters* are in fundamental agreement about foreign trade.

35. See *Correspondence*, IV 24 ff; *The Drapier's Letters*, ed. Herbert Davis (Oxford, 1935) pp. 226–8.

36. *An Essay on Trade in General; and on That of Ireland in Particular* (Dublin, 1728) p. 29.

37. *A Discourse of Trade* (1698) Preface, p. vi.

38. *A Discourse on Trade, and Other Matters* pp. 79–80. Cf. also John Pollexfen, *A Discourse of Trade and Coyn* (1697; 2nd ed. 1700) pp. 92 ff.

39. *The British Merchant*, I 3; Wood, *Survey of Trade*, pp. 224, 225.

40. *An Essay on the Trade of Ireland* (1731) part 2, pp. 41–2.

41. Part I, no. 150; part II, no. 226. For additional attacks on luxury by Irish writers, see *Dublin Journal*, no. 37 11 Dec. 1725; *Tribune*, nos. 5 and 12 (1729); *The Present State of Ireland Consider'd* (Dublin and London, 1730) pp. 21–3; Samuel Madden, *Reflections and Resolutions Proper for the Gentlemen of Ireland* (Dublin), 1738; 1816) Resolutions VIII, IX, X, XXX.

42. But see *Works*, VII 124, where he seems to combine the moral and economic arguments. The intention is economic.

43. Thomas Manley, *Usury at Six Per Cent. Examined* (1669) Preface, p. 9.

44. *Journal of the House of Commons of Ireland*, II 407. See also John Hely Hutchinson, *The Commercial Restraints of Ireland*, ed. W. G. Carroll (1888) p. 143.

45. See *Dublin Journal*, no. 25 (11 Dec. 1725); *Tribune*, no. 12 (1729); *The Present State of Ireland Consider'd* (Dublin and London, 1730) pp. 27 ff; Madden, *Reflections and Resolutions*, Resolution VIII.

46. See *The Works of Sir William Temple* (1731) I 65; John Locke, *Some Consideration of the Consequences of the Lowering of Interest, and the Raising of the Value of Money*, in *Works* (1824) IV 19–20. Cf. also Charles Davenant, *An Essay on Ways and Means of Supplying the War*, in *Political and Commercial Works* (1771) I 13; Sir Francis Brewster, *Essay on Trade and Navigation* (1695) p. 51.

47. Pollexfen, *Discourse*, pp. 80–1.

48. Cf. Harold Williams, *Dean Swift's Library* (Cambridge, 1932) Sales Catalogue, nos. 276, 288, 296, 300, 412, 436, 444.

49. *Correspondence*, III 121.

JAMES WILLIAM JOHNSON
Swift's Historical Outlook (1965)

The art and mind of Jonathan Swift have been the objects of ever greater critical attention for the last twenty or thirty years. So thoroughly have the commentators discussed Swift's attitudes and their origins that there would seem to be little left to discover about the Dean's views or why he held them or how he applied them. In respect to the role played in Swift's thought by his reading in historiography, however, and the importance of history in the conceptual bases of his writings, critics have assumed more than they have demonstrated. In spite of some useful published disquisitions – by Herbert Davis and Irvin Ehrenpreis – the implications of the importance of Swift's historical outlook have not been fully explored, nor have the formation and configuration of his historically founded beliefs been clarified and documented. The present study will attempt to explain in some detail Swift's ideas of history, where he got them, and how they affected his non-historiographical compositions.[1]

Swift's vital interest in historiography is now commonly acknowledged. The post in government he most actively tried to get was that of Historiographer Royal. Between 1714 and 1720, he devoted a good deal of time to composing his 'histories' of political activities during the Tory ministry. He essayed a history of England. His letters as well as his other works are packed with references to a multiplicity of historians drawn from disparate ages and cultures. In his library, which numbered about five hundred separate works at the time of his death, at least three fifths were historical *opera*, including diaries, memoirs, and chronologies. He wrote marginal comments in the volumes by Bodin, Echard, Daniel, Burnet, and Clarendon that indicate Swift considered his historiographical principles superior to theirs. Even in those works of his own that were overtly fiction (*A Tale of a Tub*, *Gulliver's Travels*), he assumed the part of the impartial, methodical historian, intent upon getting at the 'truth'.[2]

Literary critics, primarily interested in other matters, have been inclined to characterize Swift's historical views as those of the stereo-typical neo-classicist, who – it has been asserted by Saintsbury and others – adored the classical historians and repeated centuries-old notions of the advantages of reading history. Modern historians, pre-occupied with tracing the development of historiographical practice and theory in the pre-Gibbonian eras, find Swift a less obvious source than Bolingbroke and others. The net result has been the overlooking of an important aspect of Swiftian thought.

At first look, Swift indeed seems to belong with other eighteenth-century literary men who blandly averred the importance of historical knowledge. He was educationally indoctrinated much as the typical gentleman-scholar of his day. At Trinity College, Dublin, he got a thorough grounding in Greek and Latin historians; and later at Oxford and Moor Park he perused the standard authors, abstracting the works of Diodorus, Aelian, Florus, Herbert, Sleidan, Sarpi, Camden, and Burnet. Throughout his life he was fond of citing historical precedents for contemporary events; his published works are filled with such allusions, from the early *Of Contests and Dissensions in Athens and Rome* (1701) to the letters dated 1737.[3] It is deceptively easy to summarize Swift's historical outlook as an uncritical neo-classical reverence for antiquity coupled with a fondness for citing historical parallels to explain current situations.

That Swift reverenced classical civilization is true. That he revered all of its periods equally or uncritically is far from true. He was a little more comfortable with Rome than with Greece, partly because he found Latin the more congenial language but also because the temper of Greece was frequently expressed in art and philosophy, two disci-plines less appealing to Swift's practical tastes than history, satire, political theory, and morality.[4] But though he had an intimate know-ledge of Roman history and an enthusiasm for it, he drew a sharp line between his evaluation of Republican Rome and Imperial Rome, reserving his praise almost exclusively for the former. It is untrue that Swift – or his fellow Tories – admired Augustan Rome; on the contrary they grew to despise it.[5] Neither is it true that Swift's historically derived analogies were inexact or inappropriate. Some (for example, those in the *Examiner*) may have served partisan ends; but Swift chose them scrupulously with his own admonition in mind: 'The Value of several Circumstances in History, lessens very much by distance of Time; although some minute Circumstances are very valuable; and it requires great Judgment in a Writer to distinguish.'[6] Swift's clairvoyance in comparing the advent of the Hanovers with Caesar's dictatorship or Marlborough's venality with Crassus's may be faulted; but his confidence in the relevance of the analogies cannot be doubted. Like Addison, he knew that fourth-rate intellects often relied on historical parallels as a substitute for objective appraisal of contemporary events; he parodied such moral and intellectual laziness in *A Tritical Essay upon the Faculties of the Mind*.[7] To accuse Swift of sharing this laziness by saying that his views were the shallow ones of Chesterfield and other nominal supporters of classical history is to misunderstand Swift by denying the creativity and integrity of his intellect.

Because he never synthesized his attitudes toward historiography, history, and their interrelationship, it becomes the task of his commentator to construct Swift's purview (that is, the compass of his historical understanding) – certainly a dangerous practice. Yet, those who read Swift carefully acknowledge the importance of his implicitly historical perspective; his works are liberally sprinkled with the data that demand this acknowledgement. There are, perhaps, two practicable ways to use these data in an outline of Swift's historical purview. One is to extract from his canon everything Swift wrote about historians, historical works, and the nature of history and piece them all together in a large ideological mosaic. This method has the disadvantage of removing many statements which have historiographical significance only within their context. The other way is to read the historical works known to Swift and then construct a scholarly Road to Lilliput. This is the method basically employed by many Swift scholars including Crane and Ehrenpreis; though it can be useful and revealing, it may encourage the critic to oversimplify, to find causation where none exists, or even to impute to a writer ideas he consciously rejected.[8] However, lacking a statement by Swift himself on his theory and application of historical knowledge and perceiving that Swift implicitly held certain theories, the commentator has no alternative to using a combination of the extractive and influential techniques. His method can be tested by checking its results against the findings of other Swift scholars of varying persuasions.

To begin with, it is apparent that Swift's attraction to historical study started with his belief in its 'universal' and 'applicable' truths. No scholar today denies Swift's acceptance of the notion of 'uniformitarianism', a premise common to eighteenth-century thinkers from

Dryden to Burke. M. H. Abrams has defined this doctrine exhaustively, but it may be conveniently identified as the view that all men are essentially the same in all times and places with minor variations due to geographical and social factors. As the record of human events and personal behavior, history thus becomes an endless source of information for those interested in political science and psychology. More than that, the rhythms of historical sequence tend to repeat themselves, so that the discerning reader can find cultural paradigms by which to measure his own age and archetypal careers that bear resemblance to his own life. History thus provides models and warnings, both for the state and for the private man.[9] Johnson reflects this rationale for historical study in an aphorism: 'If we act only for ourselves, to neglect the study of history is not prudent; if we are entrusted with the care of others, it is not just.'[10] When the Queen Anne wits persistently found similarities between their age and that of Rome just before the advent of Caesar, they were not merely thinking metaphorically or belaboring an historical cliché: their reading of Livy, Trogus, Justin and, Florus in school – the 'practical stuff' of their education – had convinced them that insight into post-Restoration events demanded their awareness of Roman analogues. Even Defoe, with an inferior classical education, postulated the usefulness of drawing Roman-British parallels. This particular practice, a staple of eighteenth-century (and Swiftian) historical thought, remains common today, especially in the works of such twentieth-century English historians as Collingwood and Toynbee.[11]

The absorption of some neo-classical concepts into modern historiographical theory has prevented certain of Swift's views from passing into oblivion; but others, more important to the Dean of St Patrick's, fail to agree with modern ideology and thus are now ignored or slighted as archaic, therefore wrong. Recent literary studies have scrutinized Swift's fictional works in order to demonstrate unnecessarily the fact that Swift, a lifelong Church of England man, was a devout Christian. To point out that Swift's adherence to Christian theology affected his historical outlook might be supererogatory if the fact had not been so widely ignored. Even if theistically oriented history is presently discounted by historiographers and historical theorists, the truth is that for thousands of years intelligent men saw history in theogonic terms.[12] Swift was one of these.

Disguised though it often is by his satiric rationale and his complex irony, Swift's fundamental adherence to the idea of the pervasive

presence of God in human affairs is obvious in many of his works.[13]
Basic to his conception of a divinely ordained and controlled universe
is his postulation of a phenomenological world manifesting Providential
intent. His *Thoughts on Various Subjects* contains a succinct statement of
this:

> One argument used to the disadvantage of Providence, I take to be a very
> strong one in its defence. It is objected, that storms and tempests, unfruitful
> seasons, serpents, spiders, flies, and other noxious or troublesome animals,
> with many other instances of the same kind, discover an imperfection in
> nature, because human life would be much easier without them; but the
> design of Providence may clearly be perceived in this proceeding. The
> motions of the sun and moon, in short the whole system of the universe, as
> far as philosophers have been able to discover and observe, are in the
> utmost degree of regularity and perfection; but wherever God hath left to
> man the power of interposing a remedy by thought or labour, there he
> hath placed things in a state of imperfection, on purpose to stir up human
> industry, without which life would stagnate, or indeed could not subsist
> at all: *Curis acuuntur mortalia corda*. (*Works*, TS, I 279)

This line of argument, which ingeniously reconciles the Christian
doctrines of free will and divine omnipotence, is paralleled in *The
Sentiments of a Church of England Man* where it takes on historical
connotations:

> AMONG other Theological Arguments made use of in those Times [the
> reign of Charles II] in praise of Monarchy, and Justification of absolute
> Obedience to a Prince, there seemed to be one of a singular Nature: It was
> urged, that *Heaven* was governed by a *Monarch*, who had none to controul
> his Power, but was absolutely obeyed: Then it followed, That earthly
> Governments were the more perfect, the nearer they imitated the Govern-
> ment in Heaven. All which I look upon as the strongest Argument against
> *despotick* Power that ever was offered; since no Reason can possibly be
> assigned, why it is best for the World that God Almighty hath such a
> Power, which doth not directly prove that no Mortal Man should ever
> have the like. (*Works*, TS, I 279)[14]

Having struck down the historic principle of divine right, Swift goes on
to assert that Greek and Roman history provide many examples that
prove the validity of his premise of God as the sole ruler of man's
destiny, listing the tyrants overthrown by Him in Greece, Rome, and

England. The *Thoughts* and the *Sentiments*, one private and the other public in intent, indicate the elemental piety of Swift's outlook on the *res gestae* of historiography.[15]

Pietistic though his age was, Swift cannot be accused of uttering such sentiments out of empty convention. They appear too often, too ringingly, in his personal notebooks and private letters to be mere public pronouncements. In the *Thoughts on Religion*, he recorded his belief in historic cycles and scriptural authority (*Works*, IX 261–3). *Further Thoughts on Religion* contains his unqualified assertion that Mosaic history must be the foundation of historical thinking and that 'sacred' (Scriptural) history must take precedence over 'profane' (secular) history: 'The Scripture-system of man's creation, is what Christians are bound to believe, and seems most agreeable of all others to probability and reason.' In light of the squabbles over 'universal history', Swift's elaborate précis of the data of Genesis is irrefutable evidence of his Christian purview of history in an era when Scriptural authority was being attacked, by classicists and atheists alike.[16] His sermons provide further evidence of the belief that history manifests Providential behests and action: 'The Duty of Mutual Subjection', 'On the Testimony of Conscience', 'On Brotherly Love', 'On the Martyrdom of King Charles I', and 'On Doing Good' – all make connections between divine will and historical events. And, finally, the letters, written without guile to Pope, Pultney, Gay, Bolingbroke, and others, testify to the sincerity of Swift's pious predications about Providence and history (*Corr* I, 130; III 120 ff; V 179).

Swift's Christian theism did not negate or even modify very much his enthusiasm for the pagan historians of Greece and Rome. His Christianity transcended his classicism without superseding it. In fact, to Swift, the perspectives of neo-classicism and Christianity were hardly contradictory. Classical uniformitarianism and Christian egalitarianism were two faces of the same coin: since he believed that all men were conceived in sin and brought forth in iniquity, Swift could readily conclude that men were everywhere the same. The pagan historian presented valid evidence – theologically unenlightened though it might be – of the theogonic direction of history. Classical historiographers who postulated recurrent cycles of events could be used to support the Christian view of divinely instituted rhythms in history: in fact, Augustine, Orosius, Tertullian, Ambrose, Eusebius, Jerome, and other patristic writers known to Swift had used them for just that purpose.

Pagan historians, like Florus, who constructed the archetypal rise and fall of a civilization, confirmed the inspired prophecies of Daniel, Isaiah, and other seers, Hebrew and Christian.[17] And when sacred and profane history came into momentary conflict, preferring the Christian to the pagan version was, for Swift, a matter of simple reason and prudence. His *Letter to a Young Clergyman* and his sermons, 'On the Testimony of Conscience' and 'On the Excellency of Christianity' are clear evidence of Swift's reconciliation of secular classicism with spiritual Christianity (*Works*, IX 69 ff, 155–6, 241 ff).

Thus to Swift, history, whether pagan or Christian, could be read as confirmation of the controlling hand of God on the *res gestae* of the world. Man could not hope to comprehend the Divine Logos through scanning history, however; God maintains His mystery. But the pious student who had a 'great Judgment' might draw sacrosanct principles from history to illuminate the present state of the world and to direct his personal conduct. Like Temple and others, Swift exempted 'modern' history from his generalizations about the excellence of historiographical knowledge. Most post-Renaissance historiography he found venal, even meretricious, as the account of historians in book III of *Gulliver's Travels* shows (*Works*, IX 18–19; XI 183–4). His distrust of contemporary history, dating back to the days at Moor Park and strikingly reflected in *The Battle of the Books*, is to be found in many places, notably his essays for *The Tatler* on 15 October 1709 and 28 September 1710. It accounts for his own determination to write a history of England and his constant encouragement of Bolingbroke to do so (*Corr.* III 31 ff).[18] But with some modern history expunged, the historiographical library was a source of the wisest maxims. Swift used it as such and it determined some of his basic ideology. It is scarcely an exaggeration to say that his political principles, his personal moral code, his social criticism, his ideas of language and literature, and at last his bleakly pessimistic attitude toward the world were all strongly tinctured by his reading in history.

Though he boasted that he had never received the slightest 'hint' for his literary productions, Swift was indebted to Greek and Latin historiography for many of his basic ideas. The years of reading and abstracting classical historians left their ideological mark on the young scholar, as an examination of the historical works in Swift's library shows. Initially, it was from Graeco-Roman historians that he derived the notion of the past as a source of political and personal precepts:

Herodotus, Polybius, Dionysius of Halicarnassus, Diodorus Siculus, Livy, Justin, and Appian all espoused the belief in one form or another.[19] Moreover, though pagan, classical historians were not atheists: Xenophon, Plutarch, Cornelius Nepos, and Trogus – as well as most of those named above – countenanced the Hand of God thesis.[20] Refined by the Church historians and the Byzantine chronologers, perpetuated by such Renaissance polymaths as Bodin, Raleigh, and J. J. Scaliger, these basic ideas constantly reappeared in the historians that Swift admired.

Other constituent beliefs in his historical purview Swift derived from the humanist-classicist tradition and confirmed through first-hand knowledge of ancient historians. Since it is these beliefs that most importantly shaped his specific applications of historically gained principles, a more detailed discussion of each of four tenets is necessary. These historiographical dogmas relate to his theory of Decline, his concept of Time, his emphasis on Climate, and his attitude toward Luxury.

One of the most persistent canards in Swiftian scholarship is the idea that the Dean believed in a process of continual decline from some Saturnian golden Age of the past to the dismal condition of the brazen present. The canard springs from wrongly connecting Swift to the Renaissance tradition of the Age of the World and the Decay of Nature controversy.[21] That Swift was fully cognizant of the Decay theory and used the controversy in his *Battle of the Books* is indisputable, but the evidence is that he never subscribed to the pessimistic corollaries of mundane senility and diminution. On the contrary, he consistently spoofed them. The early *Tale of a Tub* poked cheerful fun at the small size of modern ears in contrast to the noble proportions of ancient ones with strongly prurient undertones (*Works*, I 128–9). *Gulliver's Travels* elaborately scorned the postulations of Godfrey Goodman's *The Fall of Man* (1616) in the episode of Gulliver's visit to the library of the king in Brobdingnag, where he finds a treatise that argues as proof of the age of the world the decline in size from their ancestors by the modern Brobdingnagian giants (*Works*, XI 122). Swift derided the catastrophic axiom of the Senilists in a bit of bagatelle written to Thomas Sheridan in later years (*Corr.* V 231). Thus, from 1697 to 1726 to 1735, the Dean repeatedly mocked the Decay of Nature theorists, characterizing their work as that which 'treats of the Weakness of Human kind; and is in little esteem except among Women and the Vulgar (*Works*, XI 122).

Yet, though he denied the idea of a continual decline from the past to the present, Swift emphatically held that human beings had a tendency to degenerate – morally and intellectually, if not physically. This tendency was the expression of man's innate and universal characteristic, epitomized by Swift as 'pride' and explained by the doctrine of original sin. Men were altered by the Fall so that they must eternally incline toward selfishness, sinfulness, evil, barbarity – in short, toward unalleviated Yahooism. Swift overtly confirmed his belief in original sin in the sermons and the *Further Thoughts on Religion*. He mercilessly identified innate evil in *The Last Speech and Dying Words of Ebenezor Elliston* and declared that it must be forcibly rooted out of society and individual men.[22] He saw in the events of history examples of man's perpetual tendency toward moral degeneration, which led to political and cultural decline; perhaps *The Sentiments of a Church of England Man* is the most extended exposition of this view (*Works*, II 1–23). Thus, Swift's interpretation of historic patterns was determined by his belief that human events constantly repeated mankind's aspiration to Grace and fall from it.

His basic emphasis on original sin and his equally strong belief in free will meant that Swift could not adhere to the idea that each age was progressively worse than the one before it, nor could he assume that each age was better. Every man, every group of men, must re-enact the choice of Adam, and though the same choice was made over and over, one could not – must not – assume that it was inevitable, for that would deny God's Grace and man as *capax rationis*. Thus history was the cyclic drama of attainment and failure, with the conflict between good and evil shown in groups of men and within the single man. It was a temporal process of balance and imbalance, what Herodotus and others called 'flux'. Swift's letter to Bolingbroke, on 5 April 1729, despite its irony is a fair sample of his cyclism:

> I have read my friend Congreve's verses to Lord Cobham, which end with a vile and false moral . . . that all times are equally virtuous and vicious, wherein he differs from all poets, philosophers, and Christians that ever writ. It is more probable that there may be an equal quantity of virtues always in the world, but sometimes there may be a peck of it in Asia, and hardly a thimbleful in Europe. But if there is no virtue, there is an abundance of sincerity; for I will venture all I am worth, that there is not one human creature in power, who will not be modest enough to confess that he proceeds wholly upon a principle of corruption. I say this because I have a

scheme . . . to govern England upon the principles of virtue, and when the nation is ripe for it, I desire you will send for me. (*Corr.* IV 77)

The kaleidoscopic subtleties of this passage do not obscure its vital concepts, which constantly appear in Swift's works: human behavior is the interaction of virtue and vice; these qualities increase or diminish from time to time in nations as well as men; the pattern of change can be affected by the individual's 'scheme' as well as by mass sentiment, which that scheme may help to produce, the balance or imbalance of collective vice and virtue causes the revolutions of politics. Swift was constantly preoccupied with political and moral equilibrium; in almost every instance, his use of history was to evaluate the symptomatic imbalances of his day beside the causative paradigms of recorded events, so that the balance might be restored at once (*Works*, III 161; VI 95). The Swiftian theory of Decline in human affairs may have been determinative but it was not fatalistic until the last ten years of his life. In conception it was strongly Christian.

His concept of Time, however, was not. Though Swift knew such patristic speculations about the absolute nature of Time as those of Augustine in the *Confessions*, and though he knew the fundamental assumptions about Time and history that were common to Eusebius, Jerome, and other chronologers, his practical definition of Time was not so much philosophical as metaphoric.[23] Swift's poetic – and typically neo-classical – tendency to personify Time is evident in the *Thoughts on Various Subjects*: 'No Preacher is listened to, but Time; which gives us the same Train and Turn of Thought, that elder People have tried in vain to put into our Heads before' (*Works*, I 241). Similarly, in *A Tale of a Tub*, Time becomes 'Prince Posterity', to whom the work is dedicated as one possessing accumulated wisdom and judgment (*Works*, I 22 ff). In a somewhat less anthropomorphic usage, Swift spoke of Time as the temporal process of alteration and degeneration: thus in *A Project for the Advancement of Religion* (1709), 'Abuses' were said to have crept into the Universities 'through Neglect, or Length of Time'; and the *Remarks upon a Book* (1708) declared that 'Time it hath in every Age admitted several Alterations' (*Works*, II 15, 52, 84). Leery as he was of 'airy Metaphysicks', Swift consistently avoided ontological and epistemological speculations about Time; and appalled at Hobbesian materialism, he shunned making time a function of matter, though in *A Project for the Advancement of Religion*, he came perilously close to such an attribution:

the Nature of Things is such, that if Abuses be not remedied, they will
certainly encrease, nor ever stop till they end in the Subversion of a Com-
mon-Wealth. As there must always of Necessity be some corruptions; so
in a well-instituted State, the executive Power will be always contending
against them, by *reducing Things* (as *Machiavel* speaks) *to their first Principles*;
never letting Abuses grow inveterate, or multiply so far that it will be
hard to find Remedies, and perhaps impossible to apply them. As he that
would keep his House in Repair, must attend every little Breach or Flaw,
and supply it immediately, else Time alone will bring all to Ruin; how
much more the common Accidents of Storm and Rain? (*Works*, II 63).

Beset as he was by various ideological heritages that defined
Time in differing ways, Swift apparently settled finally for the most
functional of meanings. From Marcus Aurelius and the Stoics, he
may have received a modified version of the notion, 'Time is the
enemy of man'.[24] From such Graceo-Roman historians as Herodotus,
Diodorus Siculus, and Dionysius of Halicarnassus, he educed the
historic perspective summed up in Diodorus X 10: 'Indeed there is no
noble thing among men, I suppose, which is of such a nature that the
long passage of time works it no damage or destruction.'[25] The
Church fathers – Cyprian, Orosius, Tertullian, Augustine – taught him
that 'Anything glorious that men found, they must, to make it their
own, spoil it' but that in spite of human blunderings, 'one God has
directed the course of history and . . . it is only because of His mercy
that we live at all, and that if we live in misery it is because of our own
uncontrolled passions'.[26] Such Renaissance writers as Polydore Vergil,
Samuel Daniel, and Sir John Harrington fostered the practice of
interpreting politico-historical events within a temporal pattern of
decline.[27]

As the inheritor of these views and believer in them, Swift himself
did not attempt a formal definition of 'time' but in general used it in
several ways. First, it was simply a system of measurement for sequence
and duration of events; *A Proposal for Correcting the English Tongue*
(1712), with its elaborate correlation between Roman and British
events and 'times', is an outstanding specimen of such use (*Works*, TS,
XI 8). Then, it was an abstracted, often personified agent of creation
and destruction; Swift frequently used 'Time' in this sense in 1708-9,
as was seen above. Then again, Swift thought of time as a characteristic
– or at least capacity – of matter; temporality meant ephemerality, thus
physical decay. His analogy between government and a house in the

Project for Religion is typical of this denotation. Further, Time meant 'history' or 'historic pattern' or 'historiographical data': probably Swift used 'Time' in this way in the *Thoughts on Various Subjects* quoted before. In none of these usages did the Dean bother to define the relationship of time to God, but then he did not need to. God was infinite, and Time measured the finite. If he thought of its relationship to God at all, Swift probably equated 'time' with spiders, flies, noxious animals, and other Providentially wrought imperfections intended to stimulate men to a higher state of moral if not social good.

In addition to his concepts of Decline and Time, Swift's thesis of Climate and its influence affected his historical outlook. The belief that climate was directly responsible for physical, intellectual, and cultural phenomena was a very ancient one, full expressions of it appearing in the writings of Herodotus, Hippocrates, Strabo, and their successors. It was also prevalent in Swift's time, having been prepared for by Bodin and other Renaissance thinkers who derived it from the classics. Versions of the climatic thesis influenced Clarendon, Temple, Defoe, Addison, Steele, Gay, Thompson, Fielding, Goldsmith, Boswell, and Burke. There were, of course, eighteenth-century litterateurs that scorned the notion that climate could account either for the course of history or the foibles of the single personality: chief among these were Bolingbroke and Johnson. But the countenance given the climatic thesis by such influential scientists as Dr John Arbuthnot in *An Essay Concerning the Effects of Air on Human Bodies* in the early half of the century and that of William Falconer in his *Remarks on the Influence of Climate* in the latter half helped to promote its steady popularity. Swift's thinking was strongly colored by the Climate thesis.[28]

In brief, the Climatists held that the human body was directly affected by such factors as sunlight, rainfall, wind, cloudiness, heat and cold, moisture and dryness; and they also held that the body was indirectly affected by the quality of the soil, hence the kinds of food eaten, by general topography (mountainous or level), and by presence or absence of water, salt or fresh. Intelligence also was affected by climate (heat produced quick, alert minds, and cold resulted in torpor and stupidity); therefore, personality and character were climatically influenced. Logically, it followed that national character, political systems, and military activity were climatically affected. Implicitly, the climatological views held by the Ancients had historical ramifications for the Moderns. Since the very stuff of history – politics, personal behavior, military conduct, conflict of nations – was climatically influenced, an understanding of climatic patterns aided one's understanding of history.

Though he largely ignored the physiological aspects of the climatic thesis, Swift, perhaps following Temple, fully accepted the cultural and political posits. A few instances should illustrate the relevance of these ideological données to his historical outlook. In 1708, Swift wrote:

> But although a *Church*-of-England *Man* thinks every Species of Government equally *lawful*; he doth not think them equally *expedient*; or for every Country indifferently. There may be something in the Climate, naturally disposing Men towards one Sort of Obedience; as it is manifest all over *Asia*, where we never read of any Commonwealth, except some small ones on the *Western* Coasts, established by the *Greeks*. There may be a great deal in the Situation of a Country, and in the present *Genius* of the People. It hath been observed, that the temperate Climates usually run into moderate Governments, and the Extreames into despotick Power. (*Works*, II 17–18)

He then went on to refute Hobbes and urge that 'the Authors of *Greece* and *Rome*' be read as evidence of the flourishing of democratic government in an otherwise tyrannic age and as encouragement to English democracy in a trying period.

In 1710, Swift's *Hints Towards an Essay on Conversation* suggested his doctrine of cultural imbalance in climatic terms:

> There is a sort of rude familiarity, which some people, by practising among their intimates, have introduced into their general conversation, and would have it pass for innocent freedom or humour, which is a dangerous experiment in our northern climate, where all the little decorum and politeness we have are purely forced by art, and are so ready to lapse into barbarity. (*Works*, TS, XI 72, 74)

Again, in 1712, in *A Proposal for Correcting the English Tongue*:

> For I am afraid, my lord, that with all the real good qualities of our country, we are naturally not very polite. This perpetual disposition to shorten our words . . . is nothing else but a tendency to lapse into the barbarity of those northern nations [that is, the Angles, Saxons, and Goths], from whom we are descended, and whose languages labour all under the same defect. . . . Now, as we struggle with an ill climate to improve the nobler kinds of fruits, are at the expense of walls to receive and reverberate the faint rays of the sun, and fence against the northern

blast, we sometimes, by the help of a good soil, equal the production of warmer countries, who have no need to be at so much cost and care. It is the same thing with respect to the politer arts among us; and the same defect of heat which gives a fierceness to our natures, may contribute to that roughness of our language, which bears some analogy to the harsh fruit of colder countries. For I do not reckon that we want a genius more than the rest of our neighbors. (*Works*, TS, XI 13)

Swift's omnipresent references to 'our northern genius' and 'our climate' and 'our meridian' in his works are often juxtaposed to his comments on degeneracy and time. In such combinations, his theory of Climate served to reinforce his belief that Decline, as a product of imbalance, was furthered by natural as well as moral forces, and to substantiate his notion that an abrasive Time was aided by physical factors (such as heat, cold, moisture) in working its ills. Like his other tenets, the Climate thesis did not contradict Swift's Christian postulations about history: 'Climate' was those 'storms and tempests, unfruitful seasons' that were divinely instituted. Climate, then, was one instrument through which God guided the course of history.

The fourth chief constituent of Swift's historical outlook was his conception of Luxury. This concept, essentially economic and psychological in nature, was a favorite with the humanist historians of the Renaissance and their neo-classical successors. By the eighteenth century 'Luxury', like 'Time' was often used metaphorically to express an implicit historical or moral attitude; for example, Thomas Gray's reference to the shrines of 'Luxury and Pride' heaped with incense kindled at the Muses' flame. In fact, a personified Luxury was almost a historiographical villain to English devotees of Greek and Roman history.

In ancient history, the concept of Luxury was often commingled with views of Decline, Time, and Climate. Herodotus coupled material prosperity with moral decline and military weakness as consequences of warm, fertile climates.[29] Xenophon condemned luxury as a type of self-indulgent superiority of attitude that led to laxness and moral decline.[30] Strabo scorned the luxury and sensuality of the Athenians in contrast with the economically deprived but morally exemplary barbarians.[31] Such early Roman moralists as Cato and Varro, incensed at 'unbridled luxury', blamed it as a symptom of cultural and moral decay, and thereby influenced a score of later historians.[32] Diodorus, Livy, Justin, Appian, and Florus made luxury a *bête noire* using it variously to mean material prosperity, vanity, excess profits, self-indulgence, and sensuality.[33] Such Renaissance historians as Polydore, Daniel, Holinshed, and – later – Clarendon, Burnet, Harrington, and Temple countenanced these uses, applying the luxury thesis to English history and contemporary events.[34] Temple's quasi-historical formula epitomized centuries of agreement about the role of luxury in historic patterns: 'according to the usual circle of human affairs, war ended in peace, peace in plenty and luxury, these in pride, and pride in contention, till the circle ended in new wars.'[35]

From both his classical and patristic reading, Swift drew the opinions about Luxury and history that never ceased to tint his thinking. In his comparison between the spread of Epicureanism in Augustan Rome and Restoration England, he said of the philosophical movements: 'They both seem to be corruptions occasioned by luxury and peace, and by politeness beginning to decline' (*Works*, TS, I 284; TS, XI 11). His essay *Concerning That Universal Hatred Which Prevails Against the Clergy* (1736) made luxury the enemy of the Church as well as the State: 'But, when public edifices were erected and endowed, they [the clergy] began gradually to degenerate into idleness, ignorance, avarice, ambition, and luxury, after the usual fate of all human institutions' (*Works*, III 302). And in his comments on history, English as well as Roman, he blamed luxury for its pernicious consequences. William II 'first brought in among us . . . luxury and profusion . . . a mixture of virtues and vices' with the latter predominant (*Works*, X 214). To Pope in a letter that was soon pirated and published (10 January 1721), he attributed the collapse of Rome into permanent dictatorship to the fact that 'the Virtue of the Commonwealth gave place to luxury and ambition'; and *Gulliver's Travels* (1726) in a passage on Augustan Rome remarked on 'Corruption grown so high and so quick . . . by the Force of Luxury so lately introduced' (*Works*, IX 33; XI 185–6). The sermon, 'Causes of the Wretched Condition of Ireland' (post 1720), blamed extravagance in dress, luxury, idleness, sloth, and cruelty for Ireland's economic misery and moral depravity (*Works*, IX 200–1). And one of Swift's last letters (to William Pultney, 8 March 1735) breathed out his final despair of England's future: 'But it is altogether impossible for any nation to preserve its liberty long under a tenth part of the present luxury, infidelity, and a million corruptions' (*Corr.* V 143).

Coupled with his fundamental assumption of a Providentially wrought universe and divinely guided *res gestae*, Swift's views of

Decline as a moral predisposition and a physical tendency, Time as the inexorable agent of alteration, Climate as a determinant of personal and social traits and at times as the chief cause of physical and intellectual capacity, and Luxury as an economic and psychological matrix of events – these views might well have caused Swift to be an historical fatalist. Yet he was not, until the last ten years of his life at any rate. The very body of historiography that gave him his elemental concepts provided him with counter-theses to prevent fatalism and despair. According to Greek and Roman historians, every ill had a remedy.

In the political sphere, once a polity had met its military and economic challenges and evolved a 'constitution' to regulate its subjects, its successful functioning could be assured by basing its government on a system of checks and balances that would perpetually reassert political equilibrium.[36] Polybius was the *locus classicus* of this theory for Swift and other neo-classicists; but the supplementary opinions of Dionysius, Justin, and Eutropius were also known to him.[37] Noting that the Commonwealth 'of itself is too apt to fluctuate', Swift often used Polybius to argue for the necessary maintenance of equal balance between the three governmental powers – king, nobles, and people: he did so in the *Sentiments of a Church of England Man*, *Remarks upon a Book*, and, typically, in *A Letter to a Whig Lord* (*Works*, I 25; II 17–18, 23, 83).

> FOR indeed, my Lord, your Party is much deceived, when they think to distress a Ministry for any long Time, or to any great Purpose, while those Ministers act under a Queen who is so firmly convinced of their Zeal and Ability for Her Service, and who is at the same time so thoroughly possessed of Her Peoples Hearts. Such a Weight will infallibly at length bear down the Balance: And according to the Nature of our Constitution, it ought to be so; because when any one of the Three Powers whereof our Government is composed, proves too strong for the other two, there is an End of our Monarchy. (*Works*, VI 123)

Similarly, in the *Abstract* of his proposed history of England, Swift discussed at length in his account of Henry I the origin of English balanced government, tracing it back to Polydore, and Brompton, citing Xenophon and Polybius, and examining the variations in Greece, Rome, and the Gothic states (*Works*, TS, X 225–7). Even in one of his sermons, he exegized his thesis of tri-partite balance as a preventive measure for political decline.[38]

Classical history also provided a suggestion for halting social degeneration. The pernicious effects of luxury and plenty could be minimized by the institution of a Censor, who would introduce and enforce sumptuary laws, prosecute offenders, and regulate sexual as well as economic conduct. Such ancient authorities as Livy, Dionysius of Halicarnassus, Florus, and Plutarch praised the efficacy of censorship; and Cato the Censor became the austere prototype of the regulatory moralist.[39] Confronted with a society full of the luxurious practices condemned by such classicists as Temple and Bolingbroke, Swift seriously suggested that England establish its own Censor. In *A Project for the Advancement of Religion*, after listing the numerous 'corruptions' of the age, he argued.

> I HAVE often imagined, that something parallel to the Office of Censors antiently in *Rome*, would be of mighty Use among us; and could be easily limited from running into any Exorbitances. The *Romans* understood Liberty at least as well as we; were jealous of it, and upon every Occasion as bold Assertors: Yet I do not remember to have read any great Complaints of the Abuses in that Office among them; but many Effects of it are left upon Record.

The British censor would punish 'Atheism, Drunkenness, Fraud, Avarice' and constantly inspect the nation's religion and morals (*Works*, II 49). Four years later, Swift was still supporting the office of Censor:

> The true way of multiplying Mankind to publick Advantage in such a Country as *England*, is . . . To enact and enforce Sumptuary Laws against Luxury, and all Excesses in Cloathing, Furniture, and the like: To encourage Matrimony, and reward, as the Romans did, those who have a certain Number of Children (*Works*, VI 95)

Echoes of this totalitarian notion reverberate in many of Swift's writings: in the account of the Lilliputians and their laws, the description of the council and laws of the judicious Houyhnhnms, the papers on Irish manufactures, the Drapier's Letters – even in *A Modest Proposal*.

In addition to a rigorous insistence on political balance and the exercise of moral censorship, history provided another means by which social decay and moral dissolution might be arrested: the exaltation of virtuous leaders who best exemplified the positive values of their societies. It was the happy task of historians to immortalize these paragons; historiography provided numerous instances of such conduct and its felicitous results. Xenophon enunciated the 'exemplary' thesis in his *Memorabilia*; Polybius praised the effects occasioned by virtuous behavior in a ruler; Diodorus Siculus recorded the Egyptians' regimen for instructing their princes through holding up earlier rulers as models; and the biographers – Cornelius Nepos and Plutarch in particular – justified their efforts as providing the wherewithal for moral improvement in their readers.[40]

Swift's absorption of this optimistic remedy for moral malaise may be seen in many of his works, most obviously in those dealing with Queen Anne and her reign. *A Project for the Advancement of Religion* extolled the Queen for her virtuous and pious example to her people, but Swift feared that though a vicious prince could in time corrupt an age, a virtuous one might have to exercise his authority to improve *his* age (*Works*, II 47 ff). *The History of the Last Four Years* continued to praise Anne as a model of conduct; and Swift evaluated other English rulers and praised or condemned their behavior for its effects in the *Abstract* of his history; for example, William II, Robert Earl of Gloucester, Stephen (*Works*, TS, X 206, 214, 256, 263). The sermon 'On the Testimony of Conscience' stressed the necessity of virtuous conduct in rulers if a people were to be moral (*Works*, IX 157). And Swift's letters repeatedly urged his noble correspondents to higher virtue that the common people might emulate them and benefit (*Corr.* I 252; II 239; V 179; VI 53). In his later years, he beguiled the time by making out a list 'Of Mean and Great Figures, Made by Several Persons', which catalogued those historical characters most admirable and worthy of veneration: Alexander, Socrates, Cato Uticensis, Thomas More, Charles I, and others (*Works*, TS, XI 173-4).

Underlying the theses and counter-theses which constituted Swift's historical outlook and contributing in a large way to its deterministic character was the ancient metaphor of the body politic. The time-honored analogy between body and state was common in Swift's day. Classicists knew it from the myriad translations of Aesop's fable of the Belly and the Members after 1660, from the political tracts of Plato and Aristotle, and the histories of Dionysius, Livy, and Dio Cassius.[41] Temple espoused it, and Bolingbroke used it to argue against Swift's admiration for Cato.[42] From his youth, when he was absorbing L. Annaeus Florus's vivid account of the birth, growth, maturation, and decline of Rome, to his last transcendent despair at the apparent decline of England, Swift turned to the comparison of the life span of the state with the organic development of a man.[43] He voiced it most fully in his sermon 'On the Duty of Mutual Subjection', sanctifying it with a quote from Romans xii 21: but the body-state metaphor appeared again and again in his works.

When his critic acknowledges the fact that Swift was profoundly influenced by his reading in classical history in the ways just outlined, the submerged basis for many of the satirist's intellectual constructs can be located. Swift's peculiar vantage point for criticizing his society is seen to be the detachment of the historian rather than the violent subjectivism of the thwarted politician. His literary career can be understood as a progressive series of works written to fill what Swift thought to be the needs of a society whose present course was prescribed by historic process. By this principle, Swift's works group themselves into four discernible bodies roughly corresponding to four stages in his historically oriented outlook on his society.

First came the Period of Reform (1701–14). The tracts of this period tend, like *Of Contests and Dissensions* and the *Examiner*, to comb classical history for instances that will shed light on present events and suggest what course of action is the best to follow. Swift shrugs off historical pessimism as an effect of *splendida bilis* or old age (*Works*, I 31). He smiles at those who speak of 'this critical age', for he knows that history will provide useful parallels to present problems. Thucydides and Polybius contain lessons about military conduct and balanced government. Herodotus has helpful information about the effects of climate that can be used by those who wish to establish language academies and regulate the language. Livy and Plutarch provide information about the Roman censorship that can be put into practice in England. The key to reform is understanding the past, even if history must be allegorized in the story of Peter, Martin, and Jack in *A Tale of a Tub* or satirized in *A Digression on Madness*. Whig lords who do not know how to behave in time of confusion may look to Cato for a model. These are the characteristic Swiftian posits in the time of Queen Anne.

After the Queen's death and the collapse of the Tory ministry, Swift entered his Period of Documentation (1714–20). Though some were begun earlier, the works of this era show his obsession with preserving facts, setting the historical record 'straight'. Swift's conception of himself as historiographer dominates such works as his *Enquiry into the Queen's Last Ministry* and the semi-historical *Last Four Years of the Queen*, the writing of which is demanded, Swift says in the Preface, by his duty to God and man. In this period, other works reflect the Dean's image of his place in historical sequence: the 'Verses on the Death of Dr. Swift', the letters to Pope and others, and his pleas to Bolingbroke to undertake an authentic account of what happened between 1710 and 1714 – these come from Swift's intense conviction that men's actions must be justified to posterity.

The writings after 1720 show Swift's historically fostered purview leading him to take an increasingly jaundiced outlook on contemporary events. The analogy he had drawn between Rome and England in the earlier works continued in his representation of the Hanovers as a race of despotic Caesars. The *Drapier's Letters* (1720–1) cast George I in Caesar's role, and Swift indicated in the *Letters* and his private correspondence that he no longer hoped to reform but only to impede the rate of decline. During the 1720s, as the Hanovers became entrenched and especially after George II ushered in England's nominal 'Augustan Age', Swift's works show more and more an historically cultivated resignation. The sermons of the period lament the lapse of taste, morals, and ideas. *Gulliver's Travels* increases in gloomy misanthropy from book to book, citing the history of religious and political schism in England with thinly concealed allegory in the first and third books as the data for generalized lamentations. The correspondence of this period emanates Swift's apprehensions based on his reading in history. This is the Period of Disillusionment (1720–9), the dominant chord for which was struck in Swift's letter to Pope in 1722:

> however I may have been soured by personal ill-treatment or by melancholy prospects for the public, I am too much a politician to expose my own safety by offensive words. And if my genius and spirit be sunk by increasing years, I have at least enough discretion left, not to mistake the measure of my own abilities, by attempting subjects where those talents are necessary which perhaps I have lost with my youth.

The Period of Despair (1729–40) first shows literarily in *A Modest Proposal* (1729), which ironically dismisses all practical reforms as visionary. Swift's brilliance remains but he is almost hopeless of any reformation. Such tracts as *An Essay on Modern Education* (1729), *On Abuses in Dublin* (1732), and *A Proposal to License Beggars* (1735) do not counsel plans for regeneration but advise an adjustment to degenerate realities. Swift's correspondence of this decade, typically dotted with references to historic antecedents, shows his total succumbence to the negative side of his historical outlook. Beginning in 1735, the letters show an increasingly fatalistic attitude toward England's destiny. To Pope he wrote: 'My little domestic affairs are in great confusion by the villainy of agents, and the miseries of this kingdom ... nor am I unconcerned to see all things tending toward absolute power in both nations – it is here in perfection already – although I shall not live to see it established.' To William Pultney on 8 March 1735:

> I will do an unmannerly thing, which is, to bequeath you an epitaph for forty years hence, in two words, *Ultimus Britannorum*. . . . We see the Gothic system of limited monarchy is extinguished in all the nations of Europe. It is utterly extirpated in this wretched kingdom, and yours must be the next. Such has ever been human nature, that a single man ... is able to attack twenty millions, and drag them voluntarily at his chariotwheels.

Again to Pultney on 12 May 1735, in a similar vein:

> If my health were not so bad, although my years be many, I fear I might outlive liberty in England. It has continued longer than any other monarchy, and must end as all others have done ... As to the lust of absolute power, I despair it can ever be cooled, unless Princes had capacity to read the history of the Roman Emperors; how many of them were murdered by their own army.

To Thomas Sheridan on 15 May 1736, in a bitter parody of his early satire:

> I have often given my opinion that an honest man never wished himself to be younger. My sentiment I find ought not to have been universal, because to my sorrow I have lived to change. I have seen since the death of the late Queen, who had few equals before her in every virtue since monarchy began, so great a contempt of religion, morality, learning, and common sense, among us in this kingdom; a hundred degrees beyond what I ever met with in any writer ancient or modern. I am very confident that a complete history of the foolish, wicked, weak, malicious, ruinous, factious, unaccountable, ridiculous, absurd proceedings in this kingdom would contain twelve large volumes in folio of the smallest letter in the largest paper.

At last with ultimate despair to Charles Ford on 22 June 1736: 'I am heartily sick of the worst times and peoples, and oppressions that history can show in either kingdom. . . . I have long given up all hopes of Church or Christianity.'

But if Swift despaired of the Church and the State as possible saviors, he never gave up the hope of divine intervention that could alter the course of English history. In the last of his literary products, he reiterated the providential thesis from which his historical perspective grew. As early as the fourth *Drapier's Letter*, 'To the Whole People of Ireland', Swift was stressing the thesis of the Hand of God: he quoted Bacon in the view that God governs the world by settled laws which He transcends upon highly unusual occasions: the Lord helps those who help themselves (*Works*, x 55). By the mid-1730s he believed that God alone would determine whether England, like Rome, must plummet to the nadir of decline; in 1735: 'May God work a miracle, by changing the hearts of an abandoned people, whose hearts are waxen gross, whose ears are dull of hearing, and whose eyes have been closed (*Corr.* v 179). And once more in 1735: 'I take my age with less mortification, because, if I were younger, I should probably outlive the liberty of England, which, without some unexpected assistance from Heaven, many thousand now alive will see governed by an absolute monarch (*Corr.* v 226). Swift's attitude toward English civilization and its history altered during the forty years of his writing career; but his fundamental assumptions about the essence and accidents of historical patterns never changed.

From the standpoint of modern theory, many criticisms can be made of Swift's historical outlook. According to the critic, it may be narrow, unsophisticated, overly deterministic, or metaphysically unsound. His most censorious critic must grant, nevertheless, that within his assumed premises, Swift was consistent in his historiographical beliefs. He used his wide knowledge about the past to illuminate his understanding of the affairs of his day, often to considerable advantage. He documented his profoundest beliefs with the data of history. His writings benefited constantly from the techniques and learning of historiography. In short, it is doubtful whether his broadest concepts or his specific applications can be fully grasped without a basic awareness of the importance of Swift's historical perspective.

NOTES

[Editor's Note.] Fuller notes appear in the original publication of this essay in the *Journal of British Studies*.

1. See Herbert Davis, 'The Augustan Conception of History', in *Jonathan Swift: Essays on His Satire and Other Studies* (New York, 1964); Irvin Ehrenpreis, *The Personality of Jonathan Swift* (Cambridge, Mass., 1958).

2. See Harold Williams, *Dean Swift's Library* (Cambridge, 1932) pp. 67–78; Edward Bensly, 'The Library at Moor Park', in *Notes and Queries*, CLIX (1930) 48; Harold Williams, 'Jonathan Swift and the Four Last Years of the Queen', in *Library*, XVI (1935) 61–90. Swift's pose as historian is significant in *The Battle of the Books* and *The Mechanical Operation of the Spirit* as well as other works. See Jonathan Swift, *Works*, ed. Herbert Davis (Oxford, 1939–1966) I 83, 145; I 186 ff. Future references to the *Works* will be to this edition unless the volume number is prefaced by the letters TS, which refer to the edition of Temple Scott (1910–14). See Swift, *Works*, TS, V 477; TS, XI 376–8.

3. That Swift used historical *exempla* most extensively in such works as *Contests and Dissensions*, *The Sentiments of a Church of England Man*, the essays for the *Examiner*, *The Conduct of the Allies*, and *A Proposal for Correcting the English Tongue* – all composed as exercises in persuasive logic – is probably indicative of his high seriousness. He often says so in the works themselves, obviously without ironic intent. See Swift, *Works*, I 222; II 1–2; III 29, 41–2; VI 55; TS, XI 8–10. Swift's most concentrated use of historical precedents came, understandably between 1701 and 1714, when he was most directly concerned with political matters in England.

4. Cf. Swift's eternally quoted statement: 'I have got up my Latin pretty well, and am getting up my Greek, but to enter upon causes of Philosophy is what I protest I will rather die in a ditch than go about.' Jonathan Swift, *Correspondence*, ed. F. E. Ball (1910) I 336 (references to *Corr.* are to this edition). Swift's knowledge of Greek literature should not be underestimated, however. Not only did he urge the young clergyman to read Hellenic literature; his knowledge and use of Herodotus, Thucydides, Xenophon, Homer, Hesiod, Hippocrates, Plato, Aristotle, Pindar, and Plutarch is readily demonstrable in Swift's own writings. Moreover, he owned multiple copies of Aeschylus, Sophocles, and Euripides, and he was familiar with the chief Byzantine historians and critics.

5. See Louis Bredvold, 'The Gloom of the Tory Satirists', in *Pope and His Contemporaries*, ed. J. L. Clifford and L. A. Landa (Oxford, 1949); J. W. Johnson, 'The Meaning of "Augustan"', in *Journal of the History of Ideas*, XIX (1958) 507–22. A contrary view is incorporated in J. C. Maxwell's 'Demigods and Pickpockets, The Augustan Myth in Swift and Rousseau', in *Scrutiny*, XI (1942–3) 34 ff.

6. This is only one of several aphorisms on history in the *Thoughts on Various Subjects*. See Swift, *Works*, I 241–2.

7. Addison often repeated his warning of the inapplicability of historical parallels. For one partisan example and Swift's comment on it, see Swift, *Works*, TS, X 376. The *Tritical Essay* may be found in Swift, *Works*, I 246 ff.

8. The method shows to advantage in R. S. Crane, 'The Houyhnhnms, the Yahoos, and the History of Ideas', in *Reason and Imagination*, ed. J. A. Mazzeo (New York, 1962) pp. 231–53; Irvin Ehrenpreis, *Mr. Swift and His Contemporaries* (Cambridge, 1962); and Philip Harth, *Swift and Anglican Rationalism* (Chicago, 1961).

9. Swift gave objective praise to history for these qualities in a number of later works, notably the Latin *Character of Herodotus* (Swift, *Works*, TS, XI 186), the *Vindication of Carteret* (*Works*, VII 232), *The Presbyterian's Plea of Merit* (*Works*, III 46), and *An Essay on Modern Education* in the *Intelligencer*, no. IX (1729).

10. Samuel Johnson, *Works* (1825) I 264.

11. Toynbee's capacious *The Study of History* shows a strong influence by the Augustan historiographical theorists of paradigmatic culture.

12. J. W. Thompson and Wallace Ferguson have written helpful surveys of theogonic history, before and during the Renaissance. Modern theologian-historians such as Reinhold Niebuhr and Karl Jaspers express the twentieth-century equivalent of Swift's basic position.

13. Cf. Louis Landa's Preface to Swift's Sermons. Swift, *Works*, II 19; TS, I 281.

14. *Works*, III 17–18, 19–23.

15. See also *Works*, II 75; III 49, 158–9; VII xxxiv; X 43, 126–7.

16. *Works*, IX 264. Aspects of Swift's attitude are treated in Harth's *Swift and Anglican Rationalism* and Ernest Tuveson's 'Swift and the World-Makers', in *Journal of the History of Ideas*, XI (1950) 54–74.

17. See J. W. Johnson, 'Chronology: Its Concepts and Development', in *History and Theory*, II (1962) 124–45.

18. Cf. Davis, 'Augustan Conception of History'.

19. Polybius, I 1, 35; Diodorus, I 1; Dionysius, v 74. Cf. J. W. Thompson, *A History of Historical Writing* (New York, 1942) pp. 32 ff.

20. Herodotus, I 34, 62; v 92; VI 27; Xenophon, *Memorabilia*, I 1, 4; Plutarch, 'Romulus', XXVIII. See Eduard Fueter, *Geschichte der Neueren Historiographie* (Berlin, 1911), for the influence of classical theogonic writers on Comines, de Thou, and other Renaissance historians known to Swift.

21. See R. F. Jones, *Ancients and Moderns: A Study of the Background of the Battle of the Books* (St Louis, 1936). This pioneer study has been misapplied to Swift by later critics.

22. *Works*, IX 38–41, 264. Cf. VI 78; IX 250; XI 243, 250.

23. Augustine, *Confessions*, XI. R. F. Jones, Carl Becker, J. B. Bury, and Heinrich Meyer, among others, have dealt with aspects of chronology and theories of time. See Francis C. Haber, *The Age of the World: Moses to Darwin* (Baltimore, 1959).

24. Cf. Carl Becker, *The Heavenly City of the Eighteenth Century Philosophers* (New Haven, 1932) p. 124.

25. Herodotus, I 5; Dionysius, v 77; Diodorus, I 6.

26. Tertullian, *Apology*, XIX; Paulus Orosius, *Seven Books of History Against the Pagans* (New York, 1936) p. 75; Cyprian, *Writings* (Edinburgh, 1868) pp. 423–9.

27. Cf. Victor Harris, *All Coherence Gone* (Chicago, 1949).

28. This subject is expanded in J. W. Johnson, 'Of Differing Ages and Climes', in *Journal of the History of Ideas*, XXI (1960) 465–80.

29. Herodotus, IX 122.

30. Xenophon, *Memorabilia*, I 2.

31. Strabo, VII 3.7.

32. Cato, I–VI; Varro, I–II.

33. Diodorus, VII 12; Livy, VII 32, XXIII 45, XXXIX 6; Appian, III 1; Florus, I 31.15, I 38.3; Justin, *History of the World*, in *Justin, Cornelius Nepos, and Eutropius*, ed. J. S. Watson (1884) p. 10.

34. See Polydore Vergil, *English History* (London, 1846), pp. 77, 109, 245–6; Samuel Daniel, *History* (1650) pp. 25, 166, 204–5; Lord Clarendon, *History of the Rebellion* (1826) I 4; Gilbert Burnet, *History of My Own Time* (1897) p. 330.

35. William Temple, *Works* (1757) III 93. See also I 54, 61, 136; III 74.

36. Cf. Zera Fink, *The Classical Republicans* (Evanston, 1945), for a full scale study of the 'balanced government' theory in the seventeenth century and after.

37. Polybius, IV–VI. Cf. Dionysius, II 8; also Eutropius and Justin in *Justin, Cornelius Nepos, and Eutropius*, ed. Watson, pp. 39 ff, 453 ff. Addison, in *The Freeholder*, no. 51, and Temple, in *Of Popular Discontents*, countenance the Polybian Thesis.

38. See 'Upon the Martyrdom of King Charles', in Swift, *Works*, IX 219.

39. Livy, IV 8, XXIV 1; Dionysius, IV 24; Florus, II 34; Plutarch, 'Cato', XVI.

40. Xenophon, II 1; Polybius, XI 10; Diodorus, I 94, XI 1; Justin in *Justin, Cornelius Nepos, and Eutropius*, ed. Watson, p. 68; Plutarch, 'Numa', VI. Cf. Temple, *Works*, I 54; III 43.

41. Dionysius, VI 86; Livy, II 32; Dio Cassius, IV. Each refers to the Aesopian fable.

42. Temple, *Works*, III 12–13, 458; Swift, *Corr.* III 91–2.

43. Florus, Intro. I 17, 23. The implications of the comparison to Swift are more completely dealt with in Johnson, 'Meaning of "Augustan"', in *Journal of the History of Ideas*, XIX (1958) 507–22.

F. R. LEAVIS

The Irony of Swift (1934)

SWIFT is a great English writer. For opening with this truism I have
a reason: I wish to discuss Swift's writings – to examine what they are;
and they are (as the extant commentary bears witness) of such a kind
that it is peculiarly difficult to discuss them without shifting the focus
of discussion to the kind of man that Swift was. What is most interesting
in them does not so clearly belong to the realm of things made and
detached that literary criticism, which has certainly not the less its
duties towards Swift, can easily avoid turning – unawares, and that is,
degenerating – into something else. In the attempt to say what makes
these writings so remarkable, reference to the man who wrote is
indeed necessary; but there are distinctions. For instance, one may (it
appears), having offered to discuss the nature and import of Swift's
satire, find oneself countering imputations of misanthropy with the
argument that Swift earned the love of Pope, Arbuthnot, Gay, several
other men and two women: this should not be found necessary by the
literary critic. But the irrelevancies of Thackeray and of his castigator,
the late Charles Whibley – irrelevancies not merely from the point of
view of literary criticism – are too gross to need placarding; more
insidious deviations are possible.

The reason for the opening truism is also the reason for the choice of
title. To direct the attention upon Swift's irony gives, I think, the best
chance of dealing adequately, without deviation or confusion, with
what is essential in his work. But it involves also (to anticipate an
objection) a slight to the classical status of *Gulliver's Travels*, a book
which, though it may represent Swift's most impressive achievement
in the way of complete creation – the thing achieved and detached –
does not give the best opportunities for examining his irony. And
Gulliver's Travels, one readily agrees, hasn't its classical status for nothing.
But neither is it for nothing that, suitably abbreviated, it has become a
classic for children. What for the adult reader constitutes its peculiar
force – what puts it in so different a class from *Robinson Crusoe* – resides

for the most part in the fourth book (to a less extent in the third). The adult may re-read the first two parts, as he may *Robinson Crusoe*, with great interest, but his interest, apart from being more critically conscious, will not be of a different order from the child's. He will, of course, be aware of an ingenuity of political satire in 'Lilliput', but the political satire, is unless for historians, not very much alive today. And even the more general satire characteristic of the second book will not strike him as very subtle. His main satisfaction, a great deal enhanced, no doubt, by the ironic seasoning, will be that which Swift, the student of the *Mariner's Magazine* and of travellers' relations, aimed to supply in the bare precision and the matter-of-fact realness of his narrative.

But what in Swift is most important, the disturbing characteristic of his genius, is a peculiar emotional intensity; that which, in *Gulliver*, confronts us in the Struldbrugs and the Yahoos. It is what we find ourselves contemplating when elsewhere we examine his irony. To lay the stress upon an emotional intensity should be matter of commonplace: actually, in routine usage, the accepted word for Swift is 'intellectual'. We are told, for instance, that his is pre-eminently 'intellectual satire' (though we are not told what satire is). For this formula the best reason some commentators can allege is the elaboration of analogies – their 'exact and elaborate propriety'[1] – in *Gulliver*. But a muddled perception can hardly be expected to give a clear account of itself; the stress on Swift's 'intellect' (Sir Herbert Read alludes to his 'mighty intelligence'[2]) registers, it would appear, a confused sense, not only of the mental exercise involved in his irony, but of the habitually critical attitude he maintains towards the world, and of the negative emotions he specializes in.

From 'critical' to 'negative' in this last sentence is, it will be observed, a shift of stress. There are writings of Swift where 'critical' is the more obvious word (and where 'intellectual' may seem correspondingly apt) – notably, the pamphlets or pamphleteering essays in which the irony is instrumental, directed and limited to a given end. The *Argument Against Abolishing Christianity* and the *Modest Proposal*, for instance, are discussable in the terms in which satire is commonly discussed: as the criticism of vice, folly, or other aberration, by some kind of reference to positive standards. But even here, even in the *Argument*, where Swift's ironic intensity undeniably directs itself to the defence of something that he is intensely concerned to defend, the effect is essentially negative. The positive itself appears only negatively – a kind of skeletal presence, rigid enough, but without life or body; a necessary pre-condition, as it were, of directed negation. The intensity is purely destructive.

The point may be enforced by the obvious contrast with Gibbon – except that between Swift's irony and Gibbon's the contrast is so complete that any one point is difficult to isolate. Gibbon's irony, in the fifteenth chapter, may be aimed against, instead of for, Christianity, but contrasted with Swift's it is an assertion of faith. The decorously insistent pattern of Gibbonian prose insinuates a solidarity with the reader (the implied solidarity in Swift is itself ironical – a means to betrayal), establishes an understanding and habituates to certain assumptions. The reader, it is implied, is an eighteenth-century gentleman ('rational', 'candid', 'polite', 'elegant', 'humane'); eighteen hundred years ago he would have been a pagan gentleman, living by these same standards (those of absolute civilization); by these standards (present everywhere in the stylized prose and adroitly emphasized at keypoints in such phrases as 'the polite Augustus', 'the elegant mythology of the Greeks') the Jews and early Christians are seen to have been ignorant fanatics, uncouth and probably dirty. Gibbon as a historian of Christianity had, we know, limitations; but the positive standards by reference to which his irony works represent something impressively realized in eighteenth-century civilization; impressively 'there' too in the grandiose, assured and ordered elegance of his history. (When, on the other hand, Lytton Strachey, with a Gibbonian period or phrase or word, a 'remarkable', 'oddly', or 'curious', assures us that he feels an amused superiority to these Victorian puppets, he succeeds only in conveying his personal conviction that he feels amused and superior.)

Gibbon's irony, then, habituates and reassures, ministering to a kind of judicial certitude or complacency. Swift's is essentially a matter of surprise and negation; its function is to defeat habit, to intimidate and to demoralize. What he assumes in the *Argument* is not so much a common acceptance of Christianity as that the reader will be ashamed to have to recognize how fundamentally unchristian his actual assumptions, motives and attitudes are. And in general the implication is that it would shame people if they were made to recognize themselves unequivocally. If one had to justify this irony according to the conventional notion of satire, then its satiric efficacy would be to make comfortable non-recognition, the unconsciousness of habit, impossible.

A method of surprise does not admit of description in an easy formula. Surprise is a perpetually varied accompaniment of the grave, dispassionate, matter-of-fact tone in which Swift delivers his intensities. The dissociation of emotional intensity from its usual accompaniments inhibits the automatic defence-reaction:

> He is a Presbyterian in politics, and an atheist in religion; but he chooses at present to whore with a Papist.
> What baliff would venture to arrest Mr Steele, now he has the honour to be your representative? and what bailiff ever scrupled it before?

– Or inhibits, let us say, the normal response; since 'defence' suggests that it is the 'victim' whose surprise we should be contemplating, whereas it is our own, whether Swift's butt is Wharton or the atheist or mankind in general. 'But satire, being levelled at all, is never resented for an offence by any, since every individual makes bold to understand it of others, and very wisely removes his particular part of the burden upon the shoulders of the World, which are broad enough and able to bear it.'[3] There is, of course, no contradiction here; a complete statement would be complex. But, actually, the discussion of satire in terms of offence and castigation, victim and castigator, is unprofitable, though the idea of these has to be taken into account. What we are concerned with (the reminder is especially opportune) is an arrangement of words on the page and their effects – the emotions, attitudes and ideas that they organize.

Our reaction, as Swift says, is not that of the butt or victim; nevertheless, it necessarily entails some measure of sympathetic self-projection. We more often, probably, feel the effect of the words as an intensity in the castigator than as an effect upon a victim: the dissociation of animus from the usual signs defines for our contemplation a peculiarly intense contempt or disgust. When, as sometimes we have to do, we talk in terms of effect on the victim, then 'surprise' becomes an obviously apt word; he is to be betrayed again and again, into an incipient acquiescence:

> Sixthly, This would be a great Inducement to Marriage, which all wise Nations have either encouraged by Rewards, or enforced by Laws and Penalties. It would increase the Care and Tenderness of Mothers towards their Children, when they were sure of a Settlement for Life, to the poor Babes, provided in some Sort by the Publick to their annual Profit instead of Expence; we should soon see an honest Emulation among the married Women, *which of them could bring the fattest Child to the Market*. Men would

become as *fond* of their Wives during the Time of their Pregnancy, as they are now of their *Mares* in Foal, their *Cows* in Calf, or *Sows* when they are ready to farrow, nor offer to beat or kick them (as is too *frequent* a Practice) for fear of a Miscarriage.

The implication is: 'This, as you so obligingly demonstrate, is the only kind of argument that appeals to you; here are your actual faith and morals. How, on consideration, do you like the smell of them?'

But when in reading the *Modest Proposal* we are most engaged, it is an effect directly upon ourselves that we are most disturbingly aware of. The dispassionate, matter-of-fact tone induces a feeling and a motion of assent, while the burden, at the same time, compels the feelings appropriate to rejection, and in the contrast – the tension – a remarkably disturbing energy is generated. A sense of an extraordinary energy is the general effect of Swift's irony. The intensive means just indicated are reinforced extensively in the continuous and unpredictable movement of the attack, which turns this way and that, comes now from one quarter and now from another, inexhaustibly surprising – making again an odd contrast with the sustained and level gravity of the tone. If Swift does for a moment appear to settle down to a formula it is only in order to betray; to induce a trust in the solid ground before opening the pitfall.

> His *Tale of a Tub* has little resemblance to his other pieces. It exhibits a vehemence and rapidity of mind, a copiousness of images, a vivacity of diction, such as he afterwards never possessed, or never exerted. It is of a mode so distinct and peculiar, that it must be considered by itself; what is true of that, is not true of anything else he has written.

What Johnson is really testifying to here is the degree in which the *Tale of a Tub* is characteristic and presents the qualities of Swift's genius in concentrated form. 'That he has in his works no metaphors, as has been said, is not true,' says Johnson a sentence or two later, 'but his few metaphors seem to be received rather by necessity than choice.' This last judgement may at any rate serve to enforce Johnson's earlier observation that in the *Tale of a Tub* Swift's powers function with unusual freedom. For the 'copiousness of images' that Johnson constates is, as the phrase indicates, not a matter of choice but of essential genius. And, as a matter of fact, in this 'copiousness of images' the characteristics that we noted in discussing Swift's pamphleteering irony have their supreme expression.

It is as if the gift applied in *Gulliver* to a very limiting task – directed and confined by a scheme uniting a certain consistency in analogical elaboration with verisimilitude – were here enjoying free play. For the bent expressing itself in this 'copiousness' is clearly fundamental. It shows itself in the spontaneous metaphorical energy of Swift's prose – in the image, action or blow that, leaping out of the prosaic manner, continually surprises and disconcerts the reader: 'such a man, truly wise, creams off Nature, leaving the sour and the dregs for philosophy and reason to lap up'. It appears with as convincing a spontaneity in the sardonic vivacity of comic vision that characterizes the narrative, the presentment of action and actor. If, then, the continual elaborate play of analogy is a matter of cultivated habit, it is a matter also of culti-vated natural bent, a congenial development. It is a development that would seem to bear a relation to the Metaphysical fashion in verse (Swift was born in 1667). The spirit of it is that of a fierce and insolent game, but a game to which Swift devotes himself with a creative intensity.

> And whereas the mind of man, when he gives the spur and bridle to his thoughts, does never stop, but naturally sallies out into both extremes of high and low, of good and evil, his first flight of fancy commonly trans-ports him to ideas of what is most perfect, finished, and exalted, till, having soared out of his own reach and sight, not well perceiving how near the frontiers of height and depth border upon each other, with the same course and wing he falls down plump into the lowest bottom of things, like one who travels the east into the west, or like a straight line drawn by its own length into a circle. Whether a tincture of malice in our natures makes us fond of furnishing every bright idea with its reverse, or whether reason, reflecting upon the sum of things, can, like the sun, serve only to enlighten one half of the globe, leaving the other half by necessity under shade and darkness, or whether fancy, flying up to the imagination of what is highest and best, becomes over-short, and spent, and weary, and suddenly falls, like a dead bird of paradise, to the ground . . .

One may (without difficulty) resist the temptation to make the point by saying that this is poetry; one is still tempted to say that the use to which so exuberant an energy is put is a poet's. 'Exuberant' seems, no doubt, a paradoxical word to apply to an energy used as Swift uses his; but the case is essentially one for paradoxical descrip-tions.

In his use of negative materials – negative emotions and attitudes –

there is something that it is difficult not to call creative, though the aim always is destructive. Not all the materials, of course, are negative: the 'bird of paradise' in the passage above is alive as well as dead. Effects of this kind, often much more intense, are characteristic of the *Tale of a Tub*, where surprise and contrast operate in modes that there is some point in calling poetic. 'The most heterogeneous ideas are yoked by violence together' – and in the juxtaposition intensity is generated.

'Paracelsus brought a squadron of stink-pot-flingers from the snowy mountains of Rhætia' – this (which comes actually from *The Battle of the Books*) does not represent what I have in mind; it is at once too simple and too little charged with animus. Swift's intensities are intensities of rejection and negation; his poetic juxtapositions are, characteristically, destructive in intention, and when they most seem creative of energy are most successful in spoiling, reducing, and destroying. Sustained 'copiousness' continually varying, and concentrating surprise in sudden local foci, cannot be represented in short extracts; it must suffice here to say that this kind of thing may be found at a glance on almost any page:

> Meantime it is my earnest request that so useful an undertaking may be entered upon (if their Majesties please) with all convenient speed, because I have a strong inclination before I leave the world to taste a blessing which we mysterious writers can seldom reach till we have got into our graves, whether it is that fame, being a fruit grafted on the body, can hardly grow and much less ripen till the stock is in the earth, or whether she be a bird of prey, and is lured among the rest to pursue after the scent of a carcass, or whether she conceives her trumpet sounds best and farthest when she stands on a tomb, by the advantage of a rising ground and the echo of a hollow vault.

It is, of course, possible to adduce Swift's authority for finding that his negations carry with them a complementary positive – an implicit assertion. But (*pace* Charles Whibley) the only thing in the nature of a positive that most readers will find convincingly present is self-assertion – *superbia*. Swift's way of demonstrating his superiority is to destroy, but he takes a positive delight in his power. And that the reader's sense of the negativeness of the *Tale of a Tub* is really qualified comes out when we refer to the Yahoos and the Struldbrugs for a test. The ironic detachment is of such a kind as to reassure us that this savage exhibition is mainly a game, played because it is the insolent pleasure of the author:

'demonstration of superiority' is as good a formula as any for its
prevailing spirit. Nevertheless, about a superiority that asserts itself in
this way there is something disturbingly odd, and again and again in the
Tale of a Tub we come on intensities that shift the stress decisively and
remind us how different from Voltaire Swift is, even in his most
complacent detachment.

I propose to examine in illustration a passage from the *Digression
Concerning the Original, the Use, and Improvement of Madness in a
Commonwealth* (i.e. section IX). It will have, in the nature of the case,
to be a long one, but since it exemplifies at the same time all Swift's
essential characteristics, its length will perhaps be tolerated. I shall
break up the passage for convenience of comment, but, except for the
omission of nine or ten lines in the second instalment, quotation will be
continuous:

> For the brain in its natural position and state of serenity disposeth its
> owner to pass his life in the common forms, without any thought of sub-
> duing multitudes to his own power, his reasons, or his visions, and the more
> he shapes his understanding by the pattern of human learning, the less he is
> inclined to form parties after his particular notions, because that instructs
> him in his private infirmities, as well as in the stubborn ignorance of the
> people. But when a man's fancy gets astride on his reason, when imagina-
> tion is at cuffs with the senses, and common understanding as well as com-
> mon sense is kicked out of doors, the first proselyte he makes is himself;
> and when that is once compassed, the difficulty is not so great in bringing
> over others, a strong delusion always operating from without as vigorously
> as from within. For cant and vision are to the ear and the eye the same that
> tickling is to the touch. Those entertainments and pleasures we most value
> in life are such as dupe and play the wag with the senses. For if we take an
> examination of what is generally understood by happiness, as it has
> respect either to the understanding or to the senses, we shall find all its
> properties and adjuncts will herd under this short definition, that it is a
> perpetual possession of being well deceived.

Swift's ant-like energy – the businesslike air, obsessed intentness and
unpredictable movement – have already had an effect. We are not, at the
end of this instalment, as sure that we know just what his irony is doing
as we were at the opening. Satiric criticism of sectarian 'enthusiasm'
by reference to the 'common forms' – the Augustan standards – is
something that, in Swift, we can take as very seriously meant. But in the
incessant patter of the argument we have (helped by such things as, at

the end, the suggestion of animus in that oddly concrete 'herd') a sense that direction and tone are changing. Nevertheless, the change of tone for which the next passage is most remarkable comes as a disconcerting surprise:

And first, with relation to the mind or understanding, it is manifest what mighty advantages fiction has over truth, and the reason is just at our elbow; because imagination can build nobler scenes and produce more wonderful revolutions than fortune or Nature will be at the expense to furnish. . . . Again, if we take this definition of happiness and examine it with reference to the senses, it will be acknowledged wonderfully adapt. How sad and insipid do all objects accost us that are not conveyed in the vehicle of delusion! How shrunk is everything as it appears in the glass of Nature, so that if it were not for the assistance of artificial mediums, false lights, refracted angles, varnish, and tinsel, there would be a mighty level in the felicity and enjoyments of mortal men. If this were seriously considered by the world, as I have a certain reason to suspect it hardly will, men would no longer reckon among their high points of wisdom the art of exposing weak sides and publishing infirmities – an employment, in my opinion, neither better nor worse than that of unmasking, which, I think, has never been allowed fair usage, either in the world or the playhouse.

The suggestion of changing direction does not, in the first part of this passage, bring with it anything unsettling: from ridicule of 'enthusiasm' to ridicule of human capacity for self-deception is an easy transition. The reader, as a matter of fact, begins to settle down to the habit, the steady drift of this irony, and is completely unprepared for the sudden change of tone and reversal of attitude in the two sentences beginning: 'How sad and insipid do all objects', etc. Exactly what the change means or is, it is difficult to be certain (and that is of the essence of the effect). But the tone has certainly a personal intensity and the ironic detachment seems suddenly to disappear. It is as if one found Swift in the place – at the point of view – where one expected to find his butt. But the ambiguously mocking sentence with which the paragraph ends reinforces the uncertainty.

The next paragraph keeps the reader for some time in uneasy doubt. The irony has clearly shifted its plane, but in which direction is the attack going to develop? Which, to be safe, must one dissociate oneself from, 'credulity' or 'curiosity'?

In the proportion that credulity is a more peaceful possession of the mind than curiosity, so far preferable is that wisdom which converses about the surface to that pretended philosophy which enters into the depths of things and then comes gravely back with informations and discoveries, that in the inside they are good for nothing. The two senses to which all objects first address themselves are the sight and the touch; these never examine further than the colour, the shape, the size, and whatever other qualities dwell or are drawn by art upon the outward of bodies; and then comes reason officiously, with tools for cutting, and opening, and mangling, and piercing, offering to demonstrate that they are not of the same consistence quite through. Now I take all this to be the last degree of perverting Nature, one of whose eternal laws is to put her best furniture forward. And therefore, in order to save the charges of all such expensive anatomy for the time to come, I do here think fit to inform the reader that in such conclusions as these reason is certainly in the right; and that in most corporeal beings which have fallen under my cognisance the outside hath been infinitely preferable to the in, whereof I have been further convinced from some late experiments. Last week I saw a woman flayed, and you will hardly believe how much it altered her person for the worse.

The peculiar intensity of that last sentence is, in its own way, so decisive that it has for the reader the effect of resolving uncertainty in general. The disturbing force of the sentence is a notable instance of a kind already touched on: repulsion is intensified by the momentary co-presence, induced by the tone, of incipient and incompatible feelings (or motions) of acceptance. And that Swift feels the strongest animus against 'curiosity' is now beyond all doubt. The natural corollary would seem to be that 'credulity', standing ironically for the 'common forms' – the sane, socially sustained, common-sense illusions – is the positive that the reader must associate himself with and rest on for safety. The next half-page steadily and (to all appearances) unequivocally confirms this assumption:

Yesterday I ordered the carcass of a beau to be stripped in my presence, when we were all amazed to find so many unsuspected faults under one suit of clothes. Then I laid open his brain, his heart, and his spleen, but I plainly perceived at every operation that the farther we proceeded, we found the defects increase upon us in number and bulk; from all of which I justly formed this conclusion to myself, that whatever philosopher or projector can find out an art to sodder and patch up the flaws and imper-fections of Nature, will deserve much better of mankind and teach us a much more useful science than that, so much in present esteem, of widening and exposing them (like him who held anatomy to be the ultimate end of physic). And he whose fortunes and dispositions have placed him in a convenient station to enjoy the fruits of this noble art, he that can with Epicurus content his ideas with the films and images that fly off upon his senses from the superficies of things, such a man, truly wise, creams off Nature, leaving the sour and the dregs for philosophy and reason to lap up.

Assumption has become habit, and has been so nourished that few readers note anything equivocal to trouble them in that last sentence: the concrete force of 'creams off', 'sour', 'dregs' and 'lap up' seems unmistakably to identify Swift with an intense animus against 'philosophy and reason' (understood implicitly to stand for 'curiosity' the anatomist). The reader's place, of course, is with Swift.

The trap is sprung in the last sentence of the paragraph: 'This is the sublime and refined point of felicity called the possession of being well-deceived, the serene peaceful state of being a fool among knaves.'

What is left? The next paragraph begins significantly: 'But to return to madness.' This irony may be critical, but 'critical' turns out in no very long run, to be indistinguishable from 'negative'. The positives disappear. Even when, as in the Houyhnhnms, they seem to be more substantially present, they disappear under our 'curiosity'. The Houyhnhnms, of course, stand for Reason, Truth and Nature, the Augustan positives, and it was in deadly earnest that Swift appealed to these; but how little at best they were anything solidly realized comparison with Pope brings out. Swift did his best for the Houyhnhnms, and they may have all the reason, but the Yahoos have all the life. Gulliver's master 'thought Nature and reason were sufficient guides for a reasonable animal', but nature and reason as Gulliver exhibits them are curiously negative, and the reasonable animals appear to have nothing in them to guide. 'They have no fondness for their colts or foals, but the care they take in educating them proceeds entirely from the dictates of reason.' This freedom from irrational feelings and impulses simplifies other matters too: 'their language doth not abound in variety of words, because their wants and passions are fewer than among us'. And so conversation, in this model society, is simplified: 'nothing passed but what was useful, expressed in the fewest and most significant words . . .'

Courtship, love, presents, jointures, settlements, have no place in their thoughts, or terms whereby to express them in their language. The young couple meet and are joined, merely because it is the determination of their parents and friends: it is what they see done every day, and they look upon it as one of the necessary actions of a reasonable being.

The injunction of 'temperance, industry, exercise, and cleanliness . . . the lessons enjoined to the young ones of both sexes', seems unnecessary; except possibly for exercise, the usefulness of which would not, perhaps, be immediately apparent to the reasonable young.

The clean skin of the Houyhnhnms, in short, is stretched over a void; instincts, emotions, and life, which complicate the problem of cleanliness and decency, are left for the Yahoos with the dirt and the indecorum. Reason, truth, and nature serve instead; the Houyhnhnms (who scorn metaphysics) find them adequate. Swift too scorned metaphysics, and never found anything better to contend for than a skin, a surface, an outward show. An outward show is, explicitly, all he contends for in the quite unironical *Project for the Advancement of Religion*, and the difference between the reality of religion and the show is, for the author of the *Tale of a Tub*, hardly substantial. Of Jack we are told, 'nor could all the world persuade him, as the common phrase, is to eat his victuals like a Christian'. It is characteristic of Swift that he should put in these terms, showing a complete incapacity even to guess what religious feeling might be, a genuine conviction that Jack should be made to kneel when receiving the Sacrament.

Of the intensity of this conviction there can be no doubt. The Church of England was the established 'common form', and, moreover, was Swift's Church: his insane egotism reinforced the savagery with which he fought to maintain this cover over the void, this decent surface. But what the savagery of the passage from the *Digression* shows mainly is Swift's sense of insecurity and of the undisguisable flimsiness of any surface that offered.

The case, of course, is more complex. In the passage examined the 'surface' becomes, at the most savage moment, a human skin. Swift's negative horror, at its most disturbing, becomes one with his disgust-obsession: he cannot bear to be reminded that under the skin there is blood, mess and entrails; and the skin itself, as we know from *Gulliver*, must not be seen from too close. Hypertrophy of the sense of unclean-ness, of the instinct of repulsion, is not uncommon; nor is its association with what accompanies it in Swift. What is uncommon is Swift's genius, and the paradoxical vitality with which this self-defeat of life – life turned against itself – is manifested. In the *Tale of a Tub* the defeat is also a triumph; the genius delights in its mastery, in its power to destroy, and negation is felt as self-assertion. It is only when time has confirmed Swift in disappointment and brought him to more intimate contemplation of physical decay that we get the Yahoos and the Struldbrugs.

Here, well on this side of pathology, literary criticism stops. To attempt encroachments would be absurd, and, even if one were qualified, unprofitable. No doubt psychopathology and medicine have an interesting commentary to offer, but their help is not necessary. Swift's genius belongs to literature, and its appreciation to literary criticism.

We have, then, in his writings probably the most remarkable expression of negative feelings and attitudes that literature can offer – the spectacle of creative powers (the paradoxical description seems right) exhibited consistently in negation and rejection. His verse demands an essay to itself, but fits in readily with what has been said. 'In poetry', he reports of the Houyhnhnms, 'they must be allowed to excel all other mortals; wherein the justness of their similes and the minuteness as well as exactness of their descriptions are, indeed, inimitable. Their verses abound very much in both of these. . . .' The actuality of presentment for which Swift is notable, in prose as well as verse, seems always to owe its convincing 'justness' to, at his least actively malicious, a coldly intense scrutiny, a potentially hostile attention. 'To his domesticks', says Johnson, 'he was naturally rough; and a man of rigorous temper, with that vigilance of minute attention which his works discover, must have been a master that few could bear.' *Directions to Servants* and the *Polite Conversation* enforce obviously the critical bearing and felicity of Johnson's remark.

A great writer – yes; that account still imposes itself as fitting, though his greatness is no matter of moral grandeur or human centrality; our sense of it is merely a sense of great force. And this force, as we feel it, is conditioned by frustration and constriction; the channels of life have been blocked and perverted. That we should be so often invited to regard him as a moralist and an idealist would seem to be mainly a witness to the power of vanity, and the part that vanity can play in literary appreciation: *saeva indignatio* is an indulgence that solicits us all, and the use of literature by readers and critics for the projection of nobly suffering selves is familiar. No doubt, too, it is pleasant to believe that unusual capacity for egotistic animus means unusual distinction of intellect; but, as we have seen, there is no reason to lay stress on intellect in Swift. His work does indeed exhibit an extraordinary play of mind; but it is not great intellectual force that is exhibited in his indifference to the problems raised – in, for instance, the 'Voyage to the Houyhnhnms' – by his use of the concept, or the word, 'Nature'. It is not merely that he had an Augustan contempt for metaphysics; he shared the shallowest complacencies of Augustan common sense: his irony might destroy these, but there is no conscious criticism.

He was, in various ways, curiously unaware – the reverse of clairvoyant. He is distinguished by the intensity of his feelings, not by insight into them, and he certainly does not impress us as a mind in possession of its experience.

We shall not find Swift remarkable for intelligence if we think of Blake.

NOTES

1. Churton Collins, *Jonathan Swift, A Biographical and Critical Study* (1893) p. 202.
2. *English Prose Style* (1928; new revised ed. 1952).
3. *A Tale of a Tub*: the Preface.

A. L. ROWSE

Swift as Poet (1945)

I

OF all the books that have come out in late years about Swift, there are few that are up to the subject. Middleton Murry's biography was, surprisingly, the best; but then Murry had a remarkable critical intelligence and even finer understanding, when away from his hobbies. Professor Louis Landa gave us an excellent specialist book on Swift and the Church. Professor Quintana limited himself to a study of Swift's mind and art as a writer.[1] This provides a careful survey of Swift's work, connects it up with the large body of research that has accumulated on the subject, and gives us enough of Swift's life to make it intelligible.

It is the background to Swift's thought, the various elements that entered into it from other thinkers, where they came from and how they affected him, that now need more study. There is this excuse, that there is no history of English thought in the seventeenth century, as there is of the eighteenth century, by Sir Leslie Stephen. One notices this lack most in regard to the problem of Swift's belief – or unbelief; for there was a strain of deism, or of definite unbelief, among English thinkers of that age, which must surely have left its mark on Swift's mind. Professor Quintana notices the influence of Hobbes's materialism upon Swift's view of the imagination and his aesthetics generally; but it may be that that influence went further, to affect the whole of Swift's intellectual position, to instil scepticism into a mind not naturally sceptical, to denude him of any vestige of idealism in his view of the world and experience. There is a considerable body of deistic writing contemporaneous with Swift, which is part of his intellectual background: such writers as Shaftesbury, Toland, Mandeville. Professor Quintana says that 'when the great Dean of St. Patrick's died in 1745, he had already ceased to be understood by the eighteenth century'. All the more reason to consider him historically in relation to his environment.

The question of Swift's religious convictions is central. On this point neither defence nor excuse is necessary; it is enough to understand him. 'It is not that Swift wavered in belief, nor that in conduct he failed to be guided by it,' says Professor Quintana. 'In all these matters he was rigorously consistent, rigorously in accord with his theoretical premises.' But the point is whether these premises were in accordance with orthodox Christianity. I cannot but think that Archbishop Sharp, Queen Anne, the instinct of religious believers (typified by Dr Johnson, who knew very well), were right about Swift. They scented that there was no religious belief in him. As for getting a bishopric, he was lucky to become a dean. Only an age when patronage was in the ascendant would have been so broadminded; any other age would have expected a dean to believe.

Such conception of religion as he had was of an external and institutional character; there is no sign of personal belief. Even in the 'Prayers for Stella', the nearest in expression he achieved, there is more evidence of doubt than of faith or hope; whereas he frequently gives expression to the Manichee view that life is in itself an evil to be endured. Perhaps, however, one need not take him so seriously as he took himself on this point; he clearly enjoyed some parts of his own life – the years 1709–14, for example, the exercise of power, his many friendships, writing.

Professor Quintana is at pains to rebut the charge that Swift was a misanthrope. Why shouldn't Swift be a misanthrope? Hatred of human beings is as legitimate a subject of art as love of them, and its possibilities more rarely explored. Nor need one be prudish about the scatological poems with their 'disgusting' imagery. They are often artistic successes, and are as much part of Swift's mind as the 'fine, satiric touch' – indeed more intimately part of his mind, all the more revealing of what kind of mind that was. The self-laceration of these poems may represent an excessive sensibility, turned back upon itself, turned inside out. 'I was to see Lady ——,' he wrote to Stella, 'who is just up after lying-in; and the ugliest sight I have seen, pale, dead, old and yellow, for want of her paint. *She has turned my stomach*. But she will soon be painted, and a beauty again.' In this one perceives the type of all those poems of physical disgust he wrote: they are due to a morbid degree of sensitiveness, acting upon a disillusioned temperament, to make him torture himself and others.

There was certainly an acute tension between defeatism in his view of human nature and an active temperament in himself, between reason and the emotions, in Swift's mind. He had no illusions about human nature, yet he did – perhaps unreasonably – expect men to be better than they are. He insisted always upon the moral responsibility of the person. In his outlook there was too great a dichotomy between reason and the emotions; he thought of them as simply and necessarily in conflict and this increased the strain in his inner life. The tension bore fruit in his art, but it made for unhappiness in the man. Swift believed, in accordance with the materialism of Hobbes, that 'self-love, as it is the motive to all our actions, so it is the sole cause of our grief'. It is a forbidding view to hold, repressive of the emotional life, especially with a man so self-conscious as Swift: he at any rate was not under the illusions that most people are as to their motives. He girded at *la condition humaine*, but might he not have been a little happier, if realising how little disinterestedness there was in the world or in himself, he had made it more his aim?

As it was, his intellectual position was at every point that which his interests demanded and with which his person was identified. A churchman, he saw only the interests of his own sect; a Tory, of his own party; an Irish Protestant, he stood up for the Irish Church against both Catholics and Dissenters. If he had happened to be a Dissenter, or had remained a Whig, he would have been as vehement on the other side. Professor Quintana comments, 'however ignoble his actuating impulses may have been, the ends which he achieved cannot be judged solely in terms of motive'. What is odd is Swift's consciousness of the situation and his acceptance of it. It is like his denial of any place to idealism in life, or to imagination in poetry: an abnegation springing from his fear of disillusionment. He realised all too clearly the discomfort of the latter, but did not allow for the necessity for a certain amount of illusion or even humbug to make life tolerable. As T. S. Eliot constantly enforced, human beings can bear very little reality. Swift stripped life to the bare bones.

Professor Quintana insists upon the richness and fertility of Swift's later phase. 'Nothing is further from the truth than the idea commonly entertained regarding Swift's latter years of activity. He was still the great artist, producing verse and prose of undiminished brilliance and intensity, and he remained an imperious public figure.' So often this period is treated merely as an aftermath. Yet it is in this period that he produced *Gulliver's Travels* and much of the best of his poetry. All the more reason for not agreeing that *Gulliver* is inferior to *A Tale of a Tub*. There is a universality and a range in *Gulliver* which the earlier work does not compass; it has, too, a depth of experience and conviction, where *A Tale of a Tub* is more intellectual, cold and academic. *Gulliver* is the work that the world has chosen; that kind of universal consensus is not likely to be wrong.

II

The poetry of Swift is an esoteric taste. There is hardly anyone in our literary history who has had a liking for it since his own time. Yeats is a notable exception, perhaps the only poet whose verse was directly influenced by Swift, and that is partly owing to their common Irish background, Swift's living tradition there and the cult of him in Dublin. However, contemplating and brooding over Swift was an element in making the later verse of Yeats what it became, in content and temper. But apart from Yeats, nobody. This lack of appreciation springs from the dominance of the romantic tradition in our literature – the line that runs from Spenser, Shakespeare, the Caroline poets, to the great Romantics, Wordsworth, Coleridge, Shelley and the later. But for some time such poets as Skelton, Donne, Dryden, Byron have been coming back into their own. Perhaps this definitive edition may have the effect of enabling Swift to do so too.[2]

There is so much in his poetry that should appeal to this age: its realism and ruthlessness, its exposure of the human condition, without pity or illusion, its stripping away of all pretences, its very nudity, its terse force, concentration and clarity.

Hitherto, Swift has been universally underestimated as a poet. To some extent he is himself to blame; for it has been partly due to that pride which made him careless, where Pope was so careful, about the publishing of his poems. It was Swift's foible to care more for the reputation of a gentleman than of a poet: 'I do not call him a poet that writes for his diversion,' he said, 'any more than that gentleman, a fiddler, who amuses himself with a violin.' Swift left his verse publications in indescribable confusion until Sir Harold Williams came along to bring order out of chaos, as nobody had done previously. 'No part of his writing has been so neglected and mishandled by editors,' Sir Harold says. Partly the neglect of Swift's poetry may be put down to the rapid change of fashion that came about after his death, in the latter half of the eighteenth century; and in part, too, to his consistent, half-humorous depreciation of his own verse:

> In Pope, I cannot read a Line,
> But with a Sigh I wish it Mine . . .

But it does not say much for later generations of critics that they have been so ready to take a master of irony *au pied de la lettre*. Sir Harold says that to the unhappiness of Swift's life there was added 'the misfortune of falling short of his friends, Pope, Prior and Gay, in the poetic content of his work. . . . In verse Pope was his superior. Gay and Prior had a more lyrical gift. Swift's genius lay in the succession of Samuel Butler.' Swift was a less accomplished poet than Pope, and he had altogether less charm – though he was a more astonishing apparition, a stranger genius, and this appears in his verse no less than in his prose. But fall short of Prior? or Gay? Surely not.

The truth is in force, range, persistence, he is a great poet. Swift expressed himself more fully and more continuously in his verse than in his prose. Sir Harold Williams allows that 'he was constantly turning verse as a common part of his everyday life, so much so that no part of his writing is as complete an autobiography'. He concludes: 'We are closer to Swift in his verse, and in his letters, than in his prose-writings'; and he quotes Dr Elrington Ball's summing-up, 'Without knowledge of his verse a true picture of Swift cannot be drawn. In his verse he sets forth his life as in a panorama, he shows more clearly than in his prose his peculiar turn of thought, and he reveals his character in all its phases.' He took earlier to the writing of poetry, and in an early poem, the 'Ode to Sir William Temple', describes how everything that he writes turns to verse:

> In vain all wholesome Herbs I sow,
>   Where nought but Weeds will grow.
> Whate'er I plant (like Corn on barren Earth)
>   By an equivocal Birth
> Seeds and runs up to Poetry.

That in itself is evidence of his early bent; and though there comes a break after these early poems, six years in which he is not known to have written any verse, the characteristic traits of Swift appear early. It is usual to mark a complete contrast between this first group of pindaric odes and the later poems. Yet in these first poems there is the declared intention of the satirist to lash mankind for its folly:

> My hate, whose lash just heaven has long decreed
> Shall on a day make sin and folly bleed.

There is 'that scorn of fools, by fools mistook for pride', the authentic note of contempt for mankind, the incapacity for contentment which such thoughts, in the human condition, must induce:

> Madness like this no fancy ever seiz'd,
> Still to be cheated, never to be pleas'd.

There is the inhibiting doctrine that all knowledge comes only from memory, enshrined in a remarkable passage to which Yeats drew Sir Harold Williams' attention:

> But what does our proud Ign'rance Learning call,
>   We oddly *Plato's* Paradox make good,
> Our Knowledge is but mere Remembrance all,
>   Remembrance is our Treasure and our Food;
> Nature's fair Table-book our tender Souls
> We scrawl all o'er with odd and empty Rules,
>   Stale Memorandums of the Schools;
> For Learning's mighty Treasures look
>   In that deep Grave a Book.

All this in those first few poems, the neglected odes: the poems on which Dryden is said to have commented: 'Cousin Swift, you will never be a poet.' Evidently Dryden said something of the sort; for Swift underwent some kind of crisis, was silent for six years, and then emerged with a totally different style, fully formed, from which he never afterwards departed. But the themes were continuous and receive their full development in the mature poetry.

There is a good case for holding that the more complete Swift is the Swift of the poems. There is nothing he said in prose that he did not say as well in verse; only the reputation of the author of *Gulliver* and of *A Tale of a Tub* has overshadowed the fact. There is all the savagery of the last book of *Gulliver* in 'The Legion Club'; and there are a good many things among the poems which are hardly paralleled in the prose. The good-humoured, below-stairs fun of the remarkable early poem 'Mrs. Harris's Petition' is paralleled in the late prose work, the *Directions to Servants*, but with the added note of bitterness his experience of life

had induced. It is revealing that it was in verse only that Swift expressed
the precarious ambiguity of his relations with Vanessa; nothing like it
in his prose. And how well that complex, poised state of mind, neither
wholly one thing nor the other, is described:

> But what Success Vanessa met,
> Is to the World a Secret yet:
> Whether the Nymph, to please her Swain,
> Talks in a high Romantic Strain;
> Or whether he at last descends
> To like with less Seraphick Ends;
> Or, to compound the Business, whether
> They temper Love and Books together;
> Must never to Mankind be told,
> Nor shall the conscious Muse unfold.

As to form, Swift's verse was a perfect instrument for the expression
of what he intended; it too has greater variety than is usually realised.
Even Dr Johnson, whose criticism of Swift's poems was casual and
unsympathetic, allowed this: 'They [the poetical works] are, for the
most part, what their author intended. . . . All his verses exemplify his
own definition of a good style, they consist of "proper words in proper
places".'

The ends Swift set himself were too restricted or, at a deeper level,
inhibited by his fear of giving himself away, of giving hostages to
fortune in the realm of the emotions. One can appreciate the motives
that made him repress his hopes and desires – his determination to have
his life as far as possible under his own control, a rational control; the
realisation of the insentience of the universe to the sufferings of men;
his refusal to lay himself open to experience, especially in regard to sex.
The paradox is that it is just those persons who go out of their way to
reject experience for fear of the suffering it may entail, who suffer most.
The searing irony of Swift's life is that the man who imposed so
rational a control upon his emotions should have ended by losing his
reason. Sir Harold Williams concludes that if Swift had been prepared
to let himself go, he would have been a greater poet, that 'he had something to give to English poetry that he never wholly gave'. On the other
hand, it is that very sense of restraint that gives the impression of such
power in reserve. And it is present, perfectly and precisely expressed, in
all the metres and verse-forms he chose to write in.

The real criticism against Swift's poetry is not, then, on the score of lack of variety either of subject, or of metre, but rather a lack of variety in *tone*. But may not the same be said of many other poets whom the poetic tradition recognises without demur – Spenser, Shelley, Keats – though with them the tone is a different one? It may be agreed that Swift, for a poet, wrote too much from the head, and not enough from the heart; and it is not a good thing for a poet to write wholly from the head, never to allow himself freedom from the limits consciously imposed by the intellect. That is what Swift set himself to do, and the result we have to take for what it is. It is hardly just to demand that it should be something other than it is, as so many have done, and say, 'This is not poetry.' They start from a carefully selective view of what poetry should be – one moreover which is not sanctioned by the practice of the poets – and then impose that standard upon poetry like Swift's.

Naturally, with a dominantly intellectual approach and with his experience of the world what it was, Swift's creative impulse turned mainly to satire. He might have said with his so much admired model, Juvenal: 'Difficile est non satiram scribere.' And he was well aware of the criticism that might be pointed against him:

> Perhaps I may allow, the Dean
> Had too much Satyr in his Vein;
> And seem'd determin'd not to starve it,
> Because no Age could more deserve it.

It is clear that this was the frame of mind which with him released the aesthetic impulse, that this was the psychological groove along which his inspiration and its expression ran most easily. There is a strong case for Swift's classicism, that controlled and deliberately directed emotion, as opposed to the romantic inspiration. For one thing his chief emotion was intellectual passion, a rare thing in an Englishman; which is perhaps why the English have never properly understood him or his poetry.

NOTES

1. Ricardo Quintana, *The Mind and Art of Jonathan Swift* (London and New York, 1936; 2nd ed. London, 1953)

2. *The Poems of Jonathan Swift*, ed. Harold Williams (Oxford, 1937, 2nd ed. Oxford, 1958).

HERBERT DAVIS

Literary Satire in
A Tale of a Tub (1964)

> 'Tis own'd he was a *Man of Wit* –,
> Yet many a *foolish thing* he writ –;
> And, sure he must be *deeply* learn'd –!
> That's more than ever I discern'd –;
> I know his *nearest Friends* complain
> He was too *airy* for a *Dean* –.[1]

BEFORE the publication of *A Tale of a Tub* in 1704, Swift had appeared in his own person in the world of letters only as an editor of the *Letters of Sir William Temple*. The first two volumes were printed in 1700 with a dedication in which he humbly presents them to his Most Sacred Majesty William III, describing himself as a domestic chaplain to his Excellency the Earl of Berkeley, one of the Lords Justices of Ireland. A third volume was printed in 1703. But he evidently felt that in his role as a satirist he would be hampered and restricted if he were to appear in this way, wearing a parson's gown and associated with such respectable connections. There had been, indeed, in the seventeenth century, a splendid tradition among the most reverend and eminent divines in their controversial treatises about serious matters which would seem to sanction, as Anthony Collins pointed out in his *Discourse concerning Ridicule*, the use of 'Insult, Buffoonery, Banter, Ridicule, Irony, Mockery and bitter Railing'; and after the Restoration this tendency was further encouraged by a Court audience led by 'a King who had a disposition to banter and ridicule everybody' and 'some of the greatest Droles and Wits that any Age ever produc'd'. But tastes were changing at the end of the century, and Swift himself was then under the influence of Sir William Temple, who had solemnly and vigorously denounced the taste for satire, and had probably prevented Swift from publishing *The Battle of the Books* in 1698.

At any rate we know that Swift put aside this and other satirical papers of his own which he had been working at in 1696–7, and took precautions that when they did appear he would not necessarily be involved, until he could see what sort of reception they would have. He felt that he needed for his purpose the fullest freedom to range at will over the whole field of letters, for he wished to make sport with all the foibles of the Grub-street brotherhood as well as the societies of Gresham and of Wills, the hack-writers and fashionable poets, the virtuosos and the wits, and 'to expose the numerous *Corruptions* in religion and learning, [which] might furnish Matter for a Satyr, that would be useful and diverting'. He chose therefore to appear as an unknown young gentleman of taste and learning dedicated to the high task of serving the Church and the State by diverting the attacks of the wits who occupy themselves in picking holes in the weak sides of religion and government; and in such a task – which he claimed should win him the approval of all good men – he would be justified in letting loose all his powers to expose the shams of the time and to make merry at the expense of all hypocrites and dullards. But his attack must be made 'in a manner, that should be altogether new, the World having been already too long nauseated with endless Repetitions upon every Subject' (*Prose*, I I).[2]

The author of *A Tale of a Tub* is presented to us as at the maturity of his powers – 'his Invention at the Height, and his Reading fresh in his Head, . . . a young Gentleman much in the World, and wrote to the Tast of those who were like himself' (*Prose*, I I). He is not without a certain youthful insolence, contemptuous alike of stupidity, dullness and pedantry, addressing himself to those who have enough wit to appreciate irony, and enough knowledge to recognize parody. He has had sufficient experience to know that he need not be afraid of those who will be provoked to anger and fury by his satire. They deserve only his scorn:

> There is a *Brain* that will endure but one *Scumming*: Let the Owner gather it with Discretion, and manage his little Stock with Husbandry; but of all things, let him beware of bringing it under the *Lash* of his *Betters*; because, That will make it all bubble up into Impertinence, and he will find no new Supply: Wit, without Knowledge, being a Sort of *Cream*, which gathers in a Night to the Top, and by a skilful Hand, may be soon *whipt* into *Froth*; but once scumm'd away, what appears underneath will be fit for nothing, but to be thrown to the Hogs.[3]

This is still in the manner of the seventeenth century in the true line of wit; the vivid image of the whipped cream, possibly picked up from his reading of François de Callières, who had used it simply as a symbol for writing 'large in appearance but little in substance', but here elaborated and played with and worked to the utmost, until the froth vanishes and we are left with another even more powerful image of the skimmed milk fit only for the hogs. A careful contemporary reader would have recognized the method, and might have been reminded of another fantastic image of scorn in a popular satire of the preceding generation, which the author of *A Tale of a Tub* admired and referred to, *The Rehearsal Transpros'd* by Andrew Marvell. He also is describing the brain of his adversary:

> You have, contrary to all architecture and good economy, made a snow-house in your upper roome, which indeed was philosophically done of you, seeing you bear your head so high as if it were in or above the middle region, and so you thought it secure from melting. But you did not at the same time consider that your brain is so hot, that the wit is dissolv'd by it, and is always dripping away at the icicles of your nose. But it freezes again, I confess, as soon as it falls down; and hence it proceeds that there is no passage in my Book, deep or shallow, but with a chill and key-cold conceit you can ice it in a moment, and slide shere over it without scatches.[4]

There is the same playful extravagance and exuberant gaiety in these conceits, but Swift's sentences show an economy and strength, and a power of invention – to use the phrase of the time – which seems to me to justify his claim that his wit was all his own. He speaks of having read Marvell with pleasure, and evidently took good heed of his warnings addressed to those who would take upon themselves the envious and dangerous employment of being writers.

> For indeed, whosoever he be that comes in print, whereas he might have sate at home in quiet, does either make a treat, or send a challenge to all readers; in which cases, the first, it concerns him to have no scarcity of provisions, and in the other, to be compleatly arm'd; for, if anything be amiss on either part, men are subject to scorn the weakness of the attaque, or laugh at the meanness of the entertainment.[5]

There is no scarcity of entertainment in the fare Swift provides, no lack of weapons for the attack. The manner of his attack may seem at first sight very conventional, for it was a favourite conceit of the time to refer to the custom of seamen to throw out a tub when they meet a whale to divert it from attacking the ship. It must have been well known to all Swift's readers, as it occurs in such popular books as this satire of Marvell's I have been referring to: 'I only threw it out like an empty Cask to amuse him, knowing that I had a *Whale* to deal with . . .',[6] and again in the prefatory Remarks to the Reader in Francis Osborn's *Works*, which had reached a seventh edition in 1673: '. . . in immitation of Sea-men, I may perhaps by design have cast out some empty stuff, to find play for the Whale-mouthed gapers after Levity; lest they should spoil the Voyage'.[7] Swift's parable is very obvious, where the whale symbolizes Hobbes's *Leviathan* and the ship in danger the Commonwealth, though again he does not miss the opportunity to enlarge the conceit, rather confusing the picture, as the waters round the Leviathan positively seethe with tubs, namely 'Schemes of Religion and Government, whereof a great many are hollow, and dry, and empty, and noisy, and wooden, and given to Rotation' (*Prose*, 1 24). He will himself provide for the purpose *A Tale of a Tub*. Again neither the phrase nor its use as a title is new. Instances are given in the Guthkelch and Nichol Smith edition, to which I am indebted throughout, of its common use in the sixteenth and seventeenth centuries, in the sense of 'an idle discourse', or as explained in the title of a lost work 'a gallimaufrey of merriment'.[8] Swift hooks the two ideas together and has a title for a gallimaufry of merriment in which he can make fun of everything that catches his fancy not only as he looks around him in the world of contemporary controversy, but as he looks back across the troubled waters of the Revolution and the Commonwealth and the Civil War to the serene shores of that age immediately before the troubles which he always regarded with longing and pride as the time of England's highest glory both in life and in letters.

For the real object of Swift's satire in the *Tale* is the corruption he saw in English letters during the latter half of the seventeenth century, destroying what he felt had been its finest achievements. This belief is repeatedly stated, and never modified. He first stated in it the *Tatler*, dated 28 September 1710, satirizing current affectations of language, and clearly setting forth what he regarded as the standards of good taste in English, namely that simplicity which is unaffected by modish fashions, such as 'the writings of *Hooker*, who was a Country Clergyman, and of *Parsons* the Jesuit, both in the Reign of Queen *Elizabeth* . . . much more clear and intelligible than those of Sir *H. Wooton*, Sir *Robert Naunton*, *Osborn*, *Daniel* the Historian, and several others who writ later; but being Men of the Court, and affecting the Phrases then in

Fashion; they are often either not to be understood, or appear perfectly ridiculous' (*Prose*, II 177).

He stated it very plainly in his *Letter to the Lord Treasurer*, emphasizing the corruptions in language 'from the Civil War to this present time'; first, the enthusiastic jargon prevailing during the usurpation, and then the licentiousness which entered with the Restoration, which from infecting religion and morals fell to corrupt the language, as shown in 'the Plays and other Compositions, written for Entertainment' during the next fifty years (*Prose*, IV 10 ff). He stated it again in *A Letter to a young Clergyman*, written in Ireland ten years latter, and again in a slightly different form in the *Essay on Conversation*, as, for example: 'I take the highest Period of Politeness in *England* (and it is of the same Date in *France*) to have been the peaceable Part of King *Charles* the First's Reign' (*Prose*, IV 94).

It is obvious from this on which side Swift would find himself in the controversy between the Ancients and the Moderns which had been sharpened by the recent claims for precedence made on behalf of the latest discoveries and developments in the world of science and letters. He was indeed inclined to be unduly sceptical of the importance and value of the new sciences and more aware of the corruptions than of the improvements in modern learning. He was not therefore led into the fray entirely to defend Sir William Temple against the attacks made on his *Essay upon the Ancient and Modern Learning*, although this episode provided him with an excuse to join with the Christ Church wits against Bentley and Wotton. At the same time it forced him to uphold a very weak case, as Temple had stated it in his *Essay*, and he was obliged to rely on the effectiveness of the literary devices he used to get the better of his opponents. The main device is indicated by the title – *A Full and True Account of the Battle Fought last Friday, Between the Antient and the Modern Books in St. James's Library*. This looked like an imitation of François de Callières's *Histoire poétique de la Guerre nouvellement déclarée entre les Anciens et les Modernes*, though Swift afterwards said he had never heard of it. But there were many advantages in handling the subject in a mock-heroic fashion as a battle between the actual volumes in the King's Library, which Bentley had confessed was in a state of dirt and confusion. The Homeric conflict takes place 'on the plains of St. James's Library' – a phrase which is just enough to carry us into a mock-heroic world remote from the actual controversy and the arguments over the genuineness of the Epistles of Phalaris. In

this world Swift can play with the reader as he will; he has only to
oppose Dryden to Virgil, describing Dryden's steed and his arms in
Hudibrastian fashion:

> Behold, upon a sorrel Gelding of a monstrous Size, appear'd a Foe, issuing
> from among the thickest of the Enemy's Squadrons; But his Speed was
> less than his Noise; for his Horse, old and lean, spent the Dregs of his
> Strength in a high Trot, which though it made slow Advances, yet caused
> a loud Clashing of his Armor, terrible to hear.
> . . . the Helmet was nine Times too large for the Head, which appeared
> Situate far in the hinder Part, even like the Lady in a Lobster, or like a
> Mouse under a Canopy of State or like a shrivled Beau from within the
> Penthouse of a modern Periwig. (*Prose*, 1 157)

In similar fashion he describes Bentley and Wotton 'like two Mun-
grel curs prowling around' who steal the armour of Phalaris and
Aesop while they are asleep, and the final exploit of Boyle who appears
like a young lion, and hunts the two of them until finally his lance
pierces them together:

> As, when a skilful Cook has truss'd a Brace of *Woodcocks*, He, with Iron
> Skewer, pierces the tender Sides of both, their Legs and Wings close
> pinion'd to their Ribs; So was this Pair of Friends transfix'd, till down they
> fell, joyn'd in their Lives, Join'd in their Deaths. (*Prose*, 1 164)

If this were all, however, we should feel that Swift had done no more
than provide a trivial diversion to draw attention away from the real
conflict. But again in the midst of the allegory, as in the *Tale*, he introduces a digression: and a very fitting one, as the dispute was also
concerned with Aesop, who was praised by Temple as the most ancient
of the ancients and was recognized by all ages as the greatest master in
this kind. Very fitly also in the dirt of St James's Library, Swift dis-
covers a large spider's web, in which a bee, entering through a broken
pane of the window, has become entangled. This occasions a dispute
between them which is then interpreted by Aesop, who had listened
to them 'with a world of pleasure' (*Prose*, 1 150–1).

The fable and the interpretation of it are Swift's real contribution to
the debate between the Ancients and the Moderns; and it is not surprising that a hundred and fifty years later, when the debate had taken
another form, Swift's phrase 'sweetness and light' was carried as a
banner by a young apostle of culture as he advanced against the hosts of

the Philistines. It was also a triumphant vindication of the art of Aesop, no matter what Bentley had done to his title page and half of his leaves. The fable is made out of a proverb, evidently common, as it is frequently turned to literary use in the seventeenth century: 'Where the bee sucks honey, the spider sucks poison.' Here we can observe it expanding into a lovely form, as it is dramatized in Bentley's library, and elaborated with mock-heroic language, and finally interpreted as a symbol of the dispute between the Ancients and the Moderns:

> For, pray Gentlemen, was ever any thing so *Modern* as the *Spider* in his Air, his Turns, and his Paradoxes? He argues in the Behalf of *You* his Brethren, and Himself, with many Boastings of his native Stock, and great Genius; that he Spins and Spits wholly from himself, and scorns to own any Obligation or Assistance from without. Then he displays to you his great Skill in Architecture, and Improvement in the Mathematicks . . . yet, if the materials be nothing but Dirt, spun out of your own Entrails (the Guts of *Modern* Brains) the Edifice will conclude at last in a *Cobweb*: The Duration of which, like that of other *Spiders* Webs, may be imputed to their being forgotten or neglected, or hid in a Corner. . . . As for *Us*, the *Antients*, We are content with the *Bee*, to pretend to Nothing of our own, beyond our *Wings* and our *Voice*: that is to say, our *Flights* and our *Language*; For the rest, whatever we have got, has been by infinite Labor, and search, and ranging thro' every Corner of Nature: The Difference is, that instead of *Dirt* and *Poison*, we have rather chose to fill our Hives with *Honey* and *Wax*, thus furnishing Mankind with the two Noblest of Things, which are *Sweetness* and *Light*. (*Prose*, 1 151)

It was a nice compliment to Temple to use the bee as the symbol of the Ancients; for some of Swift's readers would remember Temple's *Essay on Poetry*, where he compares the poet's art with the activities of the bees in a passage which Swift in the last sentence condensed with great precision:

> [Bees] must range through Fields, as well as Gardens, chuse such Flowers as they please, and by Proprieties and Scents they only know and distinguish: They must work up their Cells with Admirable Art, extract their Honey with infinite Labour, and sever it from the Wax, with such Distinction and Choice, as belongs to none but themselves to perform or to judge.[9]

Some of Swift's readers would also remember this passage to which Professor F. P. Wilson drew my attention, in Bacon's *Novum Organum*:

The men of experiment are like the ant; they only collect and use; the
reasoners resemble spiders, who make cobwebs out of their own substance.
But the bee takes a middle course, it gathers its material from the flowers
of the garden and of the field, but transforms and digests it by a power of
its own. Not unlike this is the true business of philosophy.

In the *Battle of the Books* Swift shows what side he is on, and he
succeeds by his wit and humour, and by the power of his style. But he
does not reveal there as he does in the *Tale* the extent of the preparation
he had undertaken so that in offering entertainment to his readers, he
should not be criticized for any scarcity of provisions. As an undergraduate at Trinity College he had had no great reputation as a scholar;
but we happen to have some interesting information about his reading
during those years when he was planning and working on the *Tale*.

The list of his studies for the year 1697 indicates the breadth and
variety of his reading including, in addition to French and English
authors, the *Iliad* and the *Odyssey*, Virgil twice, Lucretius three times,
Horace, Cicero's Epistles, Petronius, Lucius Florus three times, Diodorus Siculus, Cyprian, Irenaeus and Sleidan's commentaries. 'This', says
Professor Nichol Smith, 'gives only a fraction of the reading that went
to the making of the *Tale*', but 'it admits us, as it were, to a secret view
of Swift's habits of mind when he was gaining his full powers, and
Swift never wrote anything that gives a greater sense of sheer power
than some of the later sections of the *Tale*.'[10]
    It is unlike the rest of his writings, because it is so literary, so full of
echoes from his reading, and so concerned with the world of letters,
the world that at that time he knew best, because he had been living
entirely in it. For he had been exercising himself in the art of writing
as well as filling his mind. The *Tale* represents only a very small portion
of all that he had written during the last ten years of the century. He had
begun with a number of experiments in verse – Pindaric Odes in which
he seems to have wished to compete with Cowley and experiments in
heroic verse like the Lines addressed to Congreve, not much less
restrained in manner. He soon discovered that such forms would not
fit the kind of thing he wanted to say, and contemptuously turned
away from these poetic exercises, not even including them in any of his
later collections of verse. Nevertheless there is to be observed in them a
force and energy, struggling with the too voluminous folds of flowing

rhetoric and showing the ferment of thought in which he lived. In his attack on the extravagancies of the previous age, he benefited by these struggles in which he had won his freedom as perhaps every young writer has to do from the prevailing forces round about him, in order to shape his art to fit his own individual purpose. These Odes, addressed to the King, to Sir William Temple, to Archbishop Sancroft, and the Epistle to Mr Congreve begin in a dignified strain of compliment, and were evidently intended to serve the same purpose as those later presented by Congreve on suitable occasions as an offering to the King on his taking of Namur, or lamenting the Death of our late Gracious Queen Mary of ever blessed Memory. But unlike the cool marbled smoothness of Congreve's lines, Swift's gather a tempestuous motion and quickly become roughened by moods of anger and satire, and he breaks off apologizing for his unfitting outbursts:

> Perish the Muse's hour, thus vainly spent
> In satire, to my CONGREVE'S praises meant;
> In how ill season her resentments rule,
> What's that to her if mankind be a fool?

And in the last of these poems addressed to Temple in December 1693, he renounces the Muse as a delusion and a deceit,

> Troubling the chrystal fountain of the sight,
> Which darts on poets eyes a trembling light;
> Kindled while reason sleeps, but quickly flies,
> Like antic shapes in dreams, from waking eyes:

The experience, which he describes with such force in this poem, where he turns away forever from the fond delusions of a youthful poet's romantic dreams, is the source of the irony and gives a sort of personal colouring to the triumphant scepticism of the Digression on Madness in the *Tale*, where human happiness is defined as 'a perpetual possession of being well deceived', and the same struggle between fancy and reason is examined:

> But when a Man's Fancy gets *astride* on his Reason, when Imagination is at Cuffs with the senses, and common Understanding, as well as common Sense, is kick't out of Doors; the first Proselyte he makes, is Himself. (*Prose*, I 108)

I have tried to indicate briefly how well prepared Swift was in 1697, as a young man of thirty, for the role of the Author of *A Tale of a Tub*, not only by his hard reading and study and contemplation, but also by the vigorous exercise of his imagination and his skill in the various forms of his art. Now I should like to examine the *Tale* itself to try and show the devices he used to gather into it so much of the spirit of the century that was nearing its close, its enthusiasm, its pedantry, its shams, its conceits, and all the richness and extravagance and variety of its strange faiths and hopes and delusions. For the paradox is – and it would miss its purpose if it were not paradoxical – that the work is a product of the seventeenth century, entirely characteristic in form and manner, and at the same time a repudiation and criticism of all the most vigorous literary fashions of the previous sixty years.

For example in its outward shape and form it obviously resembles the work of those writers whom Swift repudiates, rather than the work of those like Hooker and Parsons, whose style he admired. And it is equally unlike himself, as Dr Johnson pointed out, going so far as to question indeed whether Swift could have written it: 'It has so much more thinking, more knowledge, more power, more colour, than any of the works which are indubitably his.'[11] This impression that the *Tale* is unlike Swift in having more colour, more evidence of his reading and knowledge of literature, is due to the fact that he has put into it so much material from the world of letters in order to make play with it and to shake himself free from it. It is also due to the element of parody in its whole design, a feature indeed constant in Swift's satire and he would say inevitably so, because he believed that it would be impossible for any satirist to imagine or create affectations which could serve his purpose as well as those plentifully to be found in life or literature. And parody to be perfect should be as close to the original as possible. Therefore since certain affectations in the world of letters usually appeared in certain particular places, e.g. in *Dedications*, or *Digressions*, or *Prefaces*, or *To The Readers*, what could be more fitting than to fit out the Tale with all these appendages, so that the proper place would be available to exhibit and expose such follies? In order to make sure that his method would not be misunderstood by later readers, Swift was careful in the *Apology*, which he added as a further preface in 1710, to explain exactly what he was doing and who were his victims.

There is one Thing which the judicious Reader cannot but have observed, that some of those Passages in this Discourse, which appear most liable to Objection are what they call Parodies, where the Author personates the Style and Manner of other Writers, whom he has a mind to expose. I shall produce one Instance, it is in the [42nd] Page. Dryden, L'Estrange, and some others I shall not name, are here levelled at, who having spent their Lives in Faction, and Apostacies, and all manner of Vice, pretended to be Sufferers for Loyalty and Religion. So Dryden tells us in one of his Prefaces of his Merits and Suffering, thanks God that he *possesses his Soul in Patience*: In other Places he talks at the same Rate, and L'Estrange often uses the like Style, and I believe the Reader may find more Persons to give that Passage an Application: But this is enough to direct those who may have overlook'd the Authors Intention. (*Prose*, 1 3–4)

As a sample of Dryden's complaints, I will quote a sentence from his *Discourse concerning Satire*:

But being encouraged only with fair words by King Charles II, my little salary ill paid, and no prospect of a future subsistence, I was then discouraged in the beginning of my attempt; and now age has overtaken me, and want, a more insufferable evil, through the change of the times, has wholly disenabled me.[12]

But Dryden provided even better material in his translation of the *Works of Virgil*, which appeared in the summer of 1697, while Swift was probably working on the *Tale*. The volume was printed by Tonson in a handsome folio, adorned with a hundred sculptures, and a list of names of the subscribers to the cuts, each subscription being five guineas; with a separate list of the second subscribers. It was divided into three parts, containing the Pastorals, the Georgics and the Aeneis, each part equipped not only with separate prefaces or observations, but also with separate dedications – to Lord Clifford, the Earl of Chesterfield and the Marquis of Normandy. Swift did not miss his opportunity: 'Our famous *Dryden* has ventured to proceed a Point farther, endeavouring to introduce also a Multiplicity of *God-fathers*; which is an Improvement of much more Advantage, upon a very obvious Account' (*Prose*, 1 43). It was such a good example that he would try it himself and therefore divided his treatise into forty sections and approached forty Lords of his acquaintance to stand, but they all made their excuses.

But in the Postscript to the Reader, Swift found a lovely sample of Dryden's further acknowledgments to more god-fathers for all the encouragement and aids he had received in the course of his work, starting with the assistance granted by the Almighty in the beginning, prosecution and conclusion of his studies, and ending with his obligations to the whole Faculty of medicine, especially to those two ornaments

of their profession, Dr Guibbons and Dr Hobbs. And finally he
assures the reader that his work will be judged in after ages to be no
dishonour to his native country, whose language and poetry he has
added to in the choice of words and in the harmony of numbers. This
Swift notes as an excellent method of advertisement: 'Our Great
Dryden . . . has often said to me in Confidence, that the World would
have never suspected him to be so great a Poet, if he had not assured
them so frequently in his Prefaces, that it was impossible they could
either doubt or forget it.'[13]

Finally all such affectations as are found scattered throughout these
prefaces and addresses to the reader, 'all these wonderful civilities (as
Swift calls them) that have passed of late Years between the Nation
of Authors and that of Readers' are gathered up in the extravagant
travesty of the tenth section of *A Tale of a Tub*, where the author offers
his humble thanks to his Majesty, and both Houses of Parliament, the
Lords of the Privy Council, the Judges, clergy, gentry, and yeomanry
of the land, etc. for their approbation; expresses his happiness that
Fate has flung him into so blessed an age for the mutual felicity of
authors and booksellers, who produce and sell their wares so easily, and
promises entire satisfaction for every class of readers, the superficial,
the ignorant and the learned, and ends with throwing out some bait for
the latter group, by dropping some dark hints and innuendoes of
hidden meanings and profound mysteries, in the hope – as the learned
commentator puts it in a final note – of setting curious men a-hunting
through Indexes, and enquiring for Books out of the common Road.
I may add that there are probably very few of us who have tried to edit
or comment on this *Tale* who have not been tricked in this manner,
and I can only commend to any of you who may be looking for a
subject for research with unlimited possibilities, that you should
investigate the qualities of *Acamoth*, which you may, or may not, find
illuminated in the work of the dark authors of the seventeenth century.

The method of parody is also used in the ridicule of Bentley and
Wotton, which occurs in the Digression on Critics when he sets out
gravely to search for particular descriptions of the True Critick in the
writings of the Ancients, and brings together very much in the manner
of Bentley a series of quotations proving that these Ancients generally
fixed upon the same hieroglyph, as the subject was too dangerous to be
treated except by types and figures. Thereupon the symbol of the ass is
introduced with the help of two quotations from Pausanias. 'But

Herodotus, holding the very same *Hieroglyph*, speaks much plainer and almost *in terminis*. . . . Upon which relation Ctesias yet refines, etc.' (*Prose*, 1 60). And even the three Maxims which provide a devastating close for the chapter are ornamented with a number of similitudes, in which the prevalent witty conceit is sharpened so that it may become an effective weapon for satire. I will instance only the first of these where the irony is so nicely balanced that an early compositor added a negative which has confused the sentence as it now stands in many editions:

> *Criticism*, contrary to all other Faculties of the Intellect, is ever held the truest and best, when it is the very *first* Result of the *Critick's* Mind: As Fowlers reckon the first aim for the surest, and seldom fail of missing the Mark, if they stay [not] for a Second. (*Prose*, 1 63)

I have spoken at such length about the parody in the book, because it explains its unlikeness to much of Swift's later work, and because it is, I think, the source of that extraordinary richness and variety in the style which is so much concerned with an examination of the books of the previous generation that inevitably it preserves so many of their tricks and mannerisms. But it contains also quite clearly and fully developed the qualities which most distinctively mark Swift's satire, 'an Irony which runs through the Thread of the whole Book' and a sardonic wit which is a perfect vehicle for a scepticism not less profound and not less complete than that which perhaps more plainly and nakedly reveals itself in his latest writings.

Consider for instance his answer to the problem why satire is likely to be less dull than panegyrick. The solution, he says, is easy and natural.

> For, the Materials of Panegyrick being very few in Number, have been long since exhausted: For, as Health is but one Thing and has been always the same, whereas Diseases are by thousands, besides new and daily Additions; So, all the Virtues that have been ever in Mankind, are to be counted upon a few Fingers, but his Follies and Vices are innumerable, and Time adds hourly to the Heap. (*Prose*, 1 30)

That last phrase is so characteristic. It prevents the sentence from falling flat, like some stale drab moralist's jibe. It thrusts it home, revealing the endless possibility of mankind's follies mounting higher hour by hour. It reminds us of the *Dedication to Prince Posterity*, where beneath the gay raillery of his tone as he bears witness to the actual reputation of his illustrious contemporaries at the minute he is writing, there can be heard the theme of Time and Mortality, and his sentences are caught for a moment and held by that insistent rhythm which had been dominant for a hundred years: 'I enquired after them among Readers and Booksellers, but I enquired in vain, the *Memorial of them was lost among Men, their Place was no more to be found*: and I was laughed to scorn' (*Prose*, 1 21). And then inexorably other echoes float into his mind and bring him more images for his purpose, and, as we read, his sentences are disturbed and rock a little beneath the powerful swell of this very different rhetoric:

> Sometime we see a cloud that's dragonish;
> A vapour sometime like a bear or lion,
> A tower'd citadel, a pendent rock,
> A forked mountain, or blue promontory
> With trees upon't, that nod unto the world,
> And mock our eyes with air; thou hast seen these signs;
> They are black vesper's pageants.
> > Ay, my lord.
> That which is now a horse, even with a thought
> > The rack dislimns.[14]

Here is what Swift makes of it. I do not quote it as an example of parody, but to show his mind in this way also enriched by his reading, and subduing it to his purpose.

> If I should venture in a windy Day, to affirm to *Your Highness*, that there is a large Cloud near the *Horizon* in the Form of a *Bear*, another in the *Zenith* with the Head of an *Ass*, a third to the Westward with Claws like a *Dragon*; and *Your Highness* should in a few Minutes think fit to examine the Truth, 'tis certain, they would all be changed in Figure and Position, new ones would arise, and all we could agree upon would be, that Clouds there were, but that I was grossly mistaken in the *Zoography* and *Topography* of them. (*Prose*, 1 21)

Professor Sherburn has drawn attention to a striking aspect of the *Tale*, often overlooked, as it reveals Swift's 'dislike of the deluding powers of perverted reason', or, more specifically, his dislike of proselytizing, of people who wish to force their opinions upon others.

Whoever hath *an Ambition to be heard in a Crowd* – so, with contempt, begins his Introduction to the *Tale;* and in the climactic Digression on

Madness, the lunatics are the founders of states by conquest, the founders of new systems of philosophy, and the founders of sects in religion.[15]

This is very true, but even in this there is an element of irony, which I think Swift was not unaware of, though it was at his own expense. For he also had an ambition, and a very powerful ambition, to be heard, and while he makes fun of those who exalt themselves above the crowd by mounting upon one of those three wooden machines for the use of orators who desire to talk much without interruption, he has nevertheless devised his own Tub to provide a platform for his own special wit and genius. And it cannot be denied that he has sometimes endeavoured to satisfy the 'Whale-mouthed gapers after Levity', and has taken advantage of 'the liberty of these Times, which hath afforded Wisdom a larger Passport to travel, than was ever able formerly to be obtained, when the World kept her fettered in an implicite Obedience, by the three-fold Cord of Custom, Education and Ignorance'. Even when Swift is most directly attacking the sects, and may be in part influenced by his own experience among the Presbyterians in Ireland, he is still writing not as a churchman or a politician, but as a wit and as a man of letters. That is perhaps the fundamental difference between the *Tale* and the roughest controversial satires of the bishops and their opponents. They are always at certain points protected and restrained by their official status. But the author of the *Tale* is completely free, unhampered by political or practical considerations. He is concerned with words; his wit is conceit; and he did not always realize perhaps the power and the effect of the weapons he was using.

In his handling of the allegory of the three brothers, for instance, he is inclined to dramatize their actions rather in the manner of the contemporary stage, and their language and gestures remind us of the world of Sir Novelty Fashion and Lord Foppington. And the symbol of the coats, meaning 'the Doctrine and Faith of Christianity', is full of obvious dangers, though it not only lends itself to the necessary dramatization, but also may be neatly reversed and elaborated into a satire on the real religion of the fashionable world, its god the tailor, and its system of belief according to which the universe is a large suit of Clothes and man himself but a micro-Coat, the acquirements of his mind furnishing an exact dress: 'Is not Religion a *Cloak*, Honesty a *Pair of Shoes*, worn out in the Dirt, Self-Love a *Surtout*, Vanity a *Shirt*, and Conscience a *Pair of Breeches*?' (*Prose*, 1 47). The whole of this passage is like a string of puns and conceits held together by a thread of irony. The dangers of Swift's satire on the corruptions of religion, whether in the allegory itself, or in the account of the sect of the Aeolists and the Fragment on the mechanical operation of the Spirit, arise out of the verbal play of his wit, which does not hesitate to make a sort of punning game with all the words which had become, it is true, soiled and bent by the usage they had received at the hands of hypocrites and fanatics, but which had nevertheless also been upon the lips of saints and prophets and remained for the devout Christian sacred symbols of his faith. It is not merely that the book contains 'several youthful Sallies', or that 'no one Opinion can fairly be deduced from it, which is contrary to Religion or Morality' – it is rather that the Author of *A Tale of a Tub* with an audience of 'the greatest Droles and Wits that any Age ever produced', set out to establish his reputation among them by outdistancing them all in the variety of his drollery and the reach and penetration of his wit.

In this he succeeded. None of them went farther in their probing, none of them journeyed farther in the exploration of a rationalist's complete scepticism, none of them opened their minds so freely and without prejudice to all that was being thought and said, none of them – not even Sir Thomas Browne – more eloquently expressed that experience of following the mind of man through all its magnificent and fantastic vagaries during the century. Here Swift shows what he could have done, had he wished to write like them. Here is a tour de force, a superb imitation of their most exalted rhetorical periods, soaring into the empyrean in circling parodies of their favourite cosmic images, only to burst at last into an explosive flash of wit, as he compares man's fancy to the brightly plumaged bird of paradise that was reputed to live only in the heights of the air.

AND, whereas the mind of Man, when he gives the Spur and Bridle to his Thoughts, doth never stop, but naturally sallies out into both extreams of High and Low, of Good and Evil; His first Flight of Fancy, commonly transports Him to Idea's of what is most Perfect, finished, and exalted; till having soared out of his own Reach and Sight, not well perceiving how near the Frontiers of Height and Depth, border upon each other; With the same Course and Wing, he falls down plum into the lowest Bottom of Things; like one who travels the *East* into the *West*; or like a strait Line drawn by its own length into a Circle. Whether a Tincture of Malice in our Natures, makes us fond of furnishing every bright Idea with its Reverse;

Or, whether Reason reflecting upon the Sum of Things, can, like the Sun, serve only to enlighten one half of the Globe, leaving the other half, by Necessity, under Shade and Darkness: Or, whether Fancy, flying up to the imagination of what is Highest and Best, becomes over-shot, and spent, and weary, and suddenly falls like a dead Bird of Paradise, to the Ground. (*Prose*, I 99)

But no one has more lightly tossed aside these metaphysical conjectures to argue triumphantly in the cause of reason and common sense, ironically exposing the delusions of the imagination, and the dangers of all philosophical anatomizing, and showing the wisdom of contenting ourselves with the superficies of things, only to bring us to this conclusion: 'This is the sublime and refined Point of Felicity, called, *the Possession of being well deceived*; The Serene, Peaceful State of being a Fool among Knaves' (*Prose*, I 110). And no one has gone quite so far – not even that 'absolute Lord of Wit', the Earl of Rochester, who was indeed quite unhampered in his profanity and little concerned with man's dignity – as the Author of *A Tale of a Tub* when he recommends as a very noble undertaking to Tory members of the House of Commons that they should appoint a commission (who shall be empowered to send for Persons, Papers, and Records) to examine into the merits of every student and professor in Bedlam, so that they might be properly used for all the offices in the state, ecclesiastical, civil and military. Various suitable candidates are vividly described and their special fitness for various occupations indicated; and the irony is pressed home in a characteristically thorough manner, by the evident manifestation that 'all would very much excel, and arrive at great Perfection in their several Kinds'. In case anyone should doubt this, the author of these momentous truths modestly claims to have had the happiness of being for some time a worthy member of that honourable society, and by that one plain instance clinches his argument, admitting gravely that he is 'a Person, whose Imaginations are hard-mouth'd, and exceedingly disposed to run away with his *Reason*', which he had observed 'from long experience, to be a very light Rider, and easily shook off'.

Dr Johnson relates that 'when this wild work first raised the attention of the publick, Sacheverell, meeting Smalridge, tried to flatter him by seeming to think him the author; but Smalridge answered with indignation, 'Not all that you and I have in the world nor all that ever we shall have, should hire me to write the *Tale of a Tub*''.[16] Perhaps there is some reason for such an attitude, not because the *Tale* is some-times unconventional, or even profane; but because it reveals so fully through all the parody and wit and irony the intellectual experience of the author. Though there were chasms in the manuscript, where we are told certain passages were omitted, the book as printed gives the impression of holding nothing back. It is in the tradition of the century that was closing as it was written; it is in the direct line of Wit, and it may not be altogether extravagant to say that it makes an effective epilogue, and leaves the stage clear for a new and rather different set of actors. And perhaps it almost meets on a different level the requirements of one of the most notable wits in the company for whom Swift wrote, the Duke of Buckingham, who at the end of the century challenged his generation to produce another writer of such sincerity, as he who from the beginning of the century had exercised so much influence in England, – the incomparable Montaigne. 'Yet,' he says, 'whenever any great Wit shall incline to the same free way of writing, I almost dare assure him of success; for besides the agreeableness of such a book, so very sincere a temper of mind needs not blush to be exposed as naked as possible.'[17] In spite of all their differences and in spite of the novelty and originality of *A Tale of a Tub* and the violence and exu-berance which make it so unlike the tone and manner of Montaigne, it was nevertheless written by one who was inclined to 'the same free way of writing' and of 'so very sincere a temper of mind' that it reveals as nakedly and as fearlessly as possible the intellectual experience of a man of letters, who had reached the age of thirty a little before the turn of the century together with what might not too fancifully be called the first generation of the modern world.

NOTES

1. *The Poems of Jonathan Swift*, ed. H. Williams, 2nd ed. (1958) II 547.
2. The edition referred to is *The Prose Works of Jonathan Swift*, ed. H. Davis (1939).
3. *A Tale of a Tub*, ed. A. C. Guthkelch and D. Nichol Smith, 2nd ed. (1958) pp. 215–16.
4. *The Rehearsal Transpros'd* (1673) part II, p. 255.
5. Ibid. pp. 26–7.
6. Ibid. p. 115, quoted in *A Tale of a Tub*, p. xxviii–xxx.
7. Francis Osborn, *Works* (1673) p. vi.
8. *Tale of a Tub*, pp. xxviii ff.
9. *Tale of a Tub*, p. 232 n.
10. *Tale of a Tub*, pp. lvii–lviii.

11. *Lives of the Poets*, ed. G. Birkbeck Hill (1905) III 10 (n. 6).

12. *The Essays of John Dryden*, ed. W. P. Ker (1900) II 38.

13. Dryden, op. cit. II 240–5; *Prose*, I 81–2.

14. *Antony and Cleopatra*, IV xiv 2–10.

15. George Sherburn, 'Methods in Books about Swift', in *Studies in Philology*, XXXV (Oct. 1938) 650.

16. *Lives of the Poets*, III 10–11.

17. *Miscellanea* (Haworth Press, 1933) pp. 82–3.

VIRGINIA WOOLF

Swift's *Journal to Stella* (1935)

IN any highly civilised society disguise plays so large a part, politeness is so essential, that to throw off the ceremonies and conventions and talk a 'little language' for one or two to understand, is as much a necessity as a breath of air in a hot room. The reserved, the powerful, the admired, have the most need of such a refuge. Swift himself found it so. The proudest of men coming home from the company of great men who praised him, of lovely women who flattered him, from intrigue and politics, put all that aside, settled himself comfortably in bed, pursed his severe lips into baby language and prattled to his 'two monkies', his 'dear Sirrahs', his 'naughty rogues' on the other side of the Irish Channel.

> Well, let me see you now again. My wax candle's almost out, but how-ever I'll begin. Well then don't be so tedious, Mr. Presto; what can you say to MD's letter? Make haste, have done with your preambles – why, I say, I am glad you are so often abroad.

So long as Swift wrote to Stella in that strain, carelessly, illegibly, for 'methinks when I write plain, I do not know how, but we are not alone, all the world can see us. A bad scrawl is so snug . . .', Stella had no need to be jealous. It was true that she was wearing away the flower of her youth in Ireland with Rebecca Dingley, who wore hinged spectacles, consumed large quantities of Brazil tobacco, and stumbled over her petticoats as she walked. Further, the conditions in which the two ladies lived, for ever in Swift's company when he was at home, occupying his house when he was absent, gave rise to gossip; so that though Stella never saw him except in Mrs Dingley's presence, she was one of those ambiguous women who live chiefly in the society of the other sex. But surely it was well worth while. The packets kept coming from England, each sheet written to the rim in Swift's crabbed little hand, which she imitated to perfection, full of nonsense words, and capital letters, and hints which no one but Stella could understand, and secrets which Stella was to keep, and little commissions which

Stella was to execute. Tobacco came for Dingley, and chocolate and silk aprons for Stella. Whatever people might say, surely it was well worth while.

Of this Presto, who was so different from that formidable character 't'other I', the world knew nothing. The world knew only that Swift was over in England again, soliciting the new Tory government on behalf of the Irish Church for those First Fruits which he had begged the Whigs in vain to restore. The business was soon accomplished; nothing indeed could exceed the cordiality and affection with which Harley and St John greeted him; and now the world saw what even in those days of small societies and individual pre-eminence must have been a sight to startle and amaze – the 'mad parson', who had marched up and down the coffee-houses in silence and unknown a few years ago, admitted to the inmost councils of State; the penniless boy who was not allowed to sit down at table with Sir William Temple dining with the highest ministers of the Crown, making dukes do his bidding, and so run after for his good offices that his servant's chief duty was to know how to keep people out. Addison himself forced his way up only by pretending that he was a gentleman come to pay a bill. For the time being Swift was omnipotent. Nobody could buy his services; everybody feared his pen. He went to Court, and 'am so proud I make all the lords come up to me'. The Queen wished to hear him preach; Harley and St John added their entreaties; but he refused. When Mr Secretary one night dared show his temper, Swift called upon him and warned him

> never to appear cold to me, for I would not be treated like a schoolboy. . . .
> He took all right; said I had reason . . . would have had me dine with him
> at Mrs. Masham's brother, to make up matters; but I would not. I don't
> know, but I would not.

He scribbled all this down to Stella without exultation or vanity. That he should command and dictate, prove himself the peer of great men and make rank abase itself before him, called for no comment on his part or on hers. Had she not known him years ago at Moor Park and seen him lose his temper with Sir William Temple, and guessed his greatness and heard from his own lips what he planned and hoped? Did she not know better than anyone how strangely good and bad were blent in him and all his foibles and eccentricities of temper? He scandalised the lords with whom he dined by his stinginess, picked the coals off his fire, saved halfpence on coaches; and yet by the help of these very economies he practised, she knew, the most considerate and secret of charities – he gave poor Patty Rolt 'a pistole to help her a little forward against she goes to board in the country'; he took twenty guineas to young Harrison, the sick poet, in his garret. She alone knew how he could be coarse in his speech and yet delicate in his behaviour; how he could be cynical superficially and yet cherish a depth of feeling which she had never met with in any other human being. They knew each other in and out; the good and the bad, the deep and the trivial; so that without effort or concealment he could use those precious moments late at night or the first thing on waking to pour out upon her the whole story of his day, with its charities and meannesses, its affections and ambitions and despairs, as though he were thinking aloud.

With such proof of his affection, admitted to intimacy with this Presto whom no one else in the world knew, Stella had no cause to be jealous. It was perhaps the opposite that happened. As she read the crowded pages, she could see him and hear him and imagine so exactly the impression that he must be making on all these fine people that she fell more deeply in love with him than ever. Not only was he courted and flattered by the great; everybody seemed to call upon him when they were in trouble. There was 'young Harrison'; he worried to find him ill and penniless; carried him off to Knightsbridge; took him a hundred pounds only to find that he was dead an hour before. 'Think what grief this is to me! . . . I could not dine with Lord Treasurer, nor anywhere else; but got a bit of meat toward evening.' She could imagine the strange scene, that November morning, when the Duke of Hamilton was killed in Hyde Park, and Swift went at once to the Duchess and sat with her for two hours and heard her rage and storm and rail; and took her affairs, too, on his shoulders as if it were his natural office, and none could dispute his place in the house of mourning. 'She has moved my very soul', he said. When young Lady Ashburnham died he burst out, 'I hate life when I think it exposed to such accidents; and to see so many thousand wretches burdening the earth, while such as her die, makes me think God did never intend life for a blessing.' And then, with that instinct to rend and tear his own emotions which made him angry in the midst of his pity, he would round upon the mourners, even the mother and sister of the dead woman, and part them as they cried together and complain how 'people will pretend to grieve more than they really do, and that takes off from their true grief'.

All this was poured forth freely to Stella; the gloom and the anger, the kindness and the coarseness and the genial love of little ordinary human things. To her he showed himself fatherly and brotherly; he laughed at her spelling; he scolded her about her health; he directed her business affairs. He gossiped and chatted with her. They had a fund of memories in common. They had spent many happy hours together. 'Do not you remember I used to come into your chamber and turn Stella out of her chair, and rake up the fire in a cold morning and cry *uth, uth, uth!*' She was often in his mind; he wondered if she was out walking when he was; when Prior abused one of his puns he remembered Stella's puns and how vile they were; he compared his life in London with hers in Ireland and wondered when they would be together again. And if this was the influence of Stella upon Swift in town among all the wits, the influence of Swift upon Stella marooned in an Irish village alone with Dingley was far greater. He had taught her all the little learning she had when she was a child and he a young man years ago at Moor Park. His influence was everywhere – upon her mind, upon her affections, upon the books she read and the hand she wrote, upon the friends she made and the suitors she rejected. Indeed, he was half responsible for her being.

But the woman he had chosen was no insipid slave. She had a character of her own. She was capable of thinking for herself. She was aloof, a severe critic for all her grace and sympathy, a little formidable perhaps with her love of plain speaking and her fiery temper and her fearlessness in saying what she thought. But with all her gifts she was little known. Her slender means and feeble health and dubious social standing made her way of life very modest. The society which gathered round her came for the simple pleasure of talking to a woman who listened and understood and said very little herself, but in the most agreeable of voices and generally 'the best thing that was said in the company'. For the rest she was not learned. Her health had prevented her from serious study, and though she had run over a great variety of subjects and had a fine severe taste in letters, what she did read did not stick in her mind. She had been extravagant as a girl, and flung her money about until her good sense took control of her, and now she lived with the utmost frugality. 'Five nothings on five plates of delf' made her supper. Attractive, if not beautiful with her fine dark eyes and her raven black hair, she dressed very plainly, and thus contrived to lay by enough to help the poor and to bestow upon her friends (it was an extravagance that she could not resist) 'the most agreeable presents in the world'. Swift never knew her equal in that art, 'although it be an affair of as delicate a nature as most in the course of life'. She had in addition that sincerity which Swift called 'honour', and in spite of the weakness of her body 'the personal courage of a hero'. Once when a robber came to her window, she had shot him through the body with her own hand. Such, then, was the influence which worked on Swift as he wrote; such the presence that mingled with the thought of his fruit-trees and the willows and the trout stream at Laracor when he saw the trees budding in St James's Park and heard the politicians wrangle at Westminster. Unknown to all of them, he had his retreat: and if the ministers again played him false, and once more, after making his friends' fortunes, he went empty-handed away, then after all he could retire to Ireland and to Stella and have 'no shuddering at all' at the thought.

But Stella was the last woman in the world to press her claims. None knew better than she that Swift loved power and the company of men: that though he had his moods of tenderness and his fierce spasms of disgust at society, still for the most part he infinitely preferred the dust and bustle of London to all the trout streams and cherry-trees in the world. Above all, he hated interference. If anyone laid a finger upon his liberty or hinted the least threat to his independence, were they men or women, queens or kitchen-maids, he turned upon them with a ferocity which made a savage of him on the spot. Harley once dared to offer him a bank-note; Miss Waring dared hint that the obstacles to their marriage were now removed. Both were chastised, the woman brutally. But Stella knew better than to invite such treatment. Stella had learnt patience; Stella had learnt discretion. Even in a matter like this of staying in London or coming back to Ireland she allowed him every latitude. She asked nothing for herself and therefore got more than she asked. Swift was half annoyed:

> . . . your generosity makes me mad; I know you repine inwardly at Presto's absence; you think he has broken his word, of coming in three months, and that this is always his trick: and now Stella says, she does not see possibly how I can come away in haste, and that MD is satisfied, etc. An't you a rogue to overpower me thus?

But it was thus that she kept him. Again and again he burst into language of intense affection:

Farewell dear Sirrahs, dearest lives: there is peace and quiet with MD, and nowhere else. . . . Farewell again, dearest rogues: I am never happy, but when I write or think of MD. . . . You are as welcome as my blood to every farthing I have in the world: and all that grieves me is, I am not richer, for MD's sake.

One thing alone dashed the pleasure that such words gave her. It was always in the plural that he spoke of her; it was always 'dearest Sirrahs, dearest lives'; MD stood for Stella and Mrs Dingley together. Swift and Stella were never alone. Grant that this was for form's sake merely, grant that the presence of Mrs Dingley, busy with her keys and her lap-dog and never listening to a word that was said to her, was a form too. But why should such forms be necessary? Why impose a strain that wasted her health and half spoilt her pleasure and kept 'perfect friends' who were happy only in each other's company apart? Why indeed? There was a reason; a secret that Stella knew; a secret that Stella did not impart. Divided they had to be. Since, then, no bond bound them, since she was afraid to lay the least claim upon her friend, all the more jealously must she have searched into his words and analysed his conduct to ascertain the temper of his mood and acquaint herself instantly with the least change in it. So long as he told her frankly of his 'favourites' and showed himself the bluff tyrant who required every woman to make advances to him, who lectured fine ladies and let them tease him, all was well. There was nothing in that to rouse her suspicions. Lady Berkeley might steal his hat; the Duchess of Hamilton might lay bare her agony; and Stella, who was kind to her sex, laughed with the one and grieved with the other.

But were there traces in the *Journal* of a different sort of influence – something far more dangerous because more equal and more intimate? Suppose that there were some woman of Swift's own station, a girl, like the girl that Stella herself had been when Swift first knew her, dissatisfied with the ordinary way of life, eager, as Stella put it, to know right from wrong, gifted, witty, and untaught – she indeed, if she existed, might be a rival to be feared. But was there such a rival? If so, it was plain that there would be no mention of her in the *Journal*. Instead, there would be hesitations, excuses, an occasional uneasiness and embarrassment when, in the midst of writing freely and fully, Swift was brought to a stop by something that he could not say. Indeed, he had been only a month or two in England when some such silence roused Stella's suspicions. Who was it, she asked, that boarded

near him, that he dined with now and then? 'I know no such person,'
Swift replied; 'I do not dine with boarders. What the pox! You know
whom I have dined with every day since I left you, better than I do.
What do you mean, Sirrah?' But he knew what she meant: she meant
Mrs Vanhomrigh, the widow who lived near him; she meant her
daughter Esther. 'The Vans' kept coming again and again after that in
the *Journal*. Swift was too proud to conceal the fact that he saw them,
but he sought nine times out of ten to excuse it. When he was in Suffolk
Street the Vanhomrighs were in St James's Street and thus saved him a
walk. When he was in Chelsea they were in London, and it was
convenient to keep his best gown and periwig there. Sometimes the
heat kept him there and sometimes the rain; now they were playing
cards, and young Lady Ashburnham reminded him so much of Stella
that he stayed on to help her. Sometimes he stayed out of listlessness;
again he stayed because he was very busy and they were simple people
who did not stand on ceremony. At the same time Stella had only to
hint that these Vanhomrighs were people of no consequence for him
to retort, 'Why, they keep as good female company as I do male. . . . I
saw two lady Bettys there this afternoon.' In short, to tell the whole
truth, to write whatever came into his head in the old free way, was
no longer easy.

Indeed, the whole situation was full of difficulty. No man detested
falsehood more than Swift or loved truth more whole-heartedly. Yet
here he was compelled to hedge, to hide, and to prevaricate. Again, it
had become essential to him to have some 'sluttery' or private chamber
where he could relax and unbend and be Presto and not 't'other I'.
Stella satisfied this need as no one else could. But then Stella was in
Ireland; Vanessa was on the spot. She was younger and fresher; she
too had her charms. She too could be taught and improved and scolded
into maturity as Stella had been. Obviously Swift's influence upon her
was all to the good. And so with Stella in Ireland and Vanessa in
London, why should it not be possible to enjoy what each could give
him, confer benefits on both and do no serious harm to either? It
seemed possible; at any rate he allowed himself to make the experiment.
Stella, after all, had contrived for many years to make shift with her
portion; Stella had never complained of her lot.

But Vanessa was not Stella. She was younger, more vehement, less
disciplined, less wise. She had no Mrs Dingley to restrain her. She had
no memories of the past to solace her. She had no journals coming

day by day to comfort her. She loved Swift and she knew no reason
why she should not say so. Had he not himself taught her 'to act what
was right, and not to mind what the world said'? Thus when some
obstacle impeded her, when some mysterious secret came between
them, she had the unwisdom to question him. 'Pray what can be wrong
in seeing and advising an unhappy young woman? I can't imagine.'
'You have taught me to distinguish', she burst out, 'and then you leave
me miserable.' Finally in her anguish and her bewilderment she had the
temerity to force herself upon Stella. She wrote and demanded to be
told the truth – what was Stella's connection with Swift? But it was
Swift himself who enlightened her. And when the full force of those
bright blue eyes blazed upon her, when he flung her letter on the table
and glared at her and said nothing and rode off, her life was ended. It
was no figure of speech when she said that 'his killing, killing words'
were worse than the rack to her; when she cried out that there was
'something in your look so awful that it strikes me dumb'. Within a
few weeks of that interview she was dead; she had vanished, to become
one of those uneasy ghosts who haunted the troubled background of
Stella's life, peopling its solitude with fears.

Stella was left to enjoy her intimacy alone. She lived on to practise
those sad arts by which she kept her friend at her side until, worn out
with the strain and the concealment, with Mrs Dingley and her lap-
dogs, with the perpetual fears and frustrations, she too died. As they
buried her, Swift sat in a back room away from the lights in the church-
yard and wrote an account of the character of 'the truest, most virtuous,
and valuable friend, that I, or perhaps any other person, was ever
blessed with'. Years passed; insanity overcame him; he exploded in
violent outbursts of mad rage. Then by degrees he fell silent. Once
they caught him murmuring. 'I am what I am', they heard him say.

W. B. EWALD, JR

M. B., Drapier (1954)

(a) Instruction and Exhortation

IN 1724, after ten years of residence as Dean, Swift assumed his most notable role in defence of Irish liberty. The English government had in 1722 granted William Wood, an English iron merchant, a patent to make copper money for Ireland to remedy the shortage of small coins there. A protest arose in Ireland against what was considered the introduction of a debased coinage into the country. Early in 1724 Swift entered the scene and wrote eight major tracts against Wood's coin, letters addressed to the people of Ireland (Letters I and IV), Harding the printer (II), the Irish nobility and gentry (III), Lord Viscount Molesworth (V), Lord Chancellor Midleton (VI), the Irish Parliament (VII), and the Grand Jury which was to examine the case against Harding after his printing the allegedly seditious Letter IV (*Seasonable Advice to the Grand Jury*). The last was published anonymously, and to Letter VI (this and Letter VII were first published in 1735) Swift signed his initials. But the 'author' of the other Letters was not the Dean but one 'M. B., Drapier' (frequently called 'the Drapier'), a humble but resolute Irish patriot.

Like the humble Member of the Irish Parliament, whom he recalls but whom he surpasses as an ironical device, the Drapier is not an invariably uniform character. For the Drapier's various attributes to a large extent result from the situation in which he plays a part. As spokesman for Swift he has a number of functions. Not only must he conceal superficially the identity of the true author of this dangerous set of tracts (though the authorship became an open secret). But also he must inform the uneducated as well as the educated Irish people about the nature of this coinage and the dangers it holds for Ireland. He must exhort them not to accept it. He must heap abuse on the head of Wood, who stands to profit at Ireland's expense. He must inform government officials in England and their representatives in Ireland that the Irish people will not accept the coin, and that it would be dangerous to try to introduce it. Finally, he must show both the Prime Minister, Robert Walpole, and King George I that the Irish opposition to their measure is not in any way treasonable. To accomplish all these ends Swift has to use the character of his *persona* in a number of ways.[1]

Although Swift often considered himself an Anglo-Irishman, as when he says that the low opinion the English have of the Irish brogue

> affects those among us who are not the least liable to such reproaches, farther than the misfortune of being born in Ireland, although of English parents, and whose education has been chiefly in that kingdom (*Works*, VII 346),[2]

it is fairly clear that the Drapier is interested in the welfare of Ireland as a whole. A possibly more reliable indication of Swift's whole attitude toward the Irish is found in the *Intelligencer*, XIX (1728), where Swift, writing as an Irish country gentleman and Member of Parliament, complains that the great scarcity of silver is a hardship for him. He continues:

> But the sufferings of me, and those of my rank, are trifles, in comparison of what the meaner sort undergo; such as the buyers and sellers, at fairs, and markets; the shopkeepers in every town, the farmers in general. All those who travel with fish, poultry, pedlary-ware, and other conveniences to sell. (*Works*, IX 323–4)

This passage would seem to indicate that when Swift spoke of the sufferings of the whole people of Ireland, he perhaps meant the poor as well as the more well-to-do. Swift usually wrote with a definite purpose in mind. And so when Lord Orrery said, 'The papist, the fanatic, the Tory, the Whig all listed themselves volunteers under the banners of M. B. Drapier, and were all equally zealous to serve the common cause' (*Works*, VI 8 n) it probably indicated that Swift clearly intended to speak for the whole country, not just his own group. But, of course, one cannot at this time know with absolute certainty what his attitude was.[3]

'M. B.', the Drapier, like the Member of the Irish Parliament, is basically a humble person. He is a simple tradesman, who has done some reading and thinking, who has a general intellectual alertness, but who nevertheless remains a small businessman; he enters into the serious controversy against Wood only because of his great patriotism, not because he is skilled in the intricacies of political affairs. This characterization is suggested in Letter I, as the Drapier gives extravagant examples

of what could happen if Wood's inflationary coin were brought into
Ireland: if a lady comes to 'our shops' in a coach, 'it must be followed
by a car loaden with Mr. Wood's money' (*Works*, VI 18); he will not
sell a yard of ten penny stuff for under two hundred of Wood's coins,
and he will not count them but rather weigh them in a lump. Here the
persona makes the argument concrete. Elsewhere the Drapier speaks
confidentially to his fellow tradesman: 'They say Squire Conolly has
sixteen thousand pounds a year; now if he sends for his rent to town . . .
he must have two hundred and forty horses to bring up his half year's
rent.' And the Drapier has been 'assured' that 'some great bankers'
keep forty thousand pounds by them in ready cash, a sum which, to
carry it in Wood's coin, would require twelve hundred horses. How
should a tradesman behave in such a situation? The Drapier can say for
himself:

> For my own part, I am already resolved what to do. I have a pretty good
> shop of Irish stuffs and silks, and instead of taking Mr. Wood's bad copper,
> I intend to truck with my neighbours the butchers, and bakers, and brewers,
> and the rest, goods for goods, and the little gold and silver I have, I will
> keep by me like my heart's blood till better times, or till I am just ready to
> starve, and then I will buy Mr. Wood's money as my father did the brass
> money in K. James's time, who could buy ten pound of it with a guinea,
> and I hope to get as much for a pistole, and so purchase bread from those
> who will be such fools as to sell it me.

Such an occasional long breathless sentence should probably remind the
reader that the writer (like Mrs Frances Harris?) is not a stylistic
expert (*Works*, VI 18, 20).[4]

But the Drapier is not the humblest of tradesmen. He can, in showing
how landlords will be forced to discharge their tenants and farmers,
look down upon the 'few miserable cottiers' whom the landlords will
subsequently keep on. The farmers, shopkeepers and handicraftsmen, the
Drapier adds, will be merely forced to starve; in this latter, higher,
group the Drapier includes himself. This distinction, which gives the
Drapier a certain eminence, is developed further in Letter II, where he
says that he has no worry for himself, since he has a good shop, but that
he has the public good at heart. By saying he is 'no inconsiderable
shopkeeper', that he has talked with other tradesmen, with gentlemen
of city and country, and with many farmers, cottagers and labourers,
he backs up his argument that Ireland does not need small copper. In

Letter III he introduces an anecdote as one told to him when he was in England many years ago, and in Letter VII he refers to the absentee landlords whom he knew well enough when he resided in England. Such instances show that Swift had to temper the Drapier's humility with enough eminence to make him able to carry on a convincing argument.[5]

Thus when in Letter I the Drapier, consistently with his character, writes urgently in a structure and style designed to present the most elementary facts about Wood's halfpence to the least-informed minds, he helps the common people along with specific directions: 'I will therefore first tell you the plain story of the fact; and then I will lay before you how you ought to act in common prudence, and according to the laws of your country.' He continually addresses his hearers as 'you', and like a teacher he admonishes them, 'even the wisest' among them, for not reading the works written to do them political good. To him Wood is 'a mean ordinary man, a hardware dealer'; the well-to-do merchant can share this view with the Dean of St Patrick's, who, in the sermon *Doing Good*, constantly refers to Wood as a 'mean man' and calls him 'one obscure ill-designing projector'.

Not only is Letter I 'in a style pitched studiously in the lowest key';[6] it is likely also that, as Dr Herbert Davis says, readers could hear in it the voice from the pulpit of St Patrick's Cathedral.[7] In first explaining and then exhorting, Swift is following the advice in the *Letter to a Young Clergyman* as well as the practice of his own sermons. In *Doing Good*, for example, Swift writes:

> I therefore undertake to shew you three things. First: That there are few people so weak or mean, who have it not sometimes in their power to be useful to the public. Secondly: That it is often in the power of the meanest among mankind to do mischief to the public. And, lastly: That all wilful injuries done to the public are very great and aggravated sins in the sight of God.

He then takes up each point in order. In the sermon *On the Martyrdom of King Charles I* he follows the same plan, and in the sermon 'On the Poor Man's Contentment' he frankly addresses 'you of the meaner sort'.

This style, frequent in the sermons, occurs also in Swift's secular works. In *The Conduct of the Allies*, which at least in its informative purpose is similar to the *Drapier's Letters*, Swift talks down to his audience: 'Now, to give the most ignorant reader some idea of our

present circumstances, without troubling him or myself with computations in form . . .' (*Works*, v 111). More extensively Swift assumes
the same strict didactic attitude as he instructs the young lady approaching marriage; he will indicate 'how you are to act, and what you ought
to avoid' (*Works*, xi 116). At the end of the essay he says, 'I desire you
will keep this letter in your cabinet, and often examine impartially
your whole conduct by it' (*Works*, xi 124). This advice is like the
Drapier's to the Irish at the end of Letter I: 'I desire all persons may keep
this paper carefully by them to refresh their memories whenever they
shall have farther notice of Mr. Wood's halfpence, or any other the like
imposture' (*Works*, vi 25).

But this is the Drapier, not just Swift. Although the Drapier teaches
as one who has an amount of legal and historical learning and inside
facts about contemporary life far more extensive than that of his
audience, he is still a simple tradesman. Occasionally he forgets to
list a source for his information, as when he tells the people about how
the French government calls in its money and re-coins it at a higher
value. But usually he is at some pains to cover up his superior knowledge. 'I will now go on to tell you the judgments of some great
lawyers in this matter', he says, 'whom I fee'd on purpose for your
sakes' in order to be sure about the legal grounds. That a linen draper
(who admits, in Letter VII, to more reading 'than is usual to men of my
inferior calling') should know the Bible is understandable; so without
qualification the Drapier can compare the halfpence to 'the accursed thing
which the children of Israel were forbidden to touch'. But a reference
to Phalaris's story of the eastern king who put a man into a bull of
brass, the Drapier must excuse by saying he had 'heard scholars talk' of
it. In Letter VII he refers easily to Alexander the Great and Phidias,
quotes 'the wise Lord Bacon', and paraphrases Luther briefly and aptly,
'poor Ireland maketh many rich'. Yet even in this last letter, where one
suspects Swift was being less cautious about the attributes of his
persona, the Drapier can claim he has been 'told by scholars that Caesar
said, he would rather be the first man, in I know not what village, than
the second in Rome.[8] One must accept a linen draper's talking with
scholars as one must accept his reports of conversations with members
of the nobility, eminent lawyers, and poor papist cottiers. For this
draper, by his own account, is not just an average member of his humble
profession.

Thus throughout Letter I the Drapier reveals qualities of both the

Dean and the shopkeeper. At times the Drapier shifts from one to the other. He can quote from the 'famous law-book, called *The Mirror of Justice*', since he has obtained the advice of 'great lawyers'. He can quote the 'Statute Concerning the Passing of Pence' as he 'got it translated into English, for some of our laws at that time, were, as I am told writ in Latin'. Yet he proceeds to discuss law sure-footedly, citing Parliamentary Acts to prove his points, and using such legalistic phrasing as 'pursuant to this opinion' and 'this is further manifest from the statute of the ninth year of Edward the 3d. chap. 3'. This legalistic discussion would impress the more simple people in the audience by reference to things over their heads, as well as convince the more intelligent. Even so, the Drapier is careful to summarize the results in very simple terms: 'I will now, my dear friends to save you the trouble, set before you in short, what the law obliges you to do, and what it does not oblige you to' (*Works*, VI 21–4).

This method occurs again in Letter IV, addressed to 'the whole people of Ireland'. Early in the essay the Drapier offers 'to explain to those who are ignorant, what the meaning of that word "prerogative" is'. But Swift takes his usual care to emphasize the author's humility; he explains the prerogative 'as far as a tradesman can be thought capable of explaining it'. He concludes with 'the opinion of the great Lord Bacon' that as God governs the world by the laws of nature, so the best kings govern by the laws of the kingdom and seldom make use of their prerogative. This 'quotation' (which has not been found specifically in Bacon's works) adds impressiveness to the argument of the simple unscholarly man.

The didactic method is somewhat different in the other Letters. In Letter II, intended – like I – 'for all my countrymen' and addressed 'to people of my own level and condition', the Drapier can still inform his hearers that 'N. B.' means *nota bene* or 'mark well'. He can, in a simple analogy, explain that Newton's test of Wood's coins does not prove they are good; while the Drapier admits that a gentleman buys material from him on the basis of a sample, yet he says that if he, the Drapier, were to buy a hundred sheep, he wouldn't evaluate the whole flock by a single wether. The test of Wood's coin reminds the Drapier of a man who wanted to sell his house and so carried a brick about in his pocket as a sample. It is clear, however, that this letter, unlike Letter I, is intended mainly for the Drapier's equals, not his inferiors. He urges his readers to warn 'the poor innocent people not to receive' Wood's coins. And at the end of the essay he writes up a long petition, in competent legalistic language, to be signed by several hundred of the principal men of Ireland. This petition, like the legal discussions in Letter I, is curiously prefaced by the remark that it should be drawn up by 'some skilful judicious pen'.

When the Drapier, in Letter III, addresses the Irish nobility and gentry, his humility serves a different purpose from that in I and IV. Through much of the tract Swift seems to have forgotten that he is pretending to be a simple tradesman, in his effort to make a full and convincing argument to his educated audience. He produces facts to prove the low character of Wood's three witnesses – Coleby, Browne, and Finley – who testified that Ireland needed small currency; he shows a detailed knowledge of the many types of small coins circulating in Ireland; and he knows that there would be a difference between English and Irish halfpence – because the profit to be allowed Wood for his coinage is much greater than that allowed in England. Wood's coin, contrary to Wood's claims, he proves to be no better than its predecessors. He exhibits a detailed knowledge of the history of Irish coinage since before the time of Tyrone's rebellion, and accurately discusses the difference between Wood's patents and those issued earlier to Lord Dartmouth (1680), Knox (1685), and Moore (1694). And without hesitation he quotes St Paul's distinction between things lawful and things expedient, as well as the High Priest's judgment that 'it was expedient that one Man should die for the people'.

For the most part the Drapier presents this information without citing his source as he does in the earlier letters. Only occasionally does he modestly give his authority, as when he says he has 'been told by persons eminent in the law' that the worst criminal actions may be justified by precedent, or when he says he has checked the Custom House books for details on the importation of coin into Ireland. An important purpose of the *persona's* humility in this essay is to enable Swift to present his arguments with quiet rationality, punctuated by occasional forceful understatements. Whereas in Letter II the Drapier opposed Newton's report on the value of Wood's halfpence with vivid analogies drawn from his experience as a tradesman; in Letter III, by contrast, he says persuasively that it was 'possible enough' to find Wood's coin good 'in the pieces upon which the assay was made; but Wood must have failed very much in point of dexterity' if he couldn't provide good coins especially for the test.

But most important, the Drapier's modesty in this third essay is connected cleverly with the detailed knowledge he does show. He is a simple shopkeeper, requesting the nobility for a declaration against Wood's coin. He apologizes for his 'long, undigested', repetitious paper. He is an unlearned champion, with only 'some informations from an eminent person'. Even these were not a great help:

> I am afraid I have spoiled a few by endeavouring to make them of a piece with my own productions, and the rest I was not able to manage: I was in the case of David who could not move in the armour of Saul, and therefore I rather chose to attack this 'uncircumcised Philistine (Wood I mean) with a sling, and a stone'.

He continues the analogy between Wood and Goliath: both are armed in brass. And cleverly Swift ends the passage with the Drapier as hero, yet consistently a tradesman: 'But if it happens that I prevail over him, . . . he shall never be a servant of mine, for I do not think him fit to be trusted in any honest man's shop.' The use of such humility with competent, detailed argument implies that the case of the enemy is so weak that any man of sound rationality can overcome it. 'A poor ignorant shopkeeper, utterly unskilled in law' wins his case 'by plain reason, unassisted by art, cunning, or eloquence': 'there was no great skill required to detect the many mistakes' in Newton's report.

In various ways the tradesman has informed his countrymen of Wood's vicious scheme; next, as in the sermons, he must exhort them to action. Occasionally, as in Letter II, he stands apart from his hearers and scolds them for not following his instructions:

> It is my chief endeavour to keep up your spirits and resentments. If I tell you there is a precipice under you, and that if you go forwards you will certainly break your necks . . . must I be at the trouble of repeating it every morning? Are our people's 'hearts waxed gross'? Are 'their ears dull of hearing', and have 'they closed their eyes'? (*Works,* VI 41)

His eloquence (with the powerful use of Biblical quotations) would again remind some readers of the preaching of the Dean, who believed that a strong argument ought to be presented 'in as moving a manner as the nature of the subject will properly admit'. Yet even eloquent exhortation can be introduced in keeping with the mask of a tradesman. In Letter IV the Drapier points out factually and mildly (in the manner of Letter III) that it doesn't matter whether rumours claim that the

Irish will be forced by England to accept Wood's coin: 'For in this point we have nothing to do with English ministers, and I should be sorry to lay it in their power to redress this grievance.' Then comes the most forceful sentence on liberty in all the *Letters*:

> The remedy is wholly in your own hands, and therefore I have digressed a little in order to refresh and continue that spirit so seasonably raised amongst you, and to let you see that by the laws of God, of Nature, of Nations, and of your own Country, you are and ought to be as free a people as your brethren in England. (*Works*, VI 115)

In another type of exhortation the Drapier, with none of the characteristics of the Dean, is presented as a heroic individual whom Swift sets up to lead the people by his brave example:

> Mr. Wood will *oblige* me to take fivepence halfpenny of his brass in every payment! And I will shoot Mr. Wood and his deputies through the head, like highwaymen or housebreakers, if they dare to force one farthing of their coin upon me in the payment of an hundred pounds. (*Works*, VI 39)

Such a passage could serve only to rouse the Irish people to resolute action.

In writing against Wood himself, the Drapier has an aim similar to that of exhortation: to give the Irish people an object upon which to vent their anger. Since Letter I is mainly controlled and didactic, Wood is insulted only in passing, as a 'hardware dealer', while he and his supporters are called 'blood-suckers'. This is also largely the method of Letter IV, likewise primarily didactic in purpose. Invective against Wood is limited to such phrases as 'this impostor and his crew', 'the vile accusation of Wood and his accomplices', 'the unsupportable villainy and impudence of that incorrigible wretch'. Letter II, however, which followed Newton's report, is much more violent. The first paragraph contains a direct and savage outburst against Wood for his claim that Ireland needs small coin: 'What then? If a physician prescribes to a patient a dram of physic, shall a rascal apothecary cram him with a pound, and mix it up with poison?' Such an onslaught, based on a medical metaphor, is frequent in the *Letters*. In Letter II again, Wood's remedy for Ireland's ills is 'to cure a scratch on the finger by cutting off the arm', and in Letter IV his recent threats are 'the last howls of a dog dissected alive'. The Drapier often piles up one fertile term of abuse after another. Wood, in Letter II, is 'one single, diminutive, insignificant mechanic'. His coin the Irish 'detest, abhor, and reject . . . as corrupt, fraudulent, mingled with dirt and trash'. If it were received in Ireland, the Drapier says in Letter VII, the kingdom would be 'wholly undone, destroyed, sunk, depopulated, made a scene of misery and desolation'.

Such angry outbursts, designed to overwhelm Wood by their extremeness, though they may remind us of an angry Dean, are perfectly consistent with the character of the Drapier. 'Good God! Who are his supporters, abettors, encouragers, or sharers?' he asks. Immediately afterwards, the Drapier threatens to 'shoot Wood and his deputies through the head' if they try to 'oblige' him to take their coin. There is no doubt that this is an angry shopkeeper speaking as he warns his fellows:

> Shopkeepers look to yourselves. Woods will *oblige* and force you to take fivepence halfpenny of his trash in every payment. . . . If any of you be content to deal with Mr. Woods on such conditions they may. But for my own particular, 'let his money perish with him'.

The wrath is perfectly sustained. Wood is debased, and the Drapier, consistently a shopkeeper, is much superior to him: 'It is no loss of honour to submit to the lion, but who, with the figure of a man, can think with patience of being devoured alive by a rat?' One value of having Wood overwhelmed by the Drapier instead of by Swift is obvious. To be crushed by a simple tradesman is more humiliating than to be crushed by a prominent Anglican divine. And there is added power from the humour of the shopkeeper who can (when it serves Swift's purposes) lose control of his sentences and in the first two Letters spell Wood's name 'Woods'.

The intensity of the Drapier's anger causes him to use against Wood the converse of this device: Wood and his friends are, by an inversion of values, raised to a false eminence. The Irish merchants and traders who betrayed their country by testifying that Ireland needed Wood's coin are called 'excellent witnesses'; Wood becomes 'this honest liberal hardwareman'. The Drapier says he chooses 'rather to be hanged than have all my substance taxed at seventeen shillings in the pound, at the arbitrary will and pleasure of the venerable Mr. Wood'. Of Wood's plan not to drain Ireland of its gold and silver the Drapier declares, 'This little arbitrary mock-monarch most graciously offers to "take our manufactures in exchange".' And as in direct statement the Drapier says that the struggle is between Wood on the one hand and the rights of a whole free country on the other, so in irony he says:

> But he must be surely a man of some wonderful merit. Hath he saved any other kingdom at his own expense to give him a title of reimbursing himself by the destruction of ours? Hath he discovered the longitude or the universal medicine? No. (*Works*, vi 72–3)

Indeed, the Drapier claims he has been

> sometimes tempted to wish that this project of Wood might succeed, because I reflected with some pleasure what a jolly crew it would bring over among us of lords and squires, and pensioners of both sexes, and officers civil and military, where we should live together as merry and sociable as beggars, only with this one abatement, that we should neither have meat to feed, nor manufactures to clothe us, unless we could be content to prance about in coats of mail, or eat brass as ostriches do iron. (*Work*, vi 108)

His ironic device, with its undercuts such as 'hardwareman' and 'little', is of the sort that Swift uses constantly throughout his works. Here (there is a similar use in the Irish parliamentarian's letter), it temporarily becomes a weapon in the hand of the Drapier, without modifiying his character as a tradesman.

In Letter III there are fewer of these extremes of anger. Quite often the Drapier, writing to the Irish nobility, is content to present merely factual evidence against Wood: he lost a collectorship in Shropshire; six years previously, when several bids on coinage were accepted, he made a bad offer; his coins are not milled, and so they can be 'more easily counterfeited by himself as well as others'. Wood becomes an object of burlesque humour rather than of hatred; 'Let Wood and his accomplices travel about the country with cartloads of their ware, and see who will take it off their hands, there will be no fear of his being robbed, for a highwayman would scorn to touch it.' The Drapier, too, abandons his attitude of proud scorn and as a tradesman contends with Wood, for the King has left the field open between Wood and the Irish people:

> Wood hath liberty to offer his coin, and we have law, reason, liberty and necessity to refuse it. . . . I hope the words 'voluntary' and 'willing' to receive it will be understood, and applied in their true natural meaning, as commonly understood by Protestants. For if a fierce captain comes to my shop to buy six yards of scarlet cloth, followed by a porter laden with a

sack of Wood's coin upon his shoulders . . . and thereupon seizes my cloth,
leaving me the price in his odious copper . . . : In this case I shall hardly
be brought to think I am left to my own will. (*Works*, VI 86, 88)

This is humility of another sort. This Drapier is not a triumphant hero
but an Irish shopkeeper facing a serious problem, which all his fellow
tradesmen will face, in his battle against the enemy. Like the humble
David, the Drapier has gone out to meet Wood in his armour. Wood
here is no mean and insignificant mechanic. And the outcome of the
battle is by no means certain.

After Swift came under the fire of the authorities for some of his
remarks in Letter IV, the Drapier uses this self-debasing method of
attacking Wood more than his earlier methods. In Letter VI the
Drapier says he has been told by lawyers that the first person to strike
a blow in a quarrel should be punished first; therefore the Drapier
humbly desires that Wood be hanged and 'his dross thrown into the
sea'; afterwards the Drapier would stand his own trial. In Letter VII the
lowly Drapier appears as a brave, though obscure, person, who would
suffer the most ignominious and torturing death rather than accept
Wood's coin. Such a statement sounds very unlike the Drapier's angry
promise to shoot Wood and his deputies. Yet both statements follow
from the character of the humble tradesman that Swift has created.

(b) The Drapier on Walpole, the King, and Himself

Wood was the one object of all the Drapier's anger. The problem
for Swift throughout the *Letters* was to distinguish between Wood's
evil practices and the policy of the King and his ministers. Any reference
to Walpole had to be extremely careful. But these references which in
their restraint superficially show that the Irish have no quarrel with
Walpole, at the same time carry a great deal of subtle ironical power.
In Letter III, for example, Walpole is attacked only indirectly. In the
Drapier's humble opinion the committee set up to evaluate Wood's
coin prejudged the case by calling 'the united sense of both Houses of
Parliament in Ireland "an universal clamour"'. Then he adds: 'I never
heard of a wise minister who despised the universal clamour of a
people.' In Letter IV the attacks on Walpole are much more direct.
Walpole could not have said he would force the Irish to accept Wood's
coin or eat their brogues, the Drapier, 'defending' him, says, for Walpole 'never heard of a brogue in his whole life'. Such a cutting remark

occurs in the midst of fluent declarations of esteem for the integrity of
the Prime Minister, a 'wise man, an able minister, and in all his proceedings pursuing the true interest of the King his master'. In Letter VII
also the Drapier reiterates that he 'never had the least intention' to
reflect upon the King or his ministers and that the King and his ministers intended only to benefit the Irish people. Such passages of praise
supply a background of flattery which Swift can puncture by satire.

With this flattery usually goes a remark gently critical of Wood, as
Swift tries to restrict the quarrel to one between a drapier and a hard-
ware dealer. How could Walpole be on Wood's side? The Drapier
knows he is not: 'I must beg leave in all humility to tell Mr. Wood that
he is guilty of great indiscretion by causing so honourable a name as
that of Mr. Walpole to be mentioned.' Wood should never have
reported that the Prime Minister had threatened to make the Irish
swallow the coins in fire-balls. The Drapier carefully computes the
number of Wood's coins, the number of people in Ireland, and
the number of administrators necessary to force the Irish to swallow the
coins; he 'concludes' that the scheme couldn't possibly work. Wood's
audacity shocks the simple tradesman: 'If Mr. Wood hath no better a
manner of representing his patrons, when I come to be a great man, he
shall never be suffered to attend at my levee.' In the final sentence of the
Letter Swift completes his oblique remarks on Walpole's policies:

> as his integrity is above all corruption, so is his fortune above all tempta-
> tion. I reckon therefore we are perfectly safe from that corner, and shall
> ... be left to possess our brogues and potatoes in peace as remote from
> thunder as we are from Jupiter. (*Works*, VI 119-21)

In irony similar to this against Walpole, when Swift time and again
professes the Irish loyalty to the crown and says that the English
Protestants in Ireland love their brethren across the Channel, he sets
these attitudes against satirical comments on English indifference to the
Irish people – that the English know little more of Ireland than they do
of Mexico, that Irish affairs are a topic of coffee-house conversation
when there is nothing better to talk about, and that the English,
crowding about an Irishman newly arrived in a country town, wondered 'to see him look so much better than themselves'. The Drapier
says he is sorry the English people have a false report of 'us', the Irish,
but behind this friendliness is a definite warning. In Letter I he says it
would be bad if Ireland were placed in one scale and Wood in another,

and Wood should weigh down 'this whole kingdom, by which England gets above a million of good money every year clear into their pockets, and that is more than the English do by all the world besides'. In Letter II he reminds the English that Wood's money will reduce their income, as well as that of the absentees.[9]

But sometimes the Drapier lashes out at the English with earnestness which is savage. As he attacked Wood with irony based on an inverted sense of values, so in Letter IV he says of the Irish-English relationship (speaking apparently as an Anglo-Irishman):

> One great merit I am sure we have, which those of English birth can have no pretence to, that our ancestors reduced this kingdom to the obedience of England, for which we have been rewarded with a worse climate, the privilege of being governed by laws to which we do not consent, a ruined trade, a House of Peers without Jurisdiction, almost an incapacity for all employments: and the dread of Wood's halfpence. (*Works*, VI 103-4)

In an even harsher passage, in Letter VII, representing all the unfortunate people of Ireland, he argues that Ireland deserves some indulgence from England 'not only upon the score of Christianity, natural equity, and the general rights of mankind; but chiefly on account of that immense profit they receive from us'. Everything the Drapier has said about English selfishness and ignorance of Irish affairs is outstripped in the one ironical word 'chiefly', which sets economic values above those of religion and morality. Here, as in the *Modest Proposal*, Swift is talking the cynical language of his enemies; they may not be moved to help out of decency, but even they can be aroused at once if they see they may lose a share of their income from Ireland. These passages show the Drapier, identified with the Irish people, in humble submission before the mighty English.[10]

It was even more necessary for Swift to be extremely cautious in remarks about the King. When the Drapier writes about him, he speaks as he does about the English, as an unassuming representative Irishman, not as an individual tradesman. As in his attacks on Walpole the irony is subtle. It can come in a concealed reference to the fact that the Duchess of Kendal, the King's mistress, obtained Wood's patent, as when the Drapier says in Letter III that Wood was selected 'by favour, or *something else*, or by the pretence of merit and honesty'.[11] Or the irony can be open but so clever that the King could hardly take offence at it. For instance, the Drapier says that increasing the number of pure gold coins with the King's image upon them cannot increase the Irish veneration for the King, which is already great, but it can 'very much enliven it with a mixture of comfort and satisfaction'. Such a passage emphasizes the sincerity of the Drapier's protestations that the Irish honour their King. But these protestations can be vitiated by the sort of turn used against Walpole. The Drapier observes that the King said at the end of his address to the House of Lords 'that "he will do everything in his power for the satisfaction of his people". It should seem therefore that the recalling of the patent is not to be understood as a thing in his power.'

For the most part, however, the Drapier does not rely on irony in his remarks on the King. Rather he expresses the rights of the Irish people in polite but firm terms. As in references to Walpole, the Drapier is careful not to identify the King with Wood's interests. The teacher of Letter I informs his fellow countrymen that he is sure that if the King knew the dangers of Wood's coin he would immediately recall it. At the same time, he adds, 'the laws have not given the crown a power of forcing the subject to take what money the King pleases'; for then 'if ever we should happen to live under an ill prince', he might soon manage to get all the gold and silver into his own hands. Letter II strikes angrily at Wood as the base minion who is insulting the King his master by 'raking up so much filthy dross and stamping it with His Majesty's image'. The loyal Irish who, the Drapier recalls, set up a copper statue to George I, are ashamed to see his image on Wood's coins. The King gave Wood the patent in good faith, to alleviate the troubles of Ireland; only Wood is to be blamed 'if his representation be false, and the execution of his patent be fraudulent and corrupt'.

In these passages from Letters I and II the Drapier speaks meekly for all his countrymen. When in Letter III he refers to the King's treatment of the Irish, he does so as an individual of rather slow intelligence. He is 'under some doubt' whether the gain of eight hundred pounds a year is equal to the ruin of a kingdom. He does not understand that Poyning's Act (which concerns the King's authority over Irish parliaments) deprived the Irish of their liberty. When the report of the Privy Council says that Wood's patent is obligatory, 'After long thinking, I am not able to find out what can possibly be meant here by this word "obligatory".' Again, in tentative understatement, when the report says that the patent does not invade the rights of the 'King's subjects of Ireland', the Drapier answers that in singling out 'Ireland' the report 'would seem to insinuate that we are not upon the same foot with our fellow-subjects in England'. And since no one would be 'so bold as to affirm' that in common law rights the Irish and English are not equal, 'in my humble opinion, the word "Ireland" standing in that proposition, was, in the mildest interpretation, *a lapse of the pen*'.

But the Drapier of this Letter is not all mildness. He says that the common people will never accept Wood's coin, 'I hope, and am almost confident'. In anger at the beginning of the essay he asks frankly whether, if the English Parliament and all the English people should ask the King to recall a patent for coinage, the King would debate one half-hour on what he had to do. Then follows a barrage of eleven questions about Irish equality, ending with 'Am I a freeman in England, and do I become a slave in six hours by crossing the Channel?' Bluntly he concludes, 'Let England be satisfied . . . they . . . may keep their adulterate copper at home, for we are determined not to purchase it with our manufactures.'

The fourth Letter continues this direct rejection of the threats that the King may compel the Irish to take Wood's coin. Along with every one of these rejections, however, the Drapier emphasizes his loyalty and humility. He and the other Irish people certainly have no intention at all of disputing the King's right to issue a patent for Wood to produce coins; but there is 'one small limitation': 'nobody alive is obliged to take them'. In an unusual instance of the Drapier's writing on this subject as an individual, not a representative Irishman, he stands up heroically to say that

> I, M. B. Drapier . . . next under God . . . *depend* only on the King my sovereign, and on the laws of my own country; and I am so far from *depending* upon the people of England, that if they should ever rebel against my sovereign . . . I would be ready at the first command from His Majesty to take arms against them. (*Works*, VI 114)

The shopkeeper at one stroke reaffirms both his loyalty to the King and his stubborn resolve not to let him force Wood's coin on the Irish people.[12]

But such *bravado* is less frequent in this Letter than in the first two. Primarily the Drapier uses in the fourth Letter the cringing method of the third. After a discussion of the great difference between Wood's patent and those issued earlier, the Drapier concludes, 'in my private thoughts I have sometimes made a query, whether the penner of those

words in His Majesty's most gracious answer . . . had maturely considered the several circumstances, which, in my poor opinion seem to
make a difference'. And in the midst of an argument that the Irish are a
free people, the Drapier humbly recognizes the helplessness of his
position and that of his country. For although 'in reason all government
without the consent of the governed is the very definition of slavery',
in fact

> eleven men well armed will certainly subdue one single man in his shirt.
> But I have done. For those who have used power to cramp liberty have
> gone so far as to resent even the liberty of complaining, although a man
> upon the rack was never known to be refused the liberty of roaring as
> loud as he thought fit.

The Drapier has no intention of giving up the struggle, however; for
it is in the next paragraph that he makes his most eloquent plea for
Irish liberty.

(c) Results

The Drapier's insistence on Irish freedom, as well as his barbed esteem
of Walpole and the King, got him and his printer, Harding, into
trouble. Letter VI is written privately (though it antedates Letter V,
it was not published until 1735) to Lord Chancellor Midleton, who
opposed Wood's patent, but who also signed the proclamation of the
Lord-Lieutenant and the Irish Privy Council offering a reward to
whoever discovered the author of the Fourth Letter.[13] Swift therefore
writes Letter VI in his own name, defending the Drapier against a
charge of treason. He still pretends to think of the Drapier as a real
person, and some of his vindication is such as the Drapier himself
might have made. Does not the Drapier, Swift notes, clear Walpole
'by very strong arguments' and speak of him 'with civility'? But
Swift has heard others claim that Walpole favours Wood's patent.
Besides, the Prime Minister always gets blamed for anything that
goes wrong; this was true even of Harley (Walpole would not like the
praise of the Tory leader), 'the greatest, the wisest, and the most
uncorrupt minister, I ever conversed with'. Swift feels that the Drapier
always 'meant well', though perhaps he doesn't always express himself well; the humble tradesman would never have mentioned the
King's prerogative but for Wood's claims, and, in addition, his 'invincible arguments (wherever he picked them up)' furnished proof the
Irish were not obliged to take the coin. His own abilities, Swift

confesses, are simply not enough to enable him to pick out the treason-able parts in Letter IV. Furthermore, Swift, like the Drapier, asks humbly 'whether it is utterly unlawful in any writer so much as to mention the prerogative'; for do not Coke and 'other eminent lawyers' frequently refer to it?[14]

Swift was aware, however, that Midleton knew the true identity of the Drapier. This fact is revealed as Swift says he sent 'these papers' (the *Drapier's Letters*) to an 'eminent lawyer', who assured him they were not treasonable. And Swift frankly tells Midleton that he will continue to urge the people to reject Wood's coin by lawful means. Although he will be careful to incur no criminal charges in his future writing and would certainly submit if there were a law against opposing Wood's coin, he says he has 'not yet learned to pay active obedience against my conscience, and the public safety'.

Such a policy of cautious opposition to Wood is reflected in the next Letter (V) to Lord Molesworth, a distinguished Whig and Irish patriot.[15] In large part the Drapier in this Letter repeats publicly the defence Swift had prepared in Letter VI. Writing once again under a mask, Swift has the Drapier assume an even more exaggerated attitude of humility. The anonymous defence of the Drapier and his printer, the *Seasonable Advice to the Grand Jury*, he says, could not be by the same person as the Letters, because that is the work of 'a more artful hand than that of a common Drapier'.[16] He openly claims never to have written anything for which his printer, Harding, could be prosecuted. By 'engaging in the trade of a writer', a business out of his calling, he got into difficulty. He defies any man of fifty times his understanding to avoid being trapped when the law is as meticulous as it has been made by the 'commendable acuteness' of Sir William Scroggs and when he has been pursued with 'laudable zeal and industry' by my Lord Chief Justice Whitshed. He refuses to try to clear himself of the charge that he would oppose the Pretender, because his defence would be sure to be misinterpreted. In this ironically helpless position, the Drapier pretends to be at the mercy of his enemies:

> There are, my lord, three sorts of persons with whom I am resolved never to dispute: A highway man with a pistol at my breast, a troop of dragoons who come to plunder my house, and a man of law who can make a merit of accusing me. In each of these cases, which are almost the same, the best method is to keep out of the way, and the next best is to deliver your money, surrender your house, and confess nothing.[17]

But as, Swift promised in Letter VI, the Drapier continues the fight against Wood. The attack is, as it had to be, careful. As the Drapier says, he is worried and, on the advice of 'a certain Dean', is thinking about giving up his cause, since he is in danger while other more able people are afraid to speak out. The Drapier's feeling that he has been repaid for his efforts only by persecution and ingratitude is the basis for two extended autobiographical passages. While the first ostensibly reviews the career of the wretched, unfortunate man who undertook to defend Ireland against Wood, it actually encourages his readers, who recall his former brave entreaties. Swift parallels the draper's trade and the writer's. The Drapier refers to his early 'apprenticeship' in London, whence he was forced to return to Ireland (in playful allusion to the fall of Harley and the Tory Party) 'by the deaths of some friends and the misfortunes of others'. His first Letter was made of a 'plain coarse stuff' to defend the Irish poor against 'strong easterly winds' and the fourth of 'the best Irish wool', fit to be worn by the noblest lord in the land. But for all his labour, the Drapier has gained naught, for 'of late some great folks complain . . . "that when they had it on, they felt a shuddering in their limbs"'; they have therefore condemned the cloth and 'the poor Drapier who invented it'.

Yet in this Letter, where the Drapier seems to be completely overcome, rejected by his own countrymen, Swift makes a powerful ironical appeal for liberty which equals his direct appeal of Letter IV. Though the Drapier sees that his ignorance may have led him to violate legal technicalities, he cannot admit that he actually did wrong. In addition to consulting his own conscience, he has spoken with several well-known divines and assured himself of his innocence in the sight of heaven. He goes beyond the immediate problem of the halfpence as he sees at last how absurd it was to be misled by the idea that freedom consists in government by the consent of the governed: he should never have appealed to law, liberty, and the common rights of mankind but rather indulged in 'whining, lamenting, and crying for mercy'. Why didn't he notice with whom he was yoked? Why was he not expedient in his battling?

The Drapier, in his final autobiographical account, is forced to sell his nag because snuffing the air around Brackdenstown made him an unruly lover of freedom; he himself plans to settle down harmlessly in the country reading the conservatives Hobbes, Filmer, and Bodin instead of Locke, Molyneux, and other 'dangerous authors' who argued against political slavery. The Drapier is at last cómpletely subdued, completely humbled. He assures Molesworth at the end of the essay that 'If you ever see any more of my writings upon this subject, I promise you shall find them as innocent, as insipid and without a sting as what I have now offered you.'[18] The Drapier has made his final submission.

When Swift, in Letter I, set out to instruct his countrymen about the dangers of Wood's coin, he created a character who would be equal to any emergency. Despite a few exceptions, it is with astonishing consistency that Swift continually fits his arguments to his *persona*. Even in the instances where it appears that Swift himself is speaking, using every argument at his disposal, without holding himself back to keep the Drapier a consistent dramatic character, the humble Drapier always reappears to reinforce Swift's message. The Drapier is not intended always to seem 'real' in order to make readers believe a tradesman is actually the writer. Like the member of the Irish Parliament, he is a fictitious character whose attributes can be exploited in extreme ways. He shows his humility in many forms: as a tradesman who, like his fellows, faces the dangers of Wood's coin; as an unlearned shopkeeper who instructs those even less learned than he; as a modest commoner who can exhort the nobility and gentry; as a brave private citizen who is willing to fight Wood, and who looks with contempt upon his adversary; as a loyal subject of the King; as a humble typical Irishman who expresses all that he and his countrymen have suffered at the hands of England. He is a plain man battling for his freedom and that of other plain men. Either to present a modified statement of one of Swift's sincere beliefs, or to make an ironical utterance, every one of these forms of humility had its function in the battle. One needs no more convincing proof of the success of this *persona* than the fact that the English finally had to admit their inability to force Wood's coin on Ireland.

NOTES

1. This essay analyzes Swift's method of argument rather than the economic validity of his case. Though Swift doubtless exaggerated, the Irish probably did have real objections to Wood's coin: that it would cause an outflow of foreign gold and silver coins, and that it would increase counterfeiting. For a summary, see A. Goodwin, 'Wood's Halfpence', in *English Historical Review*, LI (Oct. 1936) 647–74.

2. The edition of the *Works* referred to here and throughout text is *The Prose Works of Jonathan Swift, D.D.*, ed. Temple Scott (1897–1908).

3. Professor Landa says it is unclear whether Swift desired independence of action for all Irish or only for the English in Ireland ('Swift's Economic Views and Mercantilism', in *Journal of English Literary History*, x (1943) 316–17). See pp. 74–95 of this volume.

4. For another disjointed, trailing sentence, see the paragraph beginning: 'For suppose you go to an ale-house . . .' (*Works*, VI 17). In Harding's original text Wood's name was spelled 'Woods'; it was changed in the later editions. See *The Drapier's Letters*, ed. Herbert Davis (Oxford, 1935) pp. lxviii–lxxix; 4 n. Some of the Drapier's character is probably revealed in such punctuation and spelling in the original text. But curiously 'Woods' is the spelling in the *Seasonable Advice*, which is not by the Drapier (*Works*, VI 89, 91).

5. Few eighteenth-century readers would have considered a draper to be among the really wretched Irish. Many drapers evidently bought brown linen for cash from weavers, contracted for its bleaching and finishing, and then sold it, usually to Dublin merchants. It was thus necessary for them to travel frequently from the northern provinces to Dublin. (Conrad Gill, *The Rise of the Irish Linen Industry* (Oxford, 1925) pp. 51, 57.) Although many Catholics were engaged in the Ulster linen business (ibid. p. 23), it is still more than likely that a draper would be, like most other middle-class tradesmen, a Protestant, since no Catholics were admitted into the trade guilds. (Constantia Maxwell, *Dublin Under the Georges, 1714–1830* (1936) p. 227.) A woollen draper might carry English manufactures in his shop, though he ran the risk of having it raided by nationalist mobs. (*Dublin Evening Post*, 14 May 1734; quoted in Maxwell, op. cit. p. 123); thus Swift is perhaps wise in choosing a draper, who could conceivably be an Anglo-Irishman and whose livelihood might depend upon English trade, as a spokesman for the Irish cause. Finally, an eighteenth-century reader would have been ready to accept the idea that the Drapier was reasonably prosperous: 'The merchants, citizens, and manufacturers in Dublin are very numerous, and many of them rich and in great credit, perfectly well understanding every branch of trade, of which their linen, woollen, silk, and hair-manufactured goods are specimens' (Edward Lloyd, *A Description of the City of Dublin* (1732); quoted in Maxwell, op. cit. p. 213). These background details are reinforced by what the Drapier says of himself.

6. Churton Collins, *Jonathan Swift, a Biographical and Critical Study* (1893) pp. 177, 178.

7. The *Satire of Jonathan Swift* (New York, 1947) p. 68.

8. The Drapier's reference in Letter V to his 'learned works' is probably equivalent to his comment in the same letter that Letter IV was made out of 'the best Irish wool I could get' and 'grave and rich enough to be worn by the best lord or judge of the land'.

9. The Drapier (in Letter IV) writes with similar irony of Hugh Boulter, Archbishop of Armagh and one of Walpole's representatives in Ireland, who – the Drapier believes – 'will be as good an Irishman, upon this article, as any of his brethren, or even of us who have had the misfortune to be born in this island'; for Boulter would not want to be paid in a debased coinage. The Drapier uses a like device, though without any bitterness, against Swift's friend Carteret, who as Lord-Lieutenant of Ireland was supposed to persuade the Irish to take Wood's coin. The Drapier explains that Carteret can't be coming to help Wood, since the fight is between Wood and the Irish people, not the Irish and the King. He points out that there are few Irish public offices to be given to bribe people to support Wood's coin. And finally, he lists the methods – promises and threats – that would be used in corrupt times to force the coin on Ireland, adding that Carteret will not use these methods. Thus the Drapier gives both the Irish people and Carteret warning, while pretending merely to praise the new Lord-Lieutenant (*Works*, VI 105–12).

10. The Drapier's remarks on the Irish peerage in Letter VII are similar to his remarks on the English. He claims to be puzzled that many Irish peers prefer to live in London, where they have little or no prestige among so many others more illustrious than themselves, when they could shine in Ireland because of the scarcity of competition. This ironical

thrust at absentee ownership, which impoverished Irish farm land, he makes by way of a comment on the peers' desire to live in London where they can get the latest news earlier than they would in Dublin, add to the ring of coaches at Hyde Park, and appear at the chocolate-houses; he cannot, however, see how these persons can be led to such a life by the usual motives of human actions – pleasure, profit, and ambition. Swift achieves the irony here by endowing the simple tradesman with false wonder. He intensifies the emotion behind the irony by using the accretive style of his attacks on Wood; for in the Drapier's humble opinion 'to be wholly without power, figure, influence, honour, credit, or distinction is not ... a very amiable situation of life' (*Works*, VI 190–1). But Swift writes to his good friend Charles Ford, an absentee, that the Drapier, by opposing a debased coinage, is trying to help keep Ford and his kind in England – *The Letters of Jonathan Swift to Charles Ford*, ed. D. Nichol Smith (Oxford, 1935) pp. 111–12.

11. *Works*, VI 71. See also ibid. 84, where Swift apparently alludes to the facts that the Duchess of Kendal was receiving a yearly pension of £3000 on the Irish Establishment, and that she was to share in Wood's profits (*Drapier's Letters*, ed. Davis, p. 240 n).

12. In a clever addition to this statement, as Craik points out (*Works*, VI 114 n), the Drapier puts a suspicion of Jacobitism on his opponents by saying that if the Pretender were to become King of England, he, the Drapier, would fight to keep him from becoming King of Ireland.

13. *Works*, VI 132 n. This is the numbering of the Letters followed by Dr Herbert Davis. In the Temple Scott edition the Letter to Midleton is numbered V and the Letter to Molesworth VI.

14. Swift believes that even if the Drapier is guilty of indiscretion, his loyal intention (to defend Ireland against the Pretender in spite of the statute binding England and Ireland under one king) should be 'at least some small extenuation of his crime'. In fact, on this point Swift must confess he agrees with the Drapier.

15. *Drapier's Letters*, ed. Davis, pp. 287–9 n. Swift, writing as a moderate Whig in 1723, had praised Molesworth's 'useful hints' for improving Irish agriculture; he respects Molesworth's opinions, 'excepting in what relates to the Church' (*Some Arguments Against Enlarging the Power of Bishops*, in *Works* III 236).

16. *Works*, VI 172. Actually the *Seasonable Advice* is written in forceful, straightforward, legalistic language similar to that of the petition at the end of Letter II. It contains no pretence of humility, and its ending is blunt: 'I will conclude all with a fable, ascribed to Demosthenes' – the fable of how, once the shepherds and mastiffs were taken away, 'the wolves without all fear made havoc of the sheep' (*Works*, VI 128).

17. *Works*, VI 164–7. This cringing passage must certainly have reminded readers of a forthright one from William Molyneux: 'If a villain with a pistol at my breast makes me convey my estate to him, no one will say this gives him any right. And yet just such a title as this has an unjust conqueror who with a sword at my throat forces me into submission' *The Case of Ireland's Being Bound by Acts of Parliament in England* (Dublin, 1698) p. 18.

18. *Works*, VI 175–6. Letter VII (first published in 1735) merely continues the use of the methods already discussed, though the character of the Drapier appears somewhat less vividly than in the other essays. The Drapier restates his intention to resist Wood's coin (*Works*, VI 187). He continues to distinguish between the King, who intended the good of Ireland, and Wood, who intended Ireland's destruction. But this Letter is different from the others in its enumerating to the English Parliament the general miseries of Ireland. Even in this description, however, the humility of the tradesman can be used: the Drapier says he wishes humbly that 'the reverend the clergy' would set an example of wearing Irish manufactures, and he points out the bad practice of 'us tradesmen' in selling these manufactures.

GEORGE ORWELL

Politics *vs.* Literature: an examination of *Gulliver's Travels* (1950)

IN *Gulliver's Travels* humanity is attacked, or criticized, from at least three different angles, and the implied character of Gulliver himself necessarily changes somewhat in the process. In part I he is the typical eighteenth-century voyager, bold, practical and unromantic, his homely outlook skilfully impressed on the reader by the biographical details at the beginning, by his age (he is a man of forty, with two children, when his adventures start), and by the inventory of the things in his pockets, especially his spectacles, which make several appearances. In part II he has in general the same character, but at moments when the story demands it he has a tendency to develop into an imbecile who is capable of boasting of 'our noble Country, the Mistress of Arts and Arms, the Scourge of France', etc., etc., and at the same time of betraying every available scandalous fact about the country which he professes to love. In part III he is much as he was in part I, though, as he is consorting chiefly with courtiers and men of learning, one has the impression that he has risen in the social scale. In part IV he conceives a horror of the human race which is not apparent, or only intermittently apparent, in the earlier books, and changes into a sort of unreligious anchorite whose one desire is to live in some desolate spot where he can devote himself to meditating on the goodness of the Houyhnhnms. However, these inconsistencies are forced upon Swift by the fact that Gulliver is there chiefly to provide a contrast. It is necessary, for instance that he should appear sensible in part I and at least intermittently silly in part II, because in both books the essential manœuvre is the same, i.e. to make the human being look ridiculous by imagining him as a creature six inches high. Whenever Gulliver is not acting as a stooge there is a sort of continuity in his character, which comes out especially in his resourcefulness and his observation of physical detail. He is much the same kind of person, with the same prose style, when he bears off the warships of Blefuscu, when he rips open the belly of the monstrous rat, and when he sails away upon the ocean in his frail coracle made from the skins of Yahoos. Moreover, it is difficult not to feel that in his shrewder moments Gulliver is simply Swift himself, and there is at least one incident in which Swift seems to be venting his private grievance against contemporary Society. It will be remembered that when the Emperor of Lilliput's palace catches fire, Gulliver puts it out by urinating on it. Instead of being congratulated on his presence of mind, he finds that he has committed a capital offence by making water in the precincts of the palace, and

> I was privately assured, that the Empress, conceiving the greatest Abhorrence of what I had done, removed to the most distant Side of the Court, firmly resolved that those buildings should never be repaired for her Use; and, in the Presence of her chief Confidents, could not forbear vowing Revenge.

According to Professor G. M. Trevelyan (*England under Queen Anne*), part of the reason for Swift's failure to get preferment was that the Queen was scandalized by the *Tale of a Tub* – a pamphlet in which Swift probably felt that he had done a great service to the English Crown, since it scarifies the Dissenters and still more the Catholics, while leaving the Established Church alone. In any case no one would deny that *Gulliver's Travels* is a rancorous as well as a pessimistic book, and that especially in parts I and III it often descends into political partisanship of a narrow kind. Pettiness and magnanimity, republicanism and authoritarianism, love of reason and lack of curiosity, are all mixed up in it. The hatred of the human body with which Swift is especially associated is only dominant in part IV, but somehow this new preoccupation does not come as a surprise. One feels that all these adventures, and all these changes of mood, could have happened to the same person, and the interconnection between Swift's political loyalties and his ultimate despair is one of the most interesting features of the book.

Politically, Swift was one of those people who are driven into a sort of perverse Toryism by the follies of the progressive party of the moment. Part I of *Gulliver's Travels*, ostensibly a satire on human greatness, can be

seen, if one looks a little deeper, to be simply an attack on England, on
the dominant Whig party, and on the war with France, which – however bad the motives of the Allies may have been – did save Europe
from being tyrannized over by a single reactionary power. Swift was
not a Jacobite or strictly speaking a Tory, and his declared aim in the
war was merely a moderate peace treaty and not the outright defeat of
England. Nevertheless there is a tinge of quislingism in his attitude,
which comes out in the ending of part I and slightly interferes with the
allegory. When Gulliver flees from Lilliput (England) to Blefuscu
(France) the assumption that a human being six inches high is inherently
contemptible seems to be dropped. Whereas the people of Lilliput have
behaved towards Gulliver with the utmost treachery and meanness,
those of Blefuscu behave generously and straightforwardly, and indeed
this section of the book ends on a different note from the all-round
disillusionment of the earlier chapters. Evidently Swift's animus is, in
the first place, against *England*. It is 'your Natives' (i.e. Gulliver's
fellow-countrymen) whom the King of Brobdingnag considers to be
'the most pernicious Race of little odious vermin that Nature ever
suffered to crawl upon the surface of the Earth', and the long passage
at the end, denouncing colonization and foreign conquest, is plainly
aimed at England, although the contrary is elaborately stated. The
Dutch, England's allies and target of one of Swift's most famous
pamphlets, are also more or less wantonly attacked in part III. There is
even what sounds like a personal note in the passage in which Gulliver
records his satisfaction that the various countries he has discovered
cannot be made colonies of the British Crown:

> The *Houyhnhnms*, indeed, appear not to be so well prepared for War, a
> Science to which they are perfect Strangers, and especially against missive
> Weapons. However, supposing myself to be a Minister of State, I could
> never give my advice for invading them. . . . Imagine twenty thousand
> of them breaking into the midst of an *European* army, confounding the
> Ranks, overturning the Carriages, battering the Warrior's Faces into
> Mummy, by terrible Yerks from their hinder hoofs . . .

Considering that Swift does not waste words, that phrase, 'battering the
warriors' faces into mummy', probably indicates a secret wish to see the
invincible armies of the Duke of Marlborough treated in a like manner.
There are similar touches elsewhere. Even the country mentioned in
part III, where 'the Bulk of the People consist, in a Manner, wholly of

Discoverers, Witnesses, Informers, Accusers, Prosecutors, Evidences, Swearers, together with their several subservient and subaltern Instruments, all under the Colours, the Conduct and Pay of Ministers of State', is called Langdon, which is within one letter of being an anagram of England. (As the early editions of the book contain misprints, it may perhaps have been intended as a complete anagram.) Swift's *physical* repulsion from humanity is certainly real enough, but one has the feeling that his debunking of human grandeur, his diatribes against lords, politicians, court favourites, etc., has mainly a local application and springs from the fact that he belonged to the unsuccessful party. He denounces injustice and oppression, but he gives no evidence of liking democracy. In spite of his enormously greater powers, his implied position is very similar to that of the innumerable silly-clever Conservatives of our own day – people like Sir Alan Herbert, Professor G. M. Young, Lord Elton, the Tory Reform Committee or the long line of Catholic apologists from W. H. Mallock onwards: people who specialize in cracking neat jokes at the expense of whatever is 'modern' and 'progressive', and whose opinions are often all the more extreme because they know that they cannot influence the actual drift of events. After all, such a pamphlet as *An Argument to prove that the Abolishing of Christianity*, etc., is very like 'Timothy Shy' having a bit of clean fun with the Brains Trust, or Father Ronald Knox exposing the errors of Bertrand Russell. And the ease with which Swift has been forgiven – and forgiven, sometimes, by devout believers – for the blasphemies of *A Tale of a Tub* demonstrates clearly enough the feebleness of religious sentiments as compared with political ones.

However, the reactionary cast of Swift's mind does not show itself chiefly in his political affiliations. The important thing is his attitude towards science, and, more broadly, towards intellectual curiosity. The famous Academy of Lagado, described in part III of *Gulliver's Travels*, is, no doubt, a justified satire on most of the so-called scientists of Swift's own day. Significantly, the people at work in it are described as 'Projectors', that is, people not engaged in disinterested research but merely on the look-out for gadgets which will save labour and bring in money. But there is no sign – indeed, all through the book there are many signs to the contrary – that 'pure' science would have struck Swift as a worth-while activity. The more serious kind of scientist has already had a kick in the pants in part II, when the 'scholars' patronized by the King of Brobdingnag try to account for Gulliver's small stature:

> After much Debate, they concluded unanimously that I was only *Relplum*
> *Scalcath*, which is interpreted literally, *Lusus Naturae*; a Determination
> exactly agreeable to the modern philosophy of *Europe*, whose Professors,
> disdaining the old Evasion of *Occult Causes*, whereby the followers of
> *Aristotle* endeavoured in vain to disguise their Ignorance, have invented
> this wonderful Solution of All Difficulties, to the unspeakable Advance-
> ment of human Knowledge.

If this stood by itself one might assume that Swift is merely the enemy
of *sham* science. In a number of places, however, he goes out of his way
to proclaim the uselessness of all learning or speculation not directed
towards some practical end:

> The learning of (the Brobdingnagians) is very defective, consisting only in
> Morality, History, Poetry, and Mathematics, wherein they must be
> allowed to excel. But, the last of these is wholly applied to what may be
> useful in Life, to the improvement of Agriculture, and all mechanical Arts
> so that among us it would be little esteemed. And as to Ideas, Entities,
> Abstractions, and Transcendentals, I could never drive the least Concep-
> tion into their Heads.

The Houyhnhnms, Swift's ideal beings, are backward even in a
mechanical sense. They are unacquainted with metals, have never heard
of boats, do not, properly speaking, practise agriculture (we are told
that the oats which they live upon 'grow naturally'), and appear not to
have invented wheels.* They have no alphabet, and evidently have not
much curiosity about the physical world. They do not believe that any
inhabited country exists beside their own, and though they understand
the motions of the sun and moon, and the nature of eclipses, 'this is the
utmost progress of their *Astronomy*'. By contrast, the philosophers of the
flying island of Laputa are so continuously absorbed in mathematical
speculations that before speaking to them one has to attract their
attention by flapping them on the ear with a bladder. They have
catalogued ten thousand fixed stars, have settled the periods of ninety-
three comets, and have discovered in advance of the astronomers of
Europe, that Mars has two moons – all of which information Swift
evidently regards as ridiculous, useless and uninteresting. As one might
expect, he believes that the scientist's place, if he has a place, is in the

---

* Houyhnhnms too old to walk are described as being carried in 'sledges' or in 'a kind
of vehicle, drawn like a sledge'. Presumably these had no wheels.

laboratory, and that scientific knowledge has no bearing on political matters:

> What I . . . thought altogether unaccountable, was the strong Disposition I observed in them towards News and Politics, perpetually enquiring into Public Affairs, giving their judgments in Matters of State, and passionately disputing every inch of a Party Opinion. I have, indeed, observed the same Disposition among most of the Mathematicians I have known in *Europe*, though I could never discover the least Analogy between the two Sciences; unless those people suppose, that, because the smallest Circle hath as many Degrees as the largest, therefore the Regulation and Management of the World require no more Abilities, than the Handling and Turning of a Globe.

Is there not something familiar in that phrase 'I could never discover the least analogy between the two sciences'? It has preceisely the note of the popular Catholic apologists who profess to be astonished when a scientist utters an opinion on such questions as the existence of God or the immortality of the soul. The scientist, we are told, is an expert only in one restricted field: why should his opinions be of value in any other? The implication is that theology is just as much an exact science as, for instance, chemistry, and that the priest is also an expert whose conclusions on certain subjects must be accepted. Swift, in effect, makes the same claim for the politician, but he goes one better in that he will not allow the scientist – either the 'pure' scientist or the *ad hoc* investigator – to be a useful person in his own line. Even he if had not written part III of *Gulliver's Travels*, one could infer from the rest of the book that, like Tolstoy and like Blake, he hates the very idea of studying the processes of Nature. The 'reason' which he so admires in the Houyhnhnms does not primarily mean the power of drawing logical inferences from observed facts. Although he never defines it, it appears in most contexts to mean either common sense – i.e. acceptance of the obvious and contempt for quibbles and abstractions – or absence of passion and superstition. In general he assumes that we know all that we need to know already, and merely use our knowledge incorrectly. Medicine, for instance, is a useless science, because if we lived in a more natural way, there would be no diseases. Swift, however, is not a simple-lifer or an admirer of the Noble Savage. He is in favour of civilization and the arts of civilization. Not only does he see the value of good manners, good conversation, and even learning of a literary and historical kind, he also sees that agriculture, navigation and architecture need to be studied and could with advantages be improved. But his implied aim is a static, incurious civilization – the world of his own day, a little cleaner, a little saner, with no radical change and no poking into the unknowable. More than one would expect in anyone so free from accepted fallacies, he reveres the past, especially classical antiquity, and believes that modern man has degenerated sharply during the past hundred years.* In the island of sorcerers, where the spirits of the dead can be called up at will:

> I desired that the Senate of *Rome* might appear before me in one large chamber, and a modern Representative in Counterview, in another. The first seemed to be an Assembly of Heroes and Demy-Gods, the other a Knot of Pedlars, Pick-pockets, Highwaymen and Bullies.

Although Swift uses this section of part III to attack the truthfulness of recorded history, his critical spirit deserts him as soon as he is dealing with Greeks and Romans. He remarks, of course, upon the corruption of imperial Rome, but he has an almost unreasoning admiration for some of the leading figures of the ancient world:

> I was struck with profound Veneration at the sight of *Brutus*, and could easily discover the most consummate Virtue, the greatest Intrepidity and Firmness of Mind, the truest Love of his Country, and general Benevolence for Mankind, in every Lineament of his Countenance. . . . I had the honour to have much Conversation with *Brutus*, and was told, that his Ancestors *Junius, Socrates, Epaminondas, Cato* the younger, *Sir Thomas More*, and himself, were perpetually together: a *Sextumvirate*, to which all the Ages of the World cannot add a seventh.

It will be noticed that of these six people, only one is a Christian. This is an important point. If one adds together Swift's pessimism, his reverence for the past, his incuriosity and his horror of the human body, one arrives at an attitude common among religious reactionaries – that is, people who defend an unjust order of society by claiming that this world cannot be substantially improved and only the 'next world' matters. However, Swift shows no sign of having any religious beliefs, at least in an ordinary sense of the words. He does not appear to believe seriously in life after death, and his idea of goodness is bound up with

---

* The physical decadence which Swift claims to have observed may have been a reality at that date. He attributes it to syphilis, which was a new disease in Europe and may have been more virulent than it is now. Distilled liquors, also, were a novelty in the seventeenth century and must have led at first to a great increase in drunkenness.

republicanism, love of liberty, courage, 'benevolence' (meaning, in effect, public spirit), 'reason' and other pagan qualities. This reminds one that there is another strain in Swift, not quite congruous with his disbelief in progress and his general hatred of humanity.

To begin with, he has moments when he is 'constructive' and even 'advanced'. To be occasionally inconsistent is almost a mark of vitality in Utopia books, and Swift sometimes inserts a word of praise into a passage that ought to be purely satirical. Thus, his ideas about the education of the young are fathered on to the Lilliputians, who have much the same views on this subject as the Houyhnhnms. The Lilliputians also have various social and legal institutions (for instance, there are old-age pensions, and people are rewarded for keeping the law as well as punished for breaking it) which Swift would have liked to see prevailing in his own country. In the middle of this passage Swift remembers his satirical intention and adds: 'In relating these and the following Laws, I would only be understood to mean the original Institutions, and not the most scandalous Corruptions into which these people are fallen by the degenerate Nature of Man'; but as Lilliput is supposed to represent England, and the laws he is speaking of have never had their parallel in England, it is clear that the impulse to make constructive suggestions has been too much for him. But Swift's greatest contribution to political thought in the narrower sense of the words, is his attack, especially in part III, on what would now be called totalitarianism. He has an extraordinarily clear prevision of the spy-haunted 'police State', with its endless heresy-hunts and treason trials, all really designed to neutralize popular discontent by changing it into war hysteria. And one must remember that Swift is here inferring the whole from a quite small part, for the feeble governments of his own day did not give him illustrations ready-made. For example, there is the professor at the School of Political Projectors who 'shewed me a large Paper of Instructions for discovering Plots and Conspiracies', and who claimed that one can find people's secret thoughts by examining their excrement:

Because Men are never so serious, thoughtful, and intent, as when they are at Stool, which he found by frequent Experiment: for in such Conjunctures, when he used meerly as a trial to consider what was the best Way of murdering the King, his Ordure would have a tincture of Green; but quite different when he thought only of raising an Insurrection, or burning the Metropolis.

The professor and his theory are said to have been suggested to Swift by the – from our point of view – not particularly astonishing or disgusting fact that in a recent State trial some letters found in somebody's privy had been put in evidence. Later in the same chapter we seem to be positively in the middle of the Russian purges:

> In the Kingdom of Tribnia, by the Natives called Langdon . . . the Bulk of the People consist, in a Manner, wholly of Discoverers, Witnesses, Informers, Accusers, Prosecutors, Evidences, Swearers. . . . It is first agreed, and settled among them, what suspected Persons shall be accused of a Plot: Then, effectual Care is taken to secure all their Letters and Papers, and put the Owners in Chains. These papers are delivered to a Sett of Artists, very dexterous in finding out the mysterious Meanings of Words, Syllables, and Letters. . . . Where this method fails, they have two others more effectual, which the Learned among them call *Acrostics* and *Anagrams*. *First*, they can decypher all initial Letters into political Meanings: Thus: N shall signify a Plot, B a Regiment of Horse, L a Fleet at Sea: Or, *Secondly*, by transposing the Letters of the Alphabet in any suspected Paper, they can lay open the deepest Designs of a discontented Party. So, for Example if I should say in a Letter to a Friend, *Our Brother Tom has just got the Piles*, a skilful Decypherer would discover that the same Letters, which compose that Sentence, may be analysed in the following Words: *Resist – a Plot is brought Home – The Tour* [Tower]. And this is the anagrammatic method.

Other professors at the same school invent simplified languages, write books by machinery, educate their pupils by inscribing the lesson on a wafer and causing them to swallow it, or propose to abolish individuality altogether by cutting off part of the brain of one man and grafting it on to the head of another. There is something queerly familiar in the atmosphere of these chapters, because, mixed up with much fooling, there is a perception that one of the aims of totalitarianism is not merely to make sure that people will think the right thoughts, but actually to make them *less conscious*. Then, again, Swift's account of the Leader who is usually to be found ruling over a tribe of Yahoos, and of the 'favourite' who acts first as a dirty-worker and later as a scapegoat, fits remarkably well into the pattern of our own times. But are we to infer from all this that Swift was first and foremost an enemy of tyranny and a champion of the free intelligence? No: his own views, so far as one can discern them, are not markedly liberal. No doubt he hates lords, kings, bishops, generals, ladies of fashion, orders, titles and flummery generally, but he does not seem to think better of the common people than of their rulers, or to be in favour of increased social equality, or to be enthusiastic about representative institutions. The Houyhnhnms are organized upon a sort of caste system which is racial in character, the horses which do the menial work being of different colours from their masters and not interbreeding with them. The educational system which Swift admires in the Lilliputians takes hereditary class distinctions for granted, and the children of the poorest classes do not go to school, because 'their Business being only to till and cultivate the Earth . . . therefore their Education is of little Consequence to the Public'. Nor does he seem to have been strongly in favour of freedom of speech and the Press, in spite of the toleration which his own writings enjoyed. The King of Brobdingnag is astonished at the multiplicity of religious and political sects in England, and considers that those who hold 'opinions prejudicial to the public' (in the context this seems to mean simply heretical opinions), though they need not be obliged to change them, ought to be obliged to conceal them: for 'as it was Tyranny in any Government to require the first, so it was weakness not to enforce the second'. There is a subtler indication of Swift's own attitude in the manner in which Gulliver leaves the land of the Houyhnhnms. Intermittently, at least, Swift was a kind of anarchist, and part IV of *Gulliver's Travels* is a picture of an anarchistic society, not governed by law in the ordinary sense, but by the dictates of 'reason', which are voluntarily accepted by everyone. The General Assembly of the Houyhnhnms 'exhorts' Gulliver's master to get rid of him, and his neighbours put pressure on him to make him comply. Two reasons are given. One is that the presence of this unusual Yahoo may unsettle the rest of the tribe, and the other is that a friendly relationship between a Houhynhnm and a Yahoo is 'not agreeable to Reason or Nature, or a Thing ever heard of before among them'. Gulliver's master is somewhat unwilling to obey, but the 'exhortation' (a Houyhnhnm, we are told, is never *compelled* to do anything, he is merely 'exhorted' or 'advised') cannot be disregarded. This illustrates very well the totalitarian tendency which is explicit in the anarchist or pacifist vision of society. In a society in which there is no law, and in theory no compulsion, the only arbiter of behaviour is public opinion. But public opinion, because of the tremendous urge to conformity in gregarious animals, is less tolerant than any system of law. When human beings are governed by 'thou shalt not', the individual can practise a certain amount of eccentricity: when they are supposedly governed by 'love' or 'reason', he is under continuous pressure to make him behave and think in exactly the same way as everyone else. The Houyhnhnms, we are told, were unanimous on almost all subjects. The only question they ever *discussed* was how to deal with the Yahoos. Otherwise there was no room for disagreement among them, because the truth is always either self-evident, or else it is undiscoverable and unimportant. They had apparently no word for 'opinion' in their language, and in their conversations there was no 'difference of sentiments'. They had reached, in fact, the highest stage of totalitarian organization, the stage when conformity has become so general that there is no need for a police force. Swift approves of this kind of thing because among his many gifts neither curiosity nor good nature was included. Disagreement would always seem to him sheer perversity. 'Reason', among the Houyhnhnms, he says, 'is not a Point Problematical, as with us, where men can argue with Plausibility on both Sides of a Question; but strikes you with immediate Conviction; as it must needs do, where it is not mingled, obscured, or discoloured by Passion and Interest.' In other words, we know everything already, so why should dissident opinions be tolerated? The totalitarian society of the Houyhnhnms, where there can be no freedom and no development, follows naturally from this.

We are right to think of Swift as a rebel and iconoclast, but except in certain secondary matters, such as his insistence that women should receive the same education as men, he cannot be labelled 'Left'. He is a Tory anarchist, despising authority while disbelieving in liberty, and preserving the aristocratic outlook while seeing clearly that the existing aristocracy is degenerate and contemptible. When Swift utters one of his characteristic diatribes against the rich and powerful, one must probably, as I said earlier, write off something for the fact that he himself belonged to the less successful party, and was personally disappointed. The 'outs', for obvious reasons, are always more radical than the 'ins'.* But the most essential thing in Swift is his inability to believe

---

* At the end of the book, as typical specimens of human folly and viciousness, Swift names 'a Lawyer, a Pickpocket, a Colonel, a Fool, a Lord, a Gamester, a Politician, a Whore-master, a Physician, an Evidence, a Suborner, an Attorney, a Traitor, or the like'. One sees here the irresponsible violence of the powerless. The list lumps together those who break the conventional code and those who keep it. For instance, if you automatically condemn a colonel, as such, on what grounds do you condemn a traitor? Or again, if you want to suppress pickpockets, you must have laws, which means that you must

that life – ordinary life on the solid earth, and not some rationalized, deodorized version of it – could be made worth living. Of course, no honest person claims that happiness is *now* a normal condition among adult human beings; but perhaps it *could* be made normal, and it is upon this question that all serious political controversy really turns. Swift has much in common – more, I believe, than has been noticed – with Tolstoy, another disbeliever in the possibility of happiness. In both men you have the same anarchistic outlook covering an authoritarian cast of mind; in both a similar hostility to science, the same impatience with opponents, the same inability to see the importance of any question not interesting to themselves; and in both cases a sort of horror of the actual process of life, though in Tolstoy's case it was arrived at later and in a different way. The sexual unhappiness of the two men was not of the same kind, but there was this in common, that in both of them a sincere loathing was mixed up with a morbid fascination. Tolstoy was a reformed rake who ended by preaching complete celibacy, while continuing to practise the opposite into extreme old age. Swift was presumably impotent, and had an exaggerated horror of human dung: he also thought about it incessantly, as is evident throughout his works. Such people are not likely to enjoy even the small amount of happiness that falls to most human beings, and, from obvious motives, are not likely to admit that earthly life is capable of much improvement. Their incuriosity, and hence their intolerance, spring from the same root.

Swift's disgust, rancour and pessimism would make sense against the background of a 'next world' to which this one is the prelude. As he does not appear to believe seriously in any such thing, it becomes necessary to construct a paradise supposedly existing on the surface of the earth, but something quite different from anything we know, with all that he disapproves of – lies, folly, change, enthusiasm, pleasure, love and dirt – eliminated from it. As his ideal being he chooses the horse, an animal whose excrement is not offensive. The Houyhnhnms are dreary beasts – this is so generally admitted that the point is not worth labouring. Swift's genius can make them credible, but there can have been very few readers in whom they have excited any feeling beyond dislike. And this is not from wounded vanity at seeing animals preferred to men; for, of the two, the Houyhnhnms are much liker to

---

have lawyers. But the whole closing passage, in which the hatred is so authentic, and the reason given for it so inadequate, is somehow unconvincing. One has the feeling that personal animosity is at work.

human beings than are the Yahoos, and Gulliver's horror of the Yahoos, together with his recognition that they are the same kind of creature as himself, contains a logical absurdity. This horror comes upon him at his very first sight of them. 'I never beheld,' he says, 'in all my Travels, so disagreeable an Animal, nor one against which I naturally conceived so strong an Antipathy.' But in comparison with what are the Yahoos disgusting? Not with the Houyhnhnms, because at this time Gulliver has not seen a Houyhnhnm. It can only be in comparison with himself, i.e. with a human being. Later, however, we are to be told that the Yahoos *are* human beings, and human society becomes insupportable to Gulliver because all men are Yahoos. In that case why did he not conceive his disgust of humanity earlier? In effect we are told that the Yahoos are fantastically different from men, and yet are the same. Swift has over-reached himself in his fury, and is shouting at his fellow-creatures: 'You are filthier than you are!' However, it is impossible to feel much sympathy with the Yahoos, and it is not because they oppress the Yahoos that the Houyhnhnms are unattractive. They are unattractive because the 'reason' by which they are governed is really a desire for death. They are exempt from love, friendship, curiosity, fear, sorrow and – except in their feelings towards the Yahoos, who occupy rather the same place in their community as the Jews in Nazi Germany – anger and hatred. 'They have no Fondness for their Colts or Foles, but the Care they take, in educating them, proceeds entirely from the Dictates of *Reason.*' They lay store by 'Friendship' and 'Benevolence', but 'these are not confined to particular Objects, but universal to the whole Race'. They also value conversation, but in their conversations there are no differences of opinion, and 'nothing passed but what was useful, expressed in the fewest and most significant Words'. They practise strict birth-control, each couple producing two offspring and thereafter abstaining from sexual intercourse. Their marriages are arranged for them by their elders, on eugenic principles, and their language contains no word for 'love', in the sexual sense. When somebody dies they carry on exactly as before, without feeling any grief. It will be seen that their aim is to be as like a corpse as is possible while retaining physical life. One or two of their characteristics, it is true, do not seem to be strictly 'reasonable' in their own usage of the word. Thus, they place a great value not only on physical hardihood but on athleticism, and they are devoted to poetry. But these exceptions may be less arbitrary than they seem. Swift probably emphasizes the physical strength of the Houyhnhnms in order to make clear that they could never be conquered by the hated human race, while a taste for poetry may figure among their qualities because poetry appeared to Swift as the antithesis of science, from his point of view, the most useless of all pursuits. In part III he names 'Imagination, Fancy, and Invention' as desirable faculties in which the Laputan mathematicians (in spite of their love of music) were wholly lacking. One must remember that although Swift was an admirable writer of comic verse, the kind of poetry he thought valuable would probaby be didactic poetry. The poetry of the Houyhnhnms, he says

> must be allowed to excel [that of] all other Mortals; wherein the Justness of their Similes, and the Minuteness, as well as exactness, of their Descriptions, are, indeed, inimitable. Their Verses abound very much in both of these; and usually contain either some exalted Notions of Friendship and Benevolence, or the Praises of those who were Victors in Races, and other bodily Exercises.

Alas, not even the genius of Swift was equal to producing a specimen by which we could judge the poetry of the Houyhnhnms. But it sounds as though it were chilly stuff (in heroic couplets, presumably), and not seriously in conflict with the principles of 'reason'.

Happiness is notoriously difficult to describe, and pictures of a just and well-ordered society are seldom either attractive or convincing. Most creators of 'favourable' Utopias, however, are concerned to show what life could be like if it were lived more fully. Swift advocates a simple refusal of life, justifying this by the claim that 'reason' consists in thwarting your instincts. The Houyhnhnms, creatures without a history, continue for generation after generation to live prudently, maintaining their population at exactly the same level, avoiding all passion, suffering from no diseases, meeting death indifferently, training up their young in the same principles – and all for what? In order that the same process may continue indefinitely. The notions that life here and now is worth living, or that it could be made worth living, or that it must be sacrificed for some future good, are all absent. The dreary world of the Houyhnhnms was about as good a Utopia as Swift could construct, granting that he neither believed in a next world nor could get any pleasure out of certain normal activities. But it is not really set up as something desirable in itself, but as the justification for another attack on humanity. The aim, as usual, is to humiliate Man by reminding him that he is weak and ridiculous; and above all that he stinks; and the ultimate motive, probably, is a kind of envy, the envy of the ghost for the living, of the man who knows he cannot be happy for the others who – so he fears – may be a little happier than himself. The political expression of such an outlook must be either reactionary or nihilistic, because the person who holds it will want to prevent Society from developing in some direction in which his pessimism may be cheated. One can do this either by blowing everything to pieces, or by averting social change. Swift ultimately blew everything to pieces in the only way that was feasible before the atomic bomb – that is, he went mad – but, as I have tried to show, his political aims were on the whole reactionary ones.

From what I have written it may have seemed that I am *against* Swift, and that my object is to refute him and even to belittle him. In a political and moral sense I am against him, so far as I understand him. Yet curiously enough he is one of the writers I admire with least reserve, and *Gulliver's Travels*, in particular, is a book which it seems impossible for me to grow tired of. I read it first when I was eight – one day short of eight, to be exact, for I stole and furtively read the copy which was to be given me next day on my eighth birthday – and I have certainly read it not less than half a dozen times since. Its fascination seems inexhaustible. If I had to make a list of six books which were to be preserved when all others were destroyed, I would certainly put *Gulliver's Travels* among them. This raises the question: what is the relationship between agreement with a writer's opinions, and enjoyment of his work?

If one is capable of intellectual detachment, one can *perceive* merit in a writer whom one deeply disagrees with, but *enjoyment* is a different matter. Supposing that there is such a thing as good or bad art, then the goodness or badness must reside in the work of art itself – not independently of the observer, indeed, but independently of the mood of the observer. In one sense, therefore, it cannot be true that a poem is good on Monday and bad on Tuesday. But if one judges the poem by the appreciation it arouses, then it can certainly be true, because appreciation, or enjoyment is a subjective condition which cannot be commanded. For a great deal of his waking life, even the most cultivated person has no aesthetic feelings whatever, and the power to have aesthetic feelings is very easily destroyed. When you are frightened, or hungry, or are suffering from toothache or sea-sickness, *King Lear* is no

better from your point of view than *Peter Pan*. You may know in an
intellectual sense that it is better, but that is simply a fact which you
remember: you will not *feel* the merit of *King Lear* until you are normal
again. And aesthetic judgment can be upset just as disastrously – more
disastrously, because the cause is less readily recognized – by political or
moral disagreement. If a book angers, wounds or alarms you, then you
will not enjoy it, whatever its merits may be. If it seems to you a really
pernicious book, likely to influence other people in some undesirable
way, then you will probably construct an aesthetic theory to show
that it *has* no merits. Current literary criticism consists quite largely of
this kind of dodging to and fro between two sets of standards. And yet
the opposite process can also happen: enjoyment can overwhelm
disapproval, even though one clearly recognizes that one is enjoying
something inimical. Swift, whose world-view is so peculiarly unacceptable, but who is, nevertheless, an extremely popular writer, is a good
instance of this. Why is it that we don't mind being called Yahoos,
although firmly convinced that we are *not* Yahoos?

It is not enough to make the usual answer that of course Swift was
wrong, in fact he was insane, but he was 'a good writer'. It is true that
the literary quality of a book is to some small extent separable from its
subject-matter. Some people have a native gift for using words, as
some people have a naturally 'good eye' at games. It is largely a question of timing and of instinctively knowing how much emphasis to use.
As an example near at hand, look back at the passage I quoted earlier,
starting 'In the Kingdom of Tribnia, by the Natives called Langdon'.
It derives much of its force from the final sentence: 'And this is the
anagrammatic Method.' Strictly speaking this sentence is unnecessary,
for we have already seen the anagram deciphered, but the mock-
solemn repetition, in which one seems to hear Swift's own voice
uttering the words, drives home the idiocy of the activities described,
like the final tap to a nail. But not all the power and simplicity of
Swift's prose, nor the imaginative effort that has been able to make not
one but a whole series of impossible worlds more credible than the
majority of history books – none of this would enable us to enjoy
Swift if his world-view were truly wounding or shocking. Millions of
people, in many countries, must have enjoyed *Gulliver's Travels* while
more or less seeing its anti-human implications: and even the child who
accepts parts I and II as a simple story gets a sense of absurdity from
thinking of human beings six inches high. The explanation must be

that Swift's world-view is felt to be *not* altogether false – or it would probably be more accurate to say, not false all the time. Swift is a diseased writer. He remains permanently in a depressed mood which in most people is only intermittent, rather as though someone suffering from jaundice or the after-effects of influenza should have the energy to write books. But we all know that mood, and something in us responds to the expression of it. Take, for instance, one of his most characteristic works, 'The Lady's Dressing Room': one might add the kindred poem, 'Upon a Beautiful Young Nymph Going to Bed'. Which is truer, the viewpoint expressed in these poems, or the viewpoint implied in Blake's phrase, 'The naked female human form divine'? No doubt Blake is nearer the truth, and yet who can fail to feel a sort of pleasure in seeing that fraud, feminine delicacy, exploded for once? Swift falsifies his picture of the world by refusing to see anything in human life except dirt, folly and wickedness, but the part which he abstracts from the whole does exist, and it is something which we all know about, while shrinking from mentioning it. Part of our minds – in any normal person it is the dominant part – believes that man is a noble animal and life is worth living; but there is also a sort of inner self which at least intermittently stands aghast at the horror of existence. In the queerest way, pleasure and disgust are linked together. The human body is beautiful: it is also repulsive and ridiculous, a fact which can be verified at any swimming-pool. The sexual organs are objects of desire and also of loathing, so much so that in many languages, if not in all languages, their names are used as words of abuse. Meat is delicious, but a butcher's shop makes one feel sick: and indeed all our food springs ultimately from dung and dead bodies, the two things which of all others seem to us the most horrible. A child, when it is past the infantile stage but still looking at the world with fresh eyes, is moved by horror almost as often as by wonder – horror of snot and spittle, of the dogs' excrement on the pavement, the dying toad full of maggots, the sweaty smell of grown-ups, the hideousness of old men, with their bald heads and bulbous noses. In his endless harping on disease, dirt and deformity, Swift is not actually inventing anything, he is merely leaving something out. Human behaviour, too, especially in politics, is as he describes it, although it contains other more important factors which he refuses to admit. So far as we can see, both horror and pain are necessary to the continuance of life on this planet, and it is therefore open to pessimists like Swift to say: 'If horror and pain must always be with us, how can life be significantly improved?' His attitude is in effect the Christian attitude, minus the bribe of a 'next world' – which, however, probably has less hold upon the minds of believers than the conviction that this world is a vale of tears and the grave is a place of rest. It is, I am certain, a wrong attitude, and one which could have harmful effects upon behaviour; but something in us responds to it, as it responds to the gloomy words of the burial service and the sweetish smell of corpses in a country church.

It is often argued, at least by people who admit the importance of subject-matter, that a book cannot be 'good' if it expresses a palpably false view of life. We are told that in our own age, for instance, any book that has genuine literary merit will also be more or less 'progressive' in tendency. This ignores the fact that throughout history a similar struggle between progress and reaction has been raging, and that the best books of any one age have always been written from several different viewpoints, some of them palpably more false than others. In so far as a writer is a propagandist, the most one can ask of him is that he shall genuinely believe in what he is saying, and that it shall not be something blazingly silly. Today, for example, one can imagine a good book being written by a Catholic, a Communist, a Fascist, a pacifist, an anarchist, perhaps by an old-style Liberal or an ordinary Conservative: one cannot imagine a good book being written by a spiritualist, a Buchmanite or a member of the Ku-Klux-Klan. The views that a writer holds must be compatible with sanity, in the medical sense, and with the power of continuous thought: beyond that what we ask of him is talent, which is probably another name for conviction. Swift did not possess ordinary wisdom, but he did possess a terrible intensity of vision, capable of picking out a single hidden truth and then magnifying it and distorting it. The durability of *Gulliver's Travels* goes to show that, if the force of belief is behind it, a world-view which only just passes the test of sanity is sufficient to produce a great work of art.

MARJORIE NICOLSON AND
NORA M. MOHLER

The Scientific Background of 'Voyage to Laputa' (1937)

AMONG the travels of Gulliver, the 'Voyage to Laputa' has been most criticized and least understood. There is general agreement that in interest and literary merit it falls short of the first two voyages. It is marked by multiplicity of themes; it is episodic in character. In its reflections upon life and humanity, it lacks the philosophic intuition of the voyages to Lilliput and Brobdingnag and the power of the violent and savage attacks upon mankind in the 'Voyage to the Houyhnhnms'. Any reader sensitive to literary values must so far agree with the critics who disparage the tale. But another criticism as constantly brought against the 'Voyage to Laputa' cannot be so readily dismissed. Professor W. A. Eddy, one of the chief authorities upon the sources of *Gulliver's Travels*, has implied the usual point of view when he writes:

> There seems to be no motive for the story beyond a pointless and not too artfully contrived satire on mathematicians. . . . For this attack on theoretical science I can find no literary source or analogue, and conclude that it must have been inspired by one of Swift's literary ideocyncracies [*sic*]. Attempts have been made to detect allusions to the work of Newton and other contemporary scientists, but these, however successful, cannot greatly increase for us the slight importance of the satire on Laputa.[1]

Three themes in the 'Voyage to Laputa' have been particularly censured by modern critics. Some are repelled by the Laputans with their curious combination of mathematics and music and their dread of a comet and the sun.[2] Others are disturbed by the apparent lack of both unity and significance in the Balnibarians, particularly in the Grand Academy of Lagado (ch. 5). Most of all, the Flying Island has puzzled commentators who dismiss it as a 'piece of magical apparatus', a 'gratuitous violation of natural laws'[3] which offends the reader's sense of probability.

Yet is it conceivable that Swift, elsewhere so conscious of the un-written law of probability, should have carelessly violated it in the 'Voyage to Laputa' alone? Professor Eddy in a later work has justly said:

> The compound of magic and mathematics, of fantasy and logic, of ribaldry and gravity, is a peculiar product of the disciplined yet imagina-tive mind of Swift. There are two distinct kinds of imagination: one is creative and mystical, the other is constructive and rational. Swift had no command over the faerie architects who decree pleasure domes in Xanadu without regard to the laws of physics. His imagination, like that of Lewis Carroll, had a method in its apparent madness. . . . What seems so lawless is the product of the most rigid law.[4]

Swift's imagination, we have long recognized, was eclectic; the mark of his genius lay less in original creation than in paradoxical and brilliant new combinations of familiar materials. Indeed, one of the sources of his humour to every generation of readers has been the recognition of old and familiar themes treated in novel fashion. Pygmies and giants, animals with the power of speech, have been the perennial stuff of fairytale and legend. The novelty in *Gulliver's Travels* lies less in the material than in new combinations and the mood of treatment. The study of the sources of Swift has been particularly rewarding in showing what the 'constructive and rational' imagination may do to time-honoured themes. The very fact that the literary and political background[5] of *Gulliver's Travels* has been established so completely leads the inquisitive reader to inquire whether the unrecog-nized sources of the 'Voyage to Laputa' may not be equally capable of verification. If the most assiduous searchers into sources can find 'no literacy source or analogue' for the peculiar themes in this voyage alone, must not those sources be sought elsewhere than in the literary tradi-tions which Swift inherited?

There were other important materials accessible to writers of romance and fantasy in Swift's generation, of which many availed themselves. The attempt of this study will be to show that Swift borrowed for the 'Voyage to Laputa' even more than for the other tales, but that the sources of his borrowings were different. The mathematicians who feared the sun and comet, the projectors of the Grand Academy, the Flying Island – these came to Swift almost entirely from contemporary science.[6] The sources for nearly all the theories of the Laputans and the

Balnibarbians are to be found in the work of Swift's contemporary scientists and particularly in the *Philosophical Transactions of the Royal Society*.

I

Only during the last few years have students of literature become aware of the part played by the 'new science' in the stimulation of literary imagination in the seventeenth and eighteenth centuries. Among the various themes which have been studied, the relation of men of letters to the Royal Society has proved a rewarding field. Shadwell's *Virtuoso*, for example, takes on entirely new meaning when read in connection with experiments reported by Wilkins, Hooke, Boyle and many others,[7] and the interest of Restoration audiences in such drama becomes clear when we realize the number of men in the audience who had attended meetings of the Royal Society and had heard first-hand reports of the experiments which Shadwell satirizes through 'Sir Nicholas Gimcrack'. Wilkins, Waller, Dryden, Comenius and Evelyn in England, John Winthrop and Cotton Mather in America are among those who have been shown to have reflected in their works the discoveries of the Society. Pepys's interest may be traced through the frequent references in his diary and letters. Addison and Steele in their periodicals played to a gallery not only of gentlemen but also of ladies interested in science. No reader of *Hudibras* and of the minor poems can fail to be aware of the extent to which Butler, too, found the *virtuosi* an amusing and profitable theme. Foreign visitors to England paid particular attention to 'Gresham Colledge', sending home observations, both serious and satiric, upon collections and experiments. It has indeed been suggested that the 'early development of Anglomania' during the last years of the seventeenth century and the first quarter of the eighteenth century in France was largely the result of French interest in the Royal Society, particularly in the reports published in the *Philosophical Transactions*.[8]

The widespread interest in scientific discovery among English men of letters was in large part a natural result of the rapid strides made by science during the seventeenth and eighteenth centuries. More specifically, it was the result of the attendance at meetings of the Royal Society by men of letters, many of whom claimed the title of *virtuosi*, and of the publication of the *Philosophical Transactions*, which were widely read. In addition to the complete *Transactions*, various abridged editions were

published in the early eighteenth century. In 1705 many of the papers
were made still more accessible in an edition in three volumes under the
title *Miscellanea Curiosa*.[9] Reports of discoveries, inventions and experiments were therefore available in various ways to Jonathan Swift in
Ireland, and even more after his return to England where he 'corrected,
amended, and augmented' his voyages.[10] The influence of the *Philosophical Transactions* upon Swift appears in two ways. Both in the complete and in the abridged editions, these volumes were storehouses of
such accounts of travel as those imitated by Swift in *Gulliver's Travels*.
In addition they offered him specific sources for his scientific details in
the 'Voyage to Laputa'.

The various sources of the general idea of such 'voyages' as those of
Gulliver have been traced so often and are so obviously part of the
great interest in travel that had persisted in England since the time of
the earliest voyagers that it seems almost a work of supererogation to
suggest the *Philosophical Transactions* as still another source for the main
idea of *Gulliver's Travels*. Yet it is at least interesting to see the space
devoted in the *Transactions* – particularly between 1700 and 1720 – to
accounts of travel. From them Swift may well have gleaned many a
suggestion not only for the proper style of Captain Lemuel Gulliver,
but also for the pattern of such tales of travel and observation, for such a
pattern there was in the actual accounts. The newly discovered islands
of the Philippines, reported in the *Transactions*, must greatly have
appealed to the creator of Gulliver, who discovered so many islands,
some inhabited, some desolate; the Hottentots, as they appear in the
accounts sent to the Royal Society, are as curious a people as any
discovered by Gulliver.[11]

More specifically, Swift may well have picked up from these actual
voyages a hint for his 'men who never die', the Struldbrugs. The
authors who reported this particular group of travels to the Royal
Society showed an almost morbid interest in 'antient' men who live
too long. Mr G. Plaxton, a clergyman, who seemed to have an uncanny
affinity for livings in remote districts, reported from the parsonage of
Kinnardsey: 'I took the Number of the Inhabitants, and found that
every sixth Soul was sixty Years of Age, and upwards; some were 85,
and some 90.'[12] His next incumbency proved even more remarkable;
the number of the aged was much greater and the parishioners lived so
long that the Reverend Mr Plaxton seldom had the pleasure of burying
a member of his flock. Cotton Mather sent back from New England

'an Account of some Long-Lived Persons there', many of whom were more than a century old.[13] Closer parallels are found in 'An Account of the Bramines in the Indies': 'It is reported, that upon the Hills by Casmere there are Men that live some hundreds of Years. . . .'[14] Like the Struldbrugs, they have passed beyond curiosity, and beyond interest in life. With Tithonus they seem to have found immortal life but not immortal youth. Gulliver saw the Struldbrugs as 'the most mortifying sight I ever beheld. . . . Besides the usual deformities in extreme old age, they acquired an additional ghastliness in proportion to their number of years, which is not to be described' (p. 254). The voyager to the 'Bramines' saw his old men in much the same way: 'The Penances and Austerities that they undergo are almost incredible; Most of them, through their continual Fastings, and lying upon the parching hot Sand in the Heat of the Sun, are so lean, dry'd and wither'd, that they look like Skeletons or Shadows, and one can scarce perceive them to breathe or feel their Pulse beat.'[15]

Whether such voyages as those in the *Philosophical Transactions* combined in Swift's mind with literary sources already well established to lead him to the general idea of the travels of Gulliver, we may conjecture, though not prove. That the *Philosophical Transactions*, together with the more complete works of the *virtuosi*, were the specific source of Swift's Laputans, his projectors of the Grand Academy of Lagado, and his Flying Island, can be proved beyond the possibility of doubt.

II

The section of the 'Voyage to Laputa' which deals with the mathematical peculiarities of the Laputans has been generally recognized to be of a piece with others of Swift's pronouncements upon mathematicians.[16] Although several of the critics incline to think that such satire is peculiar to Swift, there is little in the main idea of this section that is unique. Behind the Laputans lay the rapidly growing interest of the seventeenth century in mathematics, embodied in the work of Kepler, Descartes, Leibniz and many others, and a persistent attitude of the seventeenth-century layman toward the 'uselessness' of physical and mathematical learning.[17] Bacon's discrimination between 'Experiments of Light' and 'Experiments of Fruit' had only put into pictorial language a persistent conflict between 'pure' and 'applied' science. To the layman, and particularly to the satirist of the last quarter of the seventeenth century, when the Royal Society was attracting its greatest attention, the apparent 'uselessness' of the new science was a common point of attack. Samuel Butler in *Hudibras* and in minor poems, Shadwell in the *Virtuoso*, Ned Ward in the *London Spy*, William King in the *Dialogues of the Dead* – these and a host of minor writers laughed at the impractical *virtuosi*. A close parallel for Swift's point of view in *Gulliver's Travels* may be found in the *Spectator* papers, those mirrors of the age. In spite of Addison's profound response to many of the new concepts of the day – his interest in Cartesianism, in Newtonianism, his fascination with the vastly expanded universe of astronomy and biology – he lost no chance for laughter at impractical experimenters and at absent-minded mathematicians who in their preoccupation with one subject forgot the world about them.

Swift's Laputans excel in theoretical learning; the abstractions of 'higher mathematics' are their meat and drink. They can solve equations – but they cannot build houses, because of the 'contempt they bear to practical geometry, which they despise as vulgar and mechanic' (p. 191). Unfortunately their theoretical learning is too abstruse and 'too refined for the intellectuals of their workmen'. One may well wonder whether the passage in which Swift discusses their sharp divergence between theory and practice reflects a point of view suggested by many of the theorists of the day, and expressed by Robert Boyle in these words:

> Let us now consider how far the knowledge of particular qualities, or the physical uses of things, will enable men to perform, philosophically, what is commonly done by manual operation. And here, methinks, 'tis a notable proof of human industry, as well as a great incitement thereto, that philosophy can supply the want to strength, or art, and the head prevent the drudgery of the hand.[18]

If a specific source must be found for Swift's laughter at the useless-ness of mathematical learning, it may be discovered in Fontenelle's 'Defence' of mathematical and natural philosophy and in his insistence that such publications as those of the Royal Society and the Paris Academy justified themselves. Swift's attitude toward Fontenelle is shown clearly in his earlier work *The Battle of the Books*, which was largely a reply to Fontenelle's defence of the 'moderns'. Another paper by Fontenelle so clearly suggests the position that Swift attacks in the 'Voyage to Laputa' that it seems impossible it should not have been in Swift's mind when he wrote. In 1699 Fontenelle, as part of his defence of the 'moderns', had upheld mathematical learning in a preface to the *Memoirs of the Royal Academy at Paris*, which was republished as a preface to the *Miscellanea Curiosa* in 1707.[19] The general points attacked by Swift are to be found in this preface. Fontenelle begins his defence:

> But to what purpose should People become fond of the Mathematical and Natural Philosophy? Of what use are the Transactions of the Academy? These are common Questions, which most do not barely propose as Questions, and it will not be improper to clear them. People very readily call useless, what they do not understand. It is a sort of Revenge; and as the Mathematicks and Natural Philosophy are known but by few, they are generally look'd upon as useless.

Fontenelle proceeds with a defence of such 'useless' knowledge, pointing out on the one hand that supposedly theoretical learning has resulted in practical discoveries, but, on the other hand, defending the intellectual curiosity of mathematicians and natural philosophers as an end in itself. 'Altho' the Usefulness of Mathematicks and Natural Philosophy is obscure,' he declares, 'yet it is real.'[20]

The 'contempt they bear to practical geometry' is sufficient to explain the miscalculation of the Laputan tailors in making Gulliver's clothes (p. 190). The mistaking of 'a figure in the calculations' may be intended as a satire upon Newton, as has been suggested.[21] But like the corresponding passage in the 'Voyage to Lilliput', in which tailors make clothes for the 'man mountain', the passage in the 'Voyage to Laputa' in which the tailor 'first took my altitude by a quadrant' is chiefly a satire upon the current interest in surveying and particularly upon attempts to determine the altitude of the sun, moon, stars and mountains, both lunar and terrestrial, by quadrants and other instruments.[22] Many such papers are included in the *Philosophical Transactions*; the original paper is frequently followed by a rejoinder on the part of another mathematician, pointing out errors in either method or calculation.

But the mathematical interests of the Laputans are not, as a rule, satirized alone; they are included with their interest in music, for in Laputan minds, mathematics and music are one, as they suggest in their clothing, their food and their customs. Here again Swift follows an attitude common enough in the seventeenth century, reflecting

Kepler, Descartes, Newton, Leibniz; more specifically, his ideas go back to Dr John Wallis, who contributed many papers to the Royal Society on the general subject of the analogies between music and mathematics,[23] prefacing his 'discoveries' by the suggestions that they 'may not be unacceptable to those of the Royal Society, who are Musical and Mathematical'.[24] In music and mathematics, many writers of the seventeenth century found the two eternal and immutable verities. Indeed, the mathematician and astronomer, Christian Huygens, went so far as to declare that, no matter how inhabitants of other planets might differ from man in other ways, they must agree in music and geometry, since these are 'everywhere immutably the same, and always will be so'.[25] The interest of the Laputans in music is not, as has frequently been suggested, a satire upon the interest shown in London in Swift's day in opera; the Laputan interest is diametrically opposed and shows the Laputans on the side of those who were resisting the idea that music was a handmaiden to language. Swift's main point is that the Laputans are concerned with the theory, not with the application, of both mathematics and music. Like many of Swift's contemporaries, they expressed their theory of music in mathematical formulae.[26] The Laputans, we are told, express their ideas 'perpetually in lines and figures'. Such lines and figures – almost equally divided between mathematical and musical symbols – Gulliver saw displayed upon their garments and in the king's kitchen, where 'all kinds of mathematical and musical instruments' were used to cut the food into 'rhomboides' and 'cycloids', flutes, fiddles and hautboys. It was entirely natural that, with ideas of beauty founded upon the 'Proportions' of music and mathematics, the Laputans should have transferred their figures of speech from one realm to another:

> If they would, for example, praise the beauty of a woman, or any other animal, they describe it by rhombs, circles, parallelograms, ellipses, and other geometrical terms, or by words of art drawn from music. (p. 191)[27]

No specific source is needed for such an idea; and in view of the long succession of the predecessors of the Laputans who had found evidence of eternal and perfect beauty in mathematics and music, no specific source can really be posited. Yet the musico-mathematical notions of the Laputans may be conveniently found in a paper by the Rev. T. Salmon on 'The Theory of Musick reduced to Arithmetical and Geometrical Progressions'.[28] The paper followed an earlier one in which Salmon had reported a 'Musical Experiment before the Society', the propositions of which were: 'That Music consisted in Proportions, and the more exact the Proportions, the better the Music.' In his second paper, Salmon discussed 'the Theory of Music, which is but little known in this Age, and the Practice of it which is arriv'd to a very great Excellency', both of which, he suggested, 'May be fixed upon the sure Foundations of Mathematical Certainty'. He offered in conclusion two tables 'wherein Music is set forth, first Arithmetically, and then Geometrically'. It required only one more step for the Laputans to apply the certain 'Proportions' of music and mathematics to the praise of feminine beauty.

III

More specific satire with more immediate source is found in the sections in which Swift discusses the two predominant prepossessions of the Laputans – their fear of the sun and of a comet (pp. 192–3). In spite of Swift's suggestions that the Laputans still share astrological fears, he has made them a people whose dread is founded less upon tradition than upon celestial observation. They possess 'glasses far excelling ours in goodness', by means of which they have extended 'their discoveries much further than our astronomers in Europe' (p. 200).[29] They have made important discoveries with their telescopes, none more remarkable than that of the two satellites of Mars – which actually remained hidden from all eyes but those of the Laputans until 1877![30] They are careful observers, among whom one would expect to find science rather than superstition. Yet their dread of the sun and of a comet is greater than had been their ancestors', for their fear is more profoundly rooted in contemporary science.

Three ideas of the sun particularly disturbed the Laputans:

that the earth, by the continual approaches of the sun towards it, must in course of time be absorbed or swallowed up. That the face of the sun will by degrees be encrusted with its own effluvia, and give no more light to the world. . . . That the sun daily spending its rays without any nutriment to supply them, will at last be wholly consumed and annihilated; which must be attended with the destruction of this earth, and of all the planets that receive their light from it. (p. 193)[31]

Such fears were in no way original with the Laputans; many a thoughtful man of the day found himself pondering the same possibilities.

Behind the fear that their planet might fall into the sun lay the potent influence of Newton, 'Britain's justest pride, The boast of human race'.[32] Newton's analysis of planetary motion showed that there must exist a nice balance between the velocity with which the earth is falling toward the sun and its tangential velocity at right angles to that fall. Any disturbance of this 'due proportion of velocity' would be disastrous. The most obvious possibility of disturbance is the gradual decrease of our tangential velocity, for then the earth's orbit would no longer repeat itself year after year, but would approach the sun with ever-increasing speed, eventually to fall into it. This possibility is recognized in the *Principia* by general calculations of the time required for such falls,[33] and by an estimate of the density of the material in space through which the earth spins and the retarding effect to be expected from it.[34] While Newton's conclusion was, on the whole, an optimistic one that the loss of velocity would be quite inappreciable even for 'an immense tract of time',[35] other conclusions were drawn from the same premises. The Laputans might well have found reason for their doubt in Robert Hooke, who, opposing his wave-theory to Newton's theory of light, recognized clearly that there is difficulty in describing the medium which carried these waves and that any imaginable medium would have a retarding effect upon the earth's motion.[36]

Die we must, it would seem, if we are fearful eighteenth-century Laputans. Even if we follow the conclusion of Newton in regard to our earth's falling into the sun, there still remains the warning of the sun-spots and of the consumption of the sun's energy. From the time of Galileo's first observation of sun-spots, astronomers had been concerned to explain these phenomena, and the explanations had led in many different directions. During the early years of the eighteenth century the *Philosophical Transactions* devoted much attention to the problem of these phenomena. A letter of 'Mr. Crabtrie', written in 1640, was revived and republished, and his theory debated, that the spots were 'fading Bodies. . . . no Stars, but unconstant (in regard of their Generation) and irregular Excrescences arising out of, or proceeding from the Sun's body'.[37] At the least these spots indicated 'a Smoak arising out of the Body of the Sun's.[38] At the worst, the 'Smoak' suggested volcanic action. This point of view was developed in detail by William Derham:

> From these preceding Particulars, and their Congruity to what we perceive in our own Globe, I cannot forbear to gather, That the Spots on

the Sun are caused by the Eruption of some new Vulcano therein; which at first, pouring out a prodigious Quantity of Smoak, and other opacous Matter, causeth the Spots: And as that fuliginious Matter decayeth and appendeth itself, and the Vulcano at last becomes more torrid and flaming, so the Spots decay and grow to Umbræ, and at last to Faculæ; which Faculæ I take to be no other than more flaming brighter Parts than any other Parts of the sun.[39]

The Laputans, it would seem, were incorrigible pessimists. Granted we escape, through Newton's optimism, falling into the sun, and granted too – though it seems highly improbable – that the sun-spots indicate only 'Smoak', not 'Vulcano', our fate, though different, will be as surely sealed, if the sun cools or dwindles to a vanishing point. The natural explanation of the heat of the sun, that it is a tremendous burning mass, had been made even more plausible by the discovery of those spots on the sun, which look suspiciously like smoke. Here Hooke was the chief source for concern. 'I question not', he wrote, 'but that there may be very cogent Arguments drawn to prove, that the Light of this Body of the Sun may be caused by an actual Fire, or Dissolution of the superficial Parts thereof . . . which being proved, or supposed so, all the Appearances that have been hitherto taken notice of concerning Clouds, Spots and Blazes, will be very naturally and clearly solved. . . . But some may object and say, that if this were so, certainly the Body of the Sun in so many Thousand Years would have been all consumed, at least it would have grown sensibly less. Suppose this were granted and said, that it has grown some Minutes less since it first began to give Light, none could contradict it by any Observations we have upon record.'[40]

Fear of the sun was not all; even greater than dread of such changes was the Laputan dread of comets and of one comet in particular. 'The earth very narrowly escaped a brush from the tail of the late comet, which would infallibly have reduced it to ashes', Gulliver learned in Laputa (p. 193). It is however not the 'last comet' that terrifies the Laputans so much as one that is to come 'which will probably destroy us'. Is this mere pointless satire, or is there method in this apparent madness? Swift's imagination here, as so often, is making of the real something apparently unreal. His reference – as every reader of his day must have realized – was not merely to a comet, but to 'Halley's comet' – the first comet whose period of return was definitely predicted, with resultant great excitement both to literary and to scientific imagination.[41]

Thomson, writing only a year later than Swift, shows the same response to a scientific idea, when he turns it into poetry in 'Summer':

> Lo! from the dread immensity of space
> Returning with accelerated course,
> The rushing comet to the sun descends:
> And as he sinks below the shading earth,
> With awful train projected o'er the heavens,
> The guilty nations tremble . . .
> While, from his far excursion through the wilds
> Of barren ether, faithful to his time,
> They see the blazing wonder rise anew.[42]

In this passage Swift has told us the date of composition of at least part of the 'Voyage to Laputa'. The Laputans calculated the return of their comet in 'one and thirty years'; and one and thirty years after 1726 – the date of the first publication of *Gulliver's Travels* – English laymen expected the return of Halley's comet. True, Halley himself had predicted that the comet of 1682 would return not in 1757 – as Swift's passage implies – but in 1758; but Halley's prophecy left some reason for doubt. Laymen, then as now, grasped the main point, but neglected the careful mathematics in which Halley corrected a generalization.[43] Seventy-five years had elapsed between the appearance of the comet in 1607 and its reappearance in 1682; years, not days, are important to the layman. The 'Mean period' Halley himself calculated at '75 Years and a half'.[44] The general public was not at all concerned with the careful table of Halley's 'inequalities', nor with his masterful application to his theory of comets of the explanation which he had earlier proposed for the deviation from equality in the case of Jupiter and Saturn. As he had suggested that that inequality was the result of the attraction of these planets for each other, in addition to the attraction of the sun for both, so he concluded that the inequalities in the comet's return might arise from a similar cause. The layman understood only that the comet would appear in approximately seventy-five years; and he vaguely recognized that, if it did, it would put beyond question Newton's theory of gravitation.[45]

In the period of the Renaissance, 'Comets importing change of time and states' had brandished their bloody tresses, and predicted 'disasters in the sun'. But during the seventeenth century, under the impact of the new astronomy, the attitude toward comets began gradually to change, as men questioned whether these strange phenomena, too, might not prove to have a natural place in the great cosmic scheme. There are indications in almanacs and other popular literature of the day that this was one result of Newton's discoveries. Nevertheless, old beliefs still largely dominated popular imagination.[46] As Swift himself wrote: 'Old men and comets have been reverenced for the same reasons; their long beards, and pretenses to foretell events.'[47]

The dread of the Laputans rested however less upon such superstition than upon scientific discovery. With their telescopes they had 'observed ninety-three different comets, and settled their periods with great exactness' (p. 201).[48] If therefore they feared that a comet 'one and thirty years hence' would destroy them, they must have had scientific grounds for their belief. The basis for their fear was implied even in Halley's earlier *Synopsis*, in connection with his discussion of the approach of various comets to the earth. His paper concluded with the statement: 'But what might be the Consequences of so near an appulse; or of a contact, or, lastly, of a shock of the Celestial Bodies, (which is by no means impossible to come to pass,) I leave to be discussed by the Studious of Physical matters.'[29] In his later amplification of the *Synopsis*,[50] Halley went further and expanded this section in connection with the comet of 1680:

> Now this Comet, in that part of its Orbit in which it descended towards the Sun, came so near the paths of all the Planets, that if by chance it had happened to meet any one of the Planets passing by, it must have produced very sensible effects, and the motion of the Comet would have suffered the greatest disturbance. In such case the plane and species of its Ellipsis and its periodic Time would have been very much changed, especially from meeting with Jupiter. In the late descent, the true path of this Comet left the Orbits of Saturn and Jupiter below itself a little towards the South: It approached much nearer to the paths of Venus and Mercury, and much nearer still to that of Mars. But as it was passing thro' the plane of the Ecliptic, viz., to the southern Node, it came so near the path of the Earth, that had it come towards the Sun thirty one days later than it did, it had scarce left our Globe one semidiameter of the Sun towards the North: And without doubt by its centripetal force (which with the great Newton I suppose proportional to the bulk or quantity of matter in the Comet), it would have produced some change in the situation and species of the Earth's Orbit, and in the length of the year. But may the good GOD avert such a shock or contact of such great Bodies moving with such forces (which however is manifestly by no means impossible), lest this most

beautiful order of things be intirely destroyed and reduced into its antient chaos.

Although this suggestion alone would have been sufficient to explain the Laputans' dread of the return of the comet, there is little doubt that popular imagination was even more deeply stirred by another paper which Halley presented to the Royal Society – on the subject of Noah and the Flood! This was one of many papers published in the period by important men of science in which an attempt was made to explain difficult passages in Scripture in such a way as to keep the reverence for the Bible, yet make it consistent with modern scientific thought. Straining at the gnat, Halley and others swallowed the Deluge.[51] In an earlier version of the paper, read before the Royal Society in 1694,[52] Halley had suggested 'the casual Choc of a Comet, or other transient Body' as 'an Expedient change instantly the Poles and Diurnal Rotation of the Globe'. But in the later paper he went further: 'At that Time', he says, 'I did not consider the great Agitation such a Choc must necessarily occasion in the Sea.' Halley's description of the probable consequences of such a 'Choc' was sufficient to strike terror into braver hearts than those of the Laputans. He visualizes the Deluge:

raising up Mountains where none were before, mixing the Elements into such a Heap as the Poets describe the Old Chaos; for such a Choc impelling the solid Parts would occasion the Waters, and all fluid Substances that were unconfined, as the Sea is, with one Impetus to run violently towards that Part of the Globe were [sic] the Blow was received; and that with Force sufficient to rake with it the whole Bottom of the Ocean, and to carry it upon the Land; heaping up into Mountains those earth Parts it had born away with it, in those Places where the opposite Waves balance each other, *miscens ima summis.*

Thus Halley, discovering that the comets, like the stars in their courses, obey the universal law of gravitation, established in 1705 the point of view that was to free men from their long dread of 'those stars with trains of fire and dews of blood'; but through a few sentences in a paper in which he announced the law of comets, and, most of all, through republishing in 1724 a paper largely written thirty years before on the subject of that Deluge weathered only by an ark, put into the minds of the Laputans – and many others of Swift's contemporaries – a greater dread, of the complete annihilation of this globe which we inherit.[53] Small wonder that in the morning the Laputans exchanged no trivial greetings. 'The first question is about the sun's health, how he looked at his setting and rising, and what hopes they have to avoid the stroke of the approaching comet' (p. 193). Like small boys who have listened to tales of hobgoblins, the Laputans 'dared not go to bed for fear'.

IV

After his visit to the Laputans, Gulliver descended to the mainland, Balnibarbi, and proceeded at once to the capital Lagado, whose Grand Academy was to prove one of the chief interests of his voyage. He was impressed, both in town and country, by many 'odd appearances'. The houses were 'very strangely built and most of them out of repair'. Though the fields were filled with labourers and the soil appeared excellent, he saw neither corn nor grass. As he journeyed with the 'great lord Munodi' to his country estate, he observed 'the several methods used by farmers in managing their lands, which to me were wholly unaccountable' (p. 208). Only in the privacy of the country-house did Munodi venture to explain to Gulliver the source of the evident difference between his own well-ordered estate and the 'ill contrived' buildings and 'unhappily cultivated' fields of the rest of Balnibarbi. In so far as this section of the 'Voyage to Laputa' has been studied, critics have taken for granted that the source of its satire was in contemporary politics. Balnibarbi is England, or more often Ireland, with its houses out of repair, its fields badly cultivated, its people in misery and want. Yet, though Swift undoubtedly intended some such double meaning, there is another sort of satire here also, which leads backward to Swift's part in that particular chapter of the long warfare of 'ancient' and 'modern', which Swift himself called *The Battle of the Books.*

The aspect of the old quarrel reflected in the 'Voyage to Laputa' is not the controversy between 'ancient' and 'modern' literature, but the broader implications of the quarrel which in England had become largely a scientific controversy. Munodi, with whom alone the conservative Gulliver found real sympathy, is clearly an 'ancient' and for that reason ridiculed by his 'modern' neighbours. His sympathy with the party of the 'ancients' is shown most immediately in his surroundings. His house is 'a noble structure, built according to the best rules of ancient architecture' (p. 209) and therefore, Swift slyly suggests, still standing! 'The fountains, gardens, walks, avenues, and groves were all disposed with exact judgment and taste' (p. 209). 'Everything about him was magnificent, regular, and polite' (p. 208). 'He was content to go on in the old forms, to live in the houses his ancestors had built, and act as they did in every part of life without innovation' (p. 210). Yet in the eyes of his countrymen he was not only a failure, but also an enemy to progress, an 'ill commonwealth's man'. His example would have been considered dangerous, had it not been that that example was followed only by 'such as were old, and wilful, and weak like himself' (p. 208). So strong was the pressure of public opinion that Munodi sadly faced the necessity of tearing down his noble structure to rebuild in the present ill mode.

The trouble had begun, he tells Gulliver, 'about forty years before', when certain Balnibarbians had visited progressive Laputa and, falling under the spell of Laputan philosophy, 'came back with a very small smattering in mathematics, but full of volatile spirits acquired in that airy region' (p. 209). Here, as so often, Swift's figures are significant. 'About forty years before' the composition of the 'Voyage to Laputa' – thirty-nine years if, we are to continue accepting 1726 as the year of composition of these sections – the first gun in the *Battle of the Books* had been fired by Charles Perrault's *Siècle de Louis le Grand*, followed the next year by Fontenelle's *Digression sur les anciens et les modernes* and the first volume of Perrault's *Parallèle des anciens et des modernes*, as a result of which Sir William Temple wrote his essay 'On Ancient and Modern Learning' and ultimately drew Swift into the combat. From the time of their visit to Laputa, the Balnibarbians 'fell into schemes of putting all arts, sciences, languages, and mechanics upon a new foot' (p. 209). Most of all, they had established an 'Academy of Projectors' which had come to dominate the nation – as the Royal Society dominated England. Its 'professors contrive new rules and methods of agriculture and building, and new instruments and tools for all trades and manufactures'.[54] They promised a new Utopia if their methods were followed. True, their magnificent projects had been brought to no perfection at the time of Gulliver's visit; but with Baconian optimism, they persisted in their prosecution of schemes to reform the Kingdom by science, centred in a later 'Salomon's House'.

v

It has been generally recognized that in the Grand Academy of Lagado, Swift was to some extent following a fashion, common enough in literature of the seventeenth and eighteenth centuries, of satirizing academicians in general and the Royal Society in particular; but the full extent of that satire has not been appreciated. Long before the incorporation of the Royal Society, Rabelais had introduced a somewhat similar passage in his Court of Queen Whim; Joseph Hall in 1610 described another such Academy in his *Mundus Alter et Idem*.[55] Bacon's enthusiastic proposals for his scientific Academy in the *New Atlantis* offered new fuel. The establishment of the Royal Society tended to make specific the former general satire. From the time of Samuel Sorbière's visit to London in 1663,[56] journeys, whether 'real' or 'philosophical', tended to include accounts of academies which are usually only thinly veiled pictures of the Royal Society. Ned Ward's tour of London, described in the *London Spy* in 1698,[57] led him to Gresham College as well as to the 'Colledge of Physicians'; in both institutions he examined the supposed 'rarities' and 'Philosophical Toys'. From both he went away with a poor opinion of scientists, who seemed to him only less mad than the inmates of the lunatic asylum which we also visited. Dr Martin Lister in the account of his journey to Paris,[58] paid high tribute to both French and English scientists. The subsequent parody by William King in his *Journey to London*[59] in the same year introduces satirically the theme of visits to the *virtuosi*. King carries his attack further in the Ninth Dialogue of the *Dialogues of the Dead*[60] and in the *Transactioneer*.[61] Even closer similarities to Swift's Academy may be found in Tom Brown's 'Philosophical or Virtuosi Country' in *Amusements Serious and Comical*, and in Ludwig Holberg's *Journey to a World Underground*.[62] If we are to trust the evidence of literature, Swift hardly exaggerated when he said through the lips of Munodi: 'There is not a town of any consequence . . . without such an academy' (p. 209). While there is no doubt that some of the details in the 'Voyage to Laputa' reflect such earlier works as that of Rabelais, nevertheless Swift's Grand Academy of Lagado was drawn rather from life than from literature.

On 13 December 1710 Swift himself had paid a visit to Gresham College. With many other visitors, his itinerary included other institutions often grouped together in the memory of travellers to London: 'then to Bedlam; then dined at the Chophouse behind the Exchange; then to Gresham College (but the keeper was not at home), and concluded the night at the puppet-show . . .[63] Puppet-shows, lunatic asylums, colleges for the advancement of research – they were all one to the satirists of that generation. If, in spite of the absence of the keeper,

Swift saw any of the collections of the Royal Society, we may perhaps detect reminiscences of his visit in his later references to the loadstone of the Flying Island and in his brief suggestion of projectors who were 'petrifying the hoofs of a living horse to preserve them from foundering' (p. 216). The collection of petrified objects belonging to the Royal Society was shown with pride to all visitors and was known throughout Europe. One section of their earliest catalogue was devoted to 'Animal Bodies Petrified', another to 'Vegetable Bodies Petrified'.[64] Yet on the whole Swift's Academy reflects less Swift's own visit than accounts in the *Philosophical Transactions*.

In his account of the Grand Academy, Swift first describes the institution briefly: 'This Academy is not an entire single building, but a continuation of several houses on both sides of a street, which growing waste was purchased and applied to that use' (p. 212). Gulliver later estimates that there were at least five hundred rooms in the institution. This is certainly not the Royal Society as it appeared in the years when Swift was at work on *Gulliver's Travels*. Yet it is possible that this is one of Swift's sly digs at the Society's ambition for greatly expanded quarters, which threatened to divide the Council into two factions.[65] There were those among the members who continued to entertain the noble ambition, proposed by Bacon in his description of 'Salomon's House', not only of 'great and spacious houses', but of 'deep caves . . . high towers', great lakes and artificial wells, orchards, gardens, parks and enclosures.

The members of the Academy whom Gulliver encountered were of various groups – experimental scientists, 'projectors in speculative learning', professors in the 'school of languages' and politicians. Since our concern for the moment is with the scientific background of the voyage and particularly its relation to the *Philosophical Transactions*, we may limit ourselves to the first group of experimentalists.[66] Since Swift's own larger outline cannot be followed, we may watch his subdivisions of the experiments of his projectors according to a scheme suggested by Fontenelle: 'Physick . . . is divided in the Academy into three Branches, which make three different sorts of Members of the Society, Anatomy, Chymistry, and Botanicks.'[67] The experiments of these projectors have impressed literary historians chiefly by their apparent exaggeration and have been dismissed as so obviously impossible that they become grotesque rather than humorous. Swift, the critics say, 'simply tortured his memory and his fancy to invent or recall grotesque illustrations of scientific pedantry'.[68] Yet there was humour in these passages when they were written, and humour of a sort particularly popular today. Swift's is the *reductio ad absurdum* frequently employed by modern satirists who reduce to nonsense scientific papers and doctoral dissertations, not by inventing unreal subjects of research, but – more devastatingly – by quoting actual titles of papers and theses. What, asks a modern reader, could be more absurd than 'A Study of the Bacteria Found in a Dirty Shirt'? Removed from its context, read by laymen instead of scientistis, the real serves often as a more powerful weapon against scientific research than can anything invented by fancy. Such is Swift's technique. For the most part he simply set down before his readers experiments actually performed by members of the Royal Society, more preposterous to the layman than anything imagination could invent and more devastating in their satire because of their essential truth to source. The 'invention' in Swift's passages usually consists in one of two things: sometimes he neatly combines two real experiments on different subjects – as in the case of the spiders who not only spun silk stockings, but also went one better than the scientists by colouring them naturally; at other times Swift carries a real experiment only one step further – and the added step carries us over the precipice of nonsense.

Two of the 'projects' alone seem to have had a literary source. The purposely disgusting experiment of the 'most ancient student of the Academy', who attempted to 'reduce human excrement to its original food', was based upon Rabelais' 'Archasdarpenin'.[69] The 'Ingenious architect' who built his house, like the bee and spider, by beginning at the roof and working downwards, had also a literary source, though one may suspect that Swift found at least partial authority for the idea in contemporary accounts of architectural experiments.[70] With these two possible exceptions, all of Swift's major experiments may be found in the *Philosophical Transactions* or in more complete works of members of the Royal Society.

The 'astronomer who had undertaken to place a sun-dial upon the great weather-cock on the town-house, by adjusting the annual and diurnal motions of the earth and sun, so as to answer and coincide with all accidental turnings, by the wind' (p. 214) was proposing nothing impossible. Such sun-clocks had been invented both in France and in England. Sir Christopher Wren in 1663 had contrived an automatic wind-recorder, by annexing a clock to a weather-cock and, by an ingenious combination of a pencil attached to the clock and a paper on a rundle moved by the weather-cock, procured automatic records of the wind.[71] An English correspondent of the Royal Society in 1719, taking exception to the assertion of a Frenchman that 'clocks to agree with the Sun's apparent Motion' had been invented first in France, wrote:

> [He] supposed that it was a Thing never thought of by any before himself: I shall therefore give this short Account of what I have performed in that Matter myself . . . [The account follows] . . . But these Clocks that I then made to agree with the Sun's apparent Time, were done according to the Equation Tables, which I found not to agree very exactly with the Sun's apparent Motion. . . . I made a Table myself by Observation. . . . Since then I have made many of these Clocks.[72]

Others of Swift's experiments follow actual accounts as closely. Among the many remarkable professors of Lagado was 'a man born blind, who had several apprentices in his own condition; their employment was to mix colours for painters, which their master taught them to distinguish by feeling and smelling' (p. 213).[73] One might suspect that here Swift was having his fun – as so often – with Newton, and particularly with the corpuscular theory of light, which had been reported in the *Philosophical Transactions*.[74] But the source was much more direct; not Newton, but Boyle, was the villain of this piece. Material made to his hand Swift found either in Boyle's 'Experiments and Observations upon Colours' or more probably – since Boyle's earlier reports had been made in 1663 and 1664 – in the ponderous *Philosophical Works of Robert Boyle*, which had been 'abridged, methodized, and disposed under various heads' by Peter Shaw in 1725. The blind professor whom Gulliver saw had in the preceding century been a real blind man, whose case was reported to Boyle by 'Dr. Finch, anatomist extraordinary to the great duke of Tuscany'.[75] Finch had told Boyle of 'a blind man at Maestricht, in the Low Countries, who at certain times could distinguish colours by the touch with his fingers'. After several scruples on Boyle's part, he was forced to believe in the account which he relates in these words:

> The name of the man was John Vermaasen, at that time about thirty-three years of age, who, when he was two years old, had the small pox, which render'd him absolutely blind, tho' he is at present an organist in a public choir. The doctor discoursing with him over night, the blind man affirmed, that he could distinguish colours by feeling, but not unless he

were fasting; for that any quantity of drink deprived him of that exquisite touch which is requisite to so nice a sensation. Upon this, the doctor provided against the next morning seven pieces of ribbon of these seven colours, black, white, red, blue, green, yellow, and grey; but as for mixed colours, this Vermaasen would not undertake to discern them; tho' if offer'd, he could tell that they were mixed. To discern the colour of the ribbon, he places it betwixt his thumb and his fore-finger, but his most exquisite perception is in his thumb, and much better in the right than in the left. After the man had four or five times told the doctor the several colours, whilst a napkin was tied over his eyes, the doctor observed he twice mistook, for he called the white black, and the red blue; but still before his error, he would lay them by in pairs, saying, that tho' he could easily distinguish them from all others, yet those two pair were not easily distinguishable from one another. Then the doctor desired to know what kind of difference he found in colours by his touch. To which the blind man reply'd, that all the difference he observed, was a greater or less degree of asperity: for, says he, black feels like the points of needles, or some harsh sand, whilst red feels very smooth . . .[76]

Boyle goes on to point out that before he saw the notes from which the account was taken he had believed that the blind man might have distinguished the colours not by feeling, but by smelling – another point which Swift was quick to catch. Boyle's account continues:

for some of the ingredients employ'd by dyers, have different and strong scents, which a very nice nose might distinguish; and this I the rather suspected, because he required that the ribbons he was to judge of, should be offer'd him in the morning fasting; for I have observ'd in setting-dogs, that the feeding of them greatly impairs their scent.

In others of his experiments Swift has cleverly welded together two or more accounts and has made a new combination. The cure 'of a small fit of the colic' (pp. 214–15) is of this sort. Here Swift applies to Gulliver a series of experiments which Shadwell had already made famous in the *Virtuoso*[77] and implies, in addition, various later experiments performed by members of the Royal Society on the general subject of respiration and artificial respiration. The work of Swammerdam, Hooke, Boyle and others on these subjects had long been familiar; but in addition to this general satire – in which otherwise he might be said to follow Shadwell – Swift has suggested something more specific. It is not enough that 'a large pair of bellows' should convey air into the intestines or that, when the dog dies from the treatment, artificial respiration should be used to revive it. Swift needed another element, which he found in an account of 'An extraordinary Effect of the Cholick', in which Mr St Andre had already suggested Swift's principle of 'curing that disease by contrary operations':

> The Peristaltick Motion of the Intestines is by all Anatomists supposed to be the proper Motion of those Cylindrical Tubes. The use of this Motion is to propel the Chyle into the *Vasa lactea*, and to accelerate the grosser parts of the Aliment downwards, in order to expel them, when all their nutritive Contents are extracted. This Motion, thus established, it naturally seems to follow, that an Inversion of it (call'd for that Reason an Anti-peristaltick Motion) should force the Aliments, Bile, Pancreatic Juice, and lastly the Fæces, to ascend towards the Mouth.[78]

The same trick of combining two sources is found in the remarkable experiment of the projector who was able to make silk stockings and gloves from spiders' webs. Swift's projector was found in a room 'where the walls and ceiling were all hung round with cobwebs' (p. 214). He lamented 'the fatal mistake the world had been so long in of using silk-worms, while we had such plenty of domestic insects, who infinitely excelled the former, because they knew how to weave as well as spin'. One critic has suggested that this idea went back to the proposal of a Frenchman;[79] but it has not been noticed that that Frenchman's proposal appeared in the *Philosophical Transactions*, whence it came to Swift's attention. In a paper on 'The Silk of Spiders', M. Bon in 1710 first gave an account of various sorts of spiders, which reminds the English reader of the satirical interest in these insects in Shadwell's earlier parody. Shadwell's Sir Nicholas Gimcrack had become intimately acquainted with many kinds of spiders; but M. Bon was concerned only with two: '*viz.* such as have long legs, and such as have short Ones: The latter of which furnishes the Silk I am going to speak of'. M. Bon, however, was aware, as was Sir Nicholas Gimcrack, that spiders 'are distinguished by their Colour, some being Black, others Brown, Yellow, Green, White, and others of all these Colours mixed together'. Unlike Sir Nicholas Gimcrack, M. Bon was less concerned with species of spiders than with their utilitarian value. He wrote:

> The first Thread that they wind is weak, and serves them for no other Use than to make that Sort of Web, in which they catch Flies: The second is much stronger than the first; in this they wrap up their Eggs, and by this means preserve them from the Cold, and secure them from such Insects as

would destroy them. These last Threads are wrapt very loosely about their Eggs, and resemble in Form the Bags of Silk-Worms, that have been prepared and loosened between the Fingers, in order to be put upon the Distaff. These Spiders Bags (if I may so call them) are of a grey Colour when they are new, but turn blackish when they have been long exposed to the Air. It is true, one may find several other Spiders Bags of different Colours, and that afford a better Silk, especially those of the Tarantula; but the Scarcity of them would render it very difficult to make Experiments upon them; so that we must confine ourselves to the Bags of such Spiders as are most common, which are the short-legg'd Ones. . . . And by getting together a great many of these Bags, it was that I made this new Silk, which is no-way inferior in Beauty to common Silk. It easily takes all sorts of Colours; and one may as well make large Pieces of it, as the Stockings and Gloves which I have made . . .[80]

Only one significant difference appears in Swift's account. M. Bon still found it necessary to dye his stockings and gloves in the usual way. But the projector of Lagado had had access to another paper in the *Philosophical Transactions* and was able to produce colours without added expense by a natural method:

He proposed farther that by employing spiders the charge of dyeing silks should be wholly saved, whereof I was fully convinced when he showed me a vast number of flies most beautifully coloured, wherewith he fed his spiders, assuring us that the webs would take a tincture from them; and as he had them of all hues, he hoped to fit everybody's fancy, as soon as he could find proper food for the flies, of certain gums, oils, and other glutinous matter to give a strength and consistence to the threads. (p. 214)

This trick Swift learned from another paper in the *Transactions*, of the very sort that must have delighted his ironic mind. Here Dr Wall, beginning with a discourse on amber and diamonds, concluded with gum-lac, pismires and artificial and natural dyes, and unconsciously gave rise to experimentation in Lagado:

I don't know in the Animal Kingdom any Thing but Pismires, that affords a Volatile Acid, and in the East-Indies there's a large kind of them that live on the Sap of certain Plants, affording both a Gum and a Colour, which Sap passing through the Body of those Insects and Animals, is by their Acid Spirit converted into an Animal Nature; which is the Reason, that with the Colour extracted from Gum-Lac (which Gum-Lac is nothing else but the Excrements of these Insects or Animals) almost as good, and full as lasting, Colours are made as from Cochineal: I am the more confirmed herein, because I know of an Artificial Way of converting

Vegetable Colours into an Animal Nature very much like this, by which the Colours are made much more pleasant and permanent. After the same Manner the remaining Gum, which is an Oleosum, being digested and passing through the Bodies of those Insects or Animals, is by their Volatile Acid converted into a Vegetable Animal Phosphorus or Noctiluca.[81]

The projector whom Gulliver saw 'at work to calcine ice into gun-powder' (p. 213) may have been moved by nothing more esoteric than the report of 'Haile of so great a Bigness' which 'fell at Lisle in Flanders': 'One among the rest was observed to contain a dark brown Matter, in the Middle thereof; and being thrown into the Fire, it gave a very great Report'.[82] But since Swift's projector had already written a treatise on the 'malleability of fire', and since a group of his fellow-projectors, by 'condensing the air into a dry intangible substance, by extracting the nitre, and letting the aqueous fluid particles percolate' (p. 215), showed close familiarity with the work of Boyle and his followers, it is more probable that the gunpowder-projector had been studying Boyle's 'Experiments and Observations upon Cold',[83] and had been impressed not only by the similarities between heat and cold, but also and more particularly by the long series of experiments on 'the expansive forces of congelation'[84] with their recurrent motif of explosion and violence. In all these experiments water is introduced into tubes of various types and allowed to freeze. In all, the tubes break 'with a considerable noise and violence' or 'the ball of the glass was burst to pieces with a loud report'.[85] Occasionally, 'the compress'd air flew out with a great noise, and part of the pipe . . . appear'd filled with smoke.[86] Such reports would have been enough for Swift's imagination, even if he had not also read Boyle's paper on 'The Mechanical Origins of Heat and Cold'[87] with its discussion of the apparent extravagances of 'heating cold liquors with ice'. Boyle's persistent interest in both ice and gunpowder is clear enough to the layman, so that Swift need not have entered – though he may – upon the problem of the 'effluvia' of both, which Boyle raises in this work.

Of all the experiments of Swift's projectors, none has excited more contemptuous laughter than that of the man who 'had been eight years upon a project for extracting sun-beams out of cucumbers, which were to be put into vials hermetically sealed, and let out to warm the air in raw inclement summers' (p. 212). Preposterous as this may seem, it is no more incredible than the other experiments which prove to have scientific sources – and it leads the reader into the last of the groups suggested by Fontenelle – 'Botanicks'. The basis of the project is obvious. Swift merely combined a group of experiments, adding to them little – except the cucumbers! The 'cucumber projector' may have been an assiduous student of Grew, Boyle, Hooke and Newton; he may have read a paper by Halley on 'The Circulation of Watery Vapours',[88] in which many of his ideas were suggested. But it is more likely that he was a follower of Hales, who, working upon principles laid down for him by these predecessors, made the final experiments which were imitated in the Grand Academy of Lagado. Over a period of years Hales had reported to the Royal Society experiments on the respiration of plants and animals, which he welded into a whole in 1727 in his two volumes of *Statical Essays*.[89]

Hales's work also presupposed certain conclusions made by Boyle and Newton on the nature of the 'particles of the air',[90] which gave rise to long discussion among men of science. Hales had been particularly impressed by the great quantities of air generated from certain fruits and vegetables, most of all, apples.[91] Swift's projector was familiar not only with the general principles involved in such experiments on plant respiration, but also with a series of experiments reported by Hales upon the effect of sunbeams upon the earth and with the principles by which these sunbeams were alleged to enter into plants:

> The impulse of the Sun-beams giving the moisture of the earth a brisk undulating motive, which watery particles, when separated or rarefied by heat, do descend in the form of vapour: And the vigour of warm and confined vapour . . . must be very considerable, so as to penetrate the roots with some vigour . . . 'Tis therefore probable that the roots of trees and plants are thus, by means of the Sun's warmth, constantly irrigated with fresh supplies and moisture . . . whence, by the same genial heat, in conjunction with the attraction of the capillary sap vessels, it is carried up thro' the bodies and branches of vegetables, and thence passing into the leaves, it is there most vigorously acted upon, in those thin plates, and put into an undulating motion, by the Sun's warmth, whereby it is most plentifully thrown off, and perspired thro' their surface; whence, as soon as it is disentangled, it mounts with great rapidity in the free air.[92]

Such sunbeams, sinking into the ground, as Hales reported, 'for a distance of two feet' and then rising through root and branch of the plant to be 'perspired' or 'respired', Swift's projector, like Hales, caught in his 'hermetically sealed vials'. The second step in his experiment needed only the authority of Shadwell's Sir Nicholas Gimcrack, who motivated by Boyle and Hooke collected air from all parts of the country so that his guests might choose 'Newmarket, Banstead-down, Wiltshire, Bury Air; Norwich Air; what you will';[93] when Sir Nicholas grew weary of the closeness of London and had 'a Mind to take Country Air', he sent for 'may be, forty Gallons of Bury Air, shut all my Windows and Doors close, and let it fly into my Chamber'. So Swift's projector, having collected the sunbeams, let them out 'to warm the air in raw inclement summers'.

Practical as was the application of a theory in the case of this botanist, Swift's projectors concerned with 'new methods of agriculture' were more practical still. To be sure, they had already, as Gulliver had seen, reduced the fields of Balnibarbi to desolation and were responsible for those 'wholly unaccountable' methods of managing lands which Gulliver had observed. Because of his interest in Ireland, Swift may have noticed particularly a paper 'On the Manuring of Lands by Sea-shells in Ireland, by the Archbishop of Dublin',[94] with its suggestions of the great improvements to be wrought in agriculture by this method. Swift may also have noticed the many reports on agriculture in distant countries – particularly Ceylon and China – and the proposals in the *Philosophical Transactions* for carrying over to English soil methods applicable to agriculture in very different climates. Certainly there seem to be reminiscences of such papers in the experiments of the agricultural projectors of Lagado. The professor, for example, who proposed to plough the land by driving six hundred hogs into a field, that they might 'root up the whole ground . . . at the same time manuring it with their dung' suggests that he had studied a paper on the 'Culture of Tobacco in Zeylan'.[95] The custom in Ceylon was this:

> They clear a little piece of Ground, in which they sow the Seed of Tobacco, as the Gardeners here sow Parsley and Coleworts; against the Time that this is ready for transplanting, they choose a piece of Ground, which they hedge about; when the Buffalo's begin to chew the Cud, they are put within this Hedge-Ground and let stand until they have done, and this they continue Day and Night, until the Ground be sufficiently dunged.

The 'universal artist' who devoted himself to agriculture among his various pursuits, proposed to 'sow the land with chaff, wherein he affirmed the true seminal virtue to be contained'. The 'seminal virtue' of plants had engrossed English botanists since the discovery of Nehemiah Grew that plants possessed sex. Swift needed no source for this interest in Lagado; he could have found it in Grew himself, or in such suggestions as that 'Of Manuring of Land by Sea-Sand',[96] in which the author suggests the mixing 'of these Male and Female Salts; for the Sea Salt is too lusty and active of itself'. The 'Propagation of Vegetables' from this point of view was discussed at length in another paper which, following Grew's discovery that the Farina . . . doth some way perform the Office of Male Sperm', went on to prove 'that this Farina is a Congeries of Seminal Plants, one of which must be convey'd into every Ovum before it can become prolifick'.[97]

The most specific proposal of the agriculturists of Lagado Gulliver had observed even before his visit to the Academy. On Munodi's property stood a mill, turned by the current of a river, which had for years proved satisfactory. However, some seven years before, the projectors had come to Munodi

> with proposals to destroy this mill, and build another on the side of that mountain, on the long ridge whereof a long canal must be cut for a repository of water, to be conveyed up by pipes and engines to supply the mill; because the wind and air upon a height agitated the water, and thereby made it fitter for motion; and because the water descending down a declivity would turn the mill with half the current of a river whose course is more upon a level. (pp. 210–11)

Behind this sage conclusion of the theorists of the Academy lay a long series of experiments reported to the Royal Society first by Francis Hawksbee, later by James Jurin, who from 1720 until 1727 was the editor of the *Philosophical Transactions*. Beginning with a discussion of the cause of ascent of water in capillary tubes, Jurin continued with a study of the effect on the flow of water at various heights, and finally with two papers, one in English, the other in Latin, 'Of the Motion of Running Water'.[98] Here Swift seems to have found, couched in the terms of mathematical proof which never failed to amuse and irritate him, a study of the force of running water at various heights, the effect of gravity, the mathematical ratio between 'the Altitude of the Water' and the 'Motion of the Cataract'. Here he may even have found his 'Canal'; for Jurin's experiment is in large part a study of the relation between the 'Length of the Canal', the 'Motion of the Water' and the 'Velocity of the Water'. To Jurin, to be sure, 'Canals' were only a part of laboratory equipment; but by the projectors – and by Swift – the small laboratory model was readily expanded in size and easily translated to the side of a mountain in Balnibarbi, where water flowed (or did not flow, as Munodi learned to his cost) with the same 'Force' and 'Velocity' as in Jurin's tubes.

Of all the experimenters in the Grand Academy of Lagado, there remains only that 'universal artist' who, like Bacon, believed that the end of science was the 'benefit and use of man' and who 'had been thirty years employing his thoughts for the improvement of human life' (pp. 215-16). So common were 'universal artists' in Swift's day that it is perhaps idle to seek to identify the original of a passage which is clearly intended as a satire upon the tendency of many scientists of the time to take all knowledge to be their province. Such a universal artist was the earlier Martin Scriblerus, 'this Prodigy of our Age; who may well be called The Philosopher of Ultimate Causes, since by a Sagacity peculiar to himself, he hath discover'd Effects in their very Cause; and without the trivial helps of Experiments, or Observations, hath been the Inventor of most of the modern Systems and Hypotheses'.[99] The 'universal artist' of the 'Voyage to Laputa' was, however, an experimenter; and his experiments covered many fields. He was at once a specialist on the nature of the air, on petrification, on marble, on agriculture and on the breeding of sheep. Allowing for the obvious exaggeration of the passage, we may suspect that, if Swift intended his thrust at any one man, it was at Robert Boyle, who spoke with authority on all these subjects and who, more perhaps than any other man of his age, had been a pioneer in all fields of investigation. Swift's many other references to Boyle, and his obvious familiarity with the three large volumes in which Dr Peter Shaw had treasured up his master to a life beyond life, bear out this theory. But theory it must remain; for Boyle was not alone in his encyclopaedic knowledge and in his tendency to express himself on any and every subject. If vice it was, it was, as Bacon would have said and as Swift seems to imply in his passage, less a vice of the individual than of the age.

VI

'It is highly probable', Swift wrote ironically in the 'Voyage to the Houyhnhnms', 'that such travellers who shall hereafter visit the countries described in this work of mine, may, by detecting my errors (if there be any), and adding many new discoveries of their own, justle me out of vogue, and stand in my place, making the world forget that I

was ever an author.'[100] Swift himself would have been the last to
object to the attempts of 'later travellers' to recognize the specific
sources of his satire. He, who delighted in the setting of riddles, wrote
with some regret: 'Though the present age may understand well
enough the little hints we give, the parallels we draw, and the characters we describe, yet this will all be lost the next.' Yet he added more
hopefully: 'However, if these papers should happen to live till our
grandchildren are men, I hope they may have curiosity enough to
consult annals and compare dates, in order to find out.'[101] Letters
exchanged between Swift and his contemporaries offer evidence that
Swift's own age was quick to catch the implications in the scientific
portion of the voyage. Ten days after the publication of *Gulliver's
Travels*, Gay and Pope wrote to Swift a joint letter, in which they said
that there was general agreement by the politicians that the work was
'free from particular reflections, but that the satire on general societies
of men is too severe'.[102] They added: 'Not but that we now and then
meet with people of greater perspicuity, who are in search for particular applications in every leaf, and it is highly probable we shall have
keys published to give light into Gulliver's design.'[103] Erasmus Lewis
complained that he wanted such a key.[104] Dr Arbuthnot, recognizing
the satire upon his colleagues in the Royal Society, wrote critically to
Swift: 'I tell you freely, the part of the projectors is the least brilliant';[105]
Gay and Pope reported to Swift that Arbuthnot had said 'it is ten
thousand pities he had not known it, he could have added such abundance of things upon every subject'.[106] To the joint letter Swift replied,
still pretending to preserve his anonymity, reporting other criticisms
which had come to him. He added a sentence which may well be
significant in connection with the 'Voyage to Laputa': 'I read the book
over, and in the second volume observe several passages, which appear
to be patched and altered, and the style of a different sort, unless I am
much mistaken.'[107] Various explanations may be suggested for that
self-criticism. In the light of the evidence which has been offered here,
is it not possible that Swift intended an apology for the haste with
which the scientific portions of the 'Voyage to Laputa' were completed,
after his return from Ireland?[108]

Whatever the artistic inferiorities of the 'Voyage to Laputa', Swift
has left to posterity in these chapters a record of the greatness and the
limitations of his time. No age will be a 'Century of Genuis' that does
not also appear to its coevals a century of absurdities. Perhaps the final

word on this adventure of Gulliver may best be said, not by posterity, but by one of Swift's contemporaries, John, Earl of Cork and Orrery, who wrote to his son:

> However wild the descriptions of . . . the manners, and various projects of the philosophers of Lagado may appear, yet it is a real picture embellished with much latent wit and humour. It is a satir upon those astronomers and mathematicians, who have so entirely dedicated their time to the planets, that they have been careless of their family and country, and have been chiefly anxious, about the economy and welfare of the upper worlds. But if we consider Swift's romance in a serious light, we shall find him of opinion, that those determinations in philosophy, which at present seem to the most knowing men to be perfectly well founded and understood, are in reality unsettled, or uncertain, and may perhaps some ages hence be as much decried, as the axioms of Aristotle are at this day. Sir Isaac Newton and his notions may hereafter be out of fashion. There is a kind of mode in philosophy, as well as in other things . . .[109]

NOTES

1. W. A. Eddy, *Gulliver's Travels: A Critical Study* (Princeton and London, 1923) p. 158; hereafter cited as Eddy, *Critical Study*.

2. 'Voyage to Laputa', in *Gulliver's Travels*, ed. W. A. Eddy (Oxford, 1933), ch. ii. References to the 'Voyage to Laputa' in the text are always to this edition.

3. Eddy, *Critical Study*, p. 158.

4. Introduction to *Gulliver's Travels*, ed. W. A. Eddy, p. xviii.

5. The most important study of literary sources is Eddy's *Critical Study*, which incorporates the earlier work of Borkowsky, Conant, Hönncher, Poll and others. The political satire of *Gulliver's Travels* has been definitively treated by Sir Charles Firth, 'The Political Significance of Gulliver's Travels', in *Proceedings of the British Academy*, IX (1919) 1–23.

6. An occasional commentator has recognised the scientific background of one or another of the details. M. Émile Pons, in *Gulliver's Travels [Extraits] . . . avec une introduction et des notes* (Paris, 1927) p. 204 n, remarks: 'It must be acknowledged, also, that in several of the numerous scientific hints and suggestions contained in these chapters, Swift reveals to us a remarkable and quite unexpected power of divination which is a cause of wonderment for many a scientist of our day.'

7. See Claude Lloyd, 'Shadwell and the Virtuosi', in *PMLA* XLIV (1929) 472–94.

8. Minnie M. Miller, 'Science and Philosophy as Precursors of the English Influence in France', in *PMLA* XLV (1940) 856–96.

9. *Miscellanea Curiosa. Containing a Collection of Some of the Principal Phenomena in Nature, Accounted for by the Greatest Philosophers of this Age; Being the Most Valuable Discourses, Read and Delivered to the Royal Society, for the Advancement of Physical and Mathematical Knowledge. As also a Collection of Curious Travels, Voyages, Antiquities, and Natural Histories of Countries; Presented to the same Society*. The first volumes appeared at London 1705–7;

a second edition, revised and corrected by W. Derham, was published in 1723-7. According to the catalogue of the Library of Congress, the first edition appeared under the auspices of Edmond Halley, the second under the auspices of William Derham.

10. It is clear from references in his letters that Swift was engaged upon *Gulliver's Travels* from at least 1720 until their publication in 1726. He himself points out that he completed, corrected and augmented the travels in 1726, before their publication. Critics disagree about the order of composition, the majority holding that the 'Voyage to Laputa' was the earliest and that its imperfections are to be accounted for by the fact that it was written before Swift conceived the work as a whole. One or two critics however have considered the work as the latest of the voyages. The evidence given in this paper tends to bear out the idea that a large part of the 'Voyage to Laputa' was a late composition. Several of the experiments that Swift followed most closely were performed as late as 1724. Robert Boyle's complete scientific works appeared in 1725, and though individual papers were available earlier, Swift's close following of Boyle and his many references to him seem to indicate that the complete scientific works were used. The actual dating which Swift himself gives, in the case of the comet – discussed later – and the beginning of the trouble in Balnibarbi, about forty years earlier, both point to 1726 as the most probable date of the composition of the scientific portions of the 'Voyage to Laputa'. It would seem that, while Swift was undoubtedly working upon some sections of this voyage in 1724, as references in his letters show, he put aside the more technical portions until his return to England; and that the scientific sections of the 'Voyage to Laputa' were among the latest of *Gulliver's Travels*.

11. The abridged edition of the *Transactions* from 1700 to 1720 devotes a long section (vol. v, ch. iii) to 'Travels and Voyages'. The third volume of the *Miscellanea Curiosa* is entirely devoted to 'Curious Travels, Voyages . . . and Natural Histories'. Swift's borrowing from contemporary travel tales has been pointed out particularly by W. H. Bonner, *Captain William Dampier* (Stanford, 1934) ch. ix; and by R. W. Frantz, 'Swift's Yahoos and the Voyagers', in *Modern Philology*, xxix (1931) 49-57. *Phil. Trans.* xxvi (1708) 189: 'An Extract of Two Letters from the Missionary Jesuits, concerning the Discovery of the New Phillippine-Islands, with a Map of the Same.'

12. Some Natural Observations in Natural History in Shropshire', in *Phil. Trans.* xxv (1707) 2418; abridged ed. v ii 112-15. (In general, in reference to the *Transactions*, the authors have endeavoured to give references to both the complete and the abridged editions. The first number refers to the complete edition, the second to the abridged, which is more accessible to general readers. We have used the 1749 edition of vols. ii, iii, iv and v, the 1734 edition of vols. vi and vii.)

13. 'An Extract of several Letters from Cotton Mather, D.D.', in *Phil. Trans.* xxix (1714) 62; v ii, 159-65.

14. J. Marshal, 'An Account of the Bramines in the Indies', in *Phil. Trans.* xx (1700-1) 729; v ii 165-71.

15. Account of the Bramines', v ii 169.

16. Cf. Swift, *Memoirs of Martin Scriblerus*, in *Satires and Personal Writings*, ed. W. A. Eddy (New York, 1933) p. 133: 'In his third Voyage he discover'd a whole kingdom of Philosophers, who govern by the Mathematicks.'

17. Passages which illustrate this point of view will be found in M. H. Nicolson, 'The Microscope and English Imagination', in *Smith College Studies in Modern Languages*, xvi (1935) 22-37.

18. Peter Shaw, *The Philosophical Works of the Honourable Robert Boyle, Abridged, methodized and disposed* (1725) i 131. (The pagination in this volume is duplicated in pp. 129-36.)

19. 'A Translation of Part of Monsieur Fontenelle's Preface to the Memoirs of the Royal Academy at Paris, in the Year 1699, treating of the Usefulness of Mathematical

Learning', in *Miscellanea Curiosa*, 2nd ed. (1708) I, Preface. There are striking similarities between the aspects of science defended by Fontenelle and attacked by Swift.

20. Swift possessed in his own library a copy of Fontenelle's *Histoire du renouvellement de l'Académie Royale* (Amsterdam, 1709). See *A Catalogue of Books: The Library of the late Rev. Dr. Swift* (Dublin, 1745) no. 137, p. 4. This has been republished in *Dean Swift's Library*, by Harold Williams (Cambridge, 1932).

21. G. R. Dennis, *Gulliver's Travels*, p. 167 n 1, has suggested 'an error made by New-ton's printer in adding a cipher to the distance of the earth from the sun, which drew down some ridicule upon the astronomer'.

22. R. T. Gunther, *Early Science in Oxford* (1923) I 345 ff, lists a long series of books and articles on surveying, and discusses, with illustrations, surveying instruments invented in the period, some of them as curious as those found in Laputa. The reader may well be reminded of the political significance of such toys implied in the *Spectator*, no. 262: 'The air-pump, the barometer, the quadrant, and the like inventions, were thrown out to those busy spirits [the *virtuosi*], as tubs and barrels are to a whale, that he may let the ship sail on without disturbance, while he diverts himself with those innocent amusements.'

23. See particularly Wallis, 'Imperfections in an Organ', in *Phil. Trans.* XX (1698) 249; I 612–17. Here Wallis gives an account of the work of his predecessors, and a discussion of 'the Degree of Gravity', or 'Acuteness of the one Sound to that of the other' and of the 'Proportions' in music expressed in mathematical formulae. See also 'Of the Trembling of Consonant Strings', in *Phil. Trans.*, abridged, I 606 ff.

24. 'Dr. Wallis's letter to the Publisher, concerning a new Musical Discovery', in *Phil. Trans.* XII (1677) 839.

25. C. Hugenii, ΚΟΣΜΟΘΕΩΡΟΣ, *sive de Terris cœlestibus, earumque ornatu, conjecturæ*, 1698; editio altera, 1699. The work was translated as *The Celestial Worlds Discover'd: or Conjectures Concerning the Inhabitants, Plants, and Productions of the Worlds in the Planets* (1698). The above reference is to this English translation, p. 86.

26. For such mathematical interpretations of music, see 'The Defects of a Trumpet, and Trumpet Marine' (*Phil. Trans.* XVII (1692) 559; I 660 ff), in which the author writes of the general agreement of 'all Writers on the Mathematical Part of Music'. Wallis (ibid. XX (1698) 80, 297; I 610, 618) discusses the mathematical divisions of the monochord in terms of 'Proportions of Gravity' and offers other mathematical analogies. S. Salvetti, in 'The Strange Effects reported of Musick in Former Times, examined', points out (I 618) the decadence of contemporary music, in that it was tending away from emphasis on mathematical principles and was coming to be applied merely to 'particular designs of exciting this or that particular Affection, Passion, or Temper of the Mind' – a matter, he feels, to be regretted by true musicians.

27. Cf. Fontenelle, 'Of the Usefulness of Mathematical Learning', ed. cit.: 'A Geo-metrical Genius is not so confin'd to Geometry but that it may be capable of learning other Sciences. A Tract of Morality, Politicks, or Criticism and even a Piece of Oratory, supposing the Author qualify'd otherwise for those Performances, shall be the better for being composed by a Geometrician. That Order, Perspicuity, Precision and Exactness, which some time since are found in good Books, may originally proceed from that Geometrical Genius, which is now more common than ever.'

28. *Phil. Trans.* XXIV (1705) 2072; IV i 469–74.

29. Gulliver adds: 'Although their largest telescopes do not exceed three feet, they magnify much more than those of an hundred yards among us, and at the same time show the stars with greater clearness.' This passage does not appear in the 1726 edition, but was added in 1727. The addition of the sentence may indicate the current interest in such small instruments. Cf. 'An Account of a Catadioptrick Telescope, made by Mr. J. Hadley', in *Phil. Trans.* XXXII (1723) 303; VI i 133. The telescope described was six feet long and magnified some 220 times.

30. M. Pons (*Gulliver's Travels*, p. 234 n) pays particular attention to this apparently remarkable discovery of Swift's, and points out the similarity not only in the number of satellites but in their periods to the actual discovery made in the nineteenth century. The Laputans found two satellites, 'whereof the innermost is distant from the centre of the primary planet exactly three of the diameters, and the outermost five; the former revolves in the space of ten hours, and the latter in twenty one and a half; so that the squares of their periodical times are very near in the same proportion with the cubes of their distance from the centre of Mars, which evidently shows them to be governed by the same law of gravitation, that influences the other heavenly bodies' ('Voyage to Laputa', pp. 200-1). In spite of a natural desire to agree with M. Pons and Camille Flammarion that this discovery of the satellites of Mars was 'second sight' on Swift's part, we are forced to the conclusion that it was only a happy guess. It was inevitable that many writers, scientists and laymen, should have raised the question of the satellites of Mars – see, for example, Fontenelle, *Plurality of Worlds*, trans. Glanvill (1702) pp. 120 ff. Our own planet was known to have one satellite; Galileo had discovered four about Jupiter; in Swift's time, Cassini had published his conclusions in regard to the five satellites of Saturn. (See *Phil. Trans.* abridged, I 368, 370, 377; IV 323). Swift, using no telescope but his imagination, chose two satellites for Mars, the smallest number by which he could easily indicate their obedience to Kepler's laws, a necessity clearly shown him by Cassini; this number fits neatly between the one satellite of the earth and the four of Jupiter. To indicate the Keplerian ratio, he has made one of the simplest of assumptions concerning distances and period, that of 3 : 5 for the distances, and 10 for the period of the inner satellite. It was not a difficult computation, even for a Swift who was no mathematician, to work out the necessary period of the outer satellite ($3^3 : 5^3 = 10^2 : x$). His trick proved approximately correct – though it might easily have been incorrect.

31. Cf. *Memoirs of Scriblerus*, p. 136: 'A Computation of the Duration of the Sun, and how long it will last before it be burn'd out'.

32. David Mallet, 'The Excursion', in *Poems*, ed. A. Chalmers (1810) XIV 22.

33. *Philosophiæ Naturalis Principia Mathematica* (1687), translated into English by Andrew Motte (1729). References are to the recent revision, *The Mathematical Principles*, ed. Florian Cajori (Stanford, 1934). Cf. particularly book I, sections vii and viii.

34. Ibid. book III, proposition X, theorem X: 'That the motions of the planets in the heavens may subsist an exceedingly long time.'

35. Newton goes on to prove that the life of a comet may be more rudely concluded if its approach to the sun is so near that it is slowed down by friction in the atmosphere of the sun (ibid. book III, proposition XLII, problem XXII). See below, note 53.

36. Cf. 'A Discourse of Earthquakes', in *The Posthumous Works of Robert Hooke* (1705) p. 322.

37. Crabtree's opinion in a letter to Mr Gascoigne, is included in the *Phil. Trans.* XXVII (1711) 270; IV 241 ff.

38. Ibid. XXVII (1711) 278. A series of articles on the subject will be found in the *Phil. Trans.* abridged, IV 229-47.

39. 'Spots on the Sun from 1703 to 1708', by Mr W. Derham, in ibid. IV 235.

40. 'Lectures of Light', in *Posthumous Works of Robert Hooke*, p. 94.

41. Swift had already satirized the popular excitement occasioned by the prediction of a comet's return in 'A True and Faithful Narrative of What Passed in London' (*Satires and Personal Writings*, p. 90): 'But on Wednesday morning (I believe to the exact Calculation of Mr. Whitson) the Comet appear'd: For at three Minutes after five, by my own Watch, I saw it. He, indeed, foretold that it would be seen at five Minutes after Five, but as the best Watches may be a Minute or too [*sic*] slow, I am apt to think his Calculation Just to a Minute.'

42. *Poems*, ed. Chalmers, XII 434-5.

43. Halley's earliest complete publication on the periods of comets appeared as the 'Astronomiæ Cometicæ Synopsis', published in the *Phil. Trans.* for 1705. An English translation, published at Oxford, appeared in the same year. The latter paper may be found appended to *The Elements of Astronomy, Physical and Geometrical*, by David Gregory (1715) II 881–905. The inclusion of this paper in Gregory's volume seems to have escaped the notice of Halley's bibliographers. It is not mentioned in the 'Halleiana' in *Correspondence and Papers of Edmond Halley*, ed. E. F. MacPike (Oxford, 1932) pp. 272–8, although the later Latin edition of the 1726 in Gregory's volume is noted, p. 278.

44. In the later edition of the *Synopsis* Halley wrote: 'Now it is manifest that two periods of this Comet are finished in 150 Years nearly, and that each alternately, the greater and the less, are compleated in about 76 and 75 Years; wherefore, taking the mean period, to be 75 Years and a half . . .'

45. Halley himself was incorrect in his computations, as events proved, since the theory of perturbations was not sufficiently advanced for him to make exact prophecy; in addition, Uranus and Neptune were unknown to his generation. The comet passed perihelion on 13 March 1759, though it was observed on Christmas night, 1758.

46. For the popular attitude towards comets in this period see C. P. Oliver, *Comets* (Baltimore, 1930) ch. i.

47. *Prose Works*, ed. T. Scott, I 281.

48. This is characteristic Laputan exaggeration. No such number of comets had been observed; and the periods of only three had been fully calculated by Halley. Gulliver adds characteristically: 'It is much to be wished that the observations were made public, whereby the theory of comets, which at present is very lame and defective, might be brought to the same perfection with other parts of astronomy.' Among the advantages which Gulliver at first thought might come from the immortality of the Struldbrugs, he suggested (p. 250): 'What wonderful discoveries should we make in astronomy, by outliving and confirming our own predictions, by observing the progress and return of comets, with the changes of motion in the sun, moon, and stars.'

49. *The Elements of Astronomy*, II 905. Cf. *Memoirs of Scriblerus*, p. 136. One of the 'Philosophical and Mathematical Works' of Martin Scriblerus was 'Tide-Tables for a Comet, that is to approximate towards the Earth'.

50. There is no mention in the 'Halleiana' referred to above of the fact that Halley published a later edition of the *Synopsis*, with several corrections and additions. Such a paper appeared however in *Astronomical Tables with Præcepts Both in English and Latin, For Computing the Places of the Sun, Moon, Planets, and Comets*, by Edmond Halley (1752). The volume is not paginated. The editor states that the tables were 'sent to the press in 1717 and printed off in 1719'. The chief changes are in the tables; the rest follows the original until the conclusion, to which we refer, which is expanded.

51. Cf. *Memoires of Scriblerus*, p. 135: 'To him we owe all the observations of the Parallax of the Pole-Star, and all the new Theories of the Deluge.'

52. 'Some Considerations about the Cause of the Universal Deluge', in *Phil. Trans.* abridged, VI ii 1–5. The original paper, which differed in several important respects, was read before the Society on 12 Dec. 1694. The later paper was read in 1724. To some extent the ideas suggested in the earlier paper were intended as a confutation of Thomas Burnet's *Sacred Theory of the Earth*, 2 vols (1681–2), a copy of which, containing annotations in his own hand, was in Swift's library. See *A Catalogue of Books*, no. 375.

53. The Laputans may also have found reason for their fear of a collision in Newton's passage (referred to above, note 35) in the *Principia*, book III, proposition XLII, problem XXII: 'The comet which appeared in the year 1680 was in its perihelion less distant from the sun than by a sixth part of the sun's diameter; and because of its extreme velocity in that proximity to the sun, and some density of the sun's atmosphere, it must have suffered some resistance and retardation; and therefore, being attracted something nearer to the

sun in every revolution, will at last fall down upon the body of the sun.' After a discussion of the appearance and disappearance of *novæ*, Newton concludes: 'The vapours which arise from the sun, the fixed stars, and the tails of the comets, may meet at last with, and fall into, the atmospheres of the planets by their gravity . . .'

54. The terminology here recalls that of the Royal Society. Cf. *The History of the Royal Society of London, For the Improving of Natural Knowledge*, by Tho. Sprat, 3rd ed. (1722) p. 190: 'They have propounded the composing a Catalogue of all Trades, Works, and Manufactures, wherein Men are employ'd . . . by taking notice of all the physical Receipts or Secrets, the Instruments, Tools, and Engines . . . and whatever else belongs to the Operations, of all Trades'. The interest of the Society in 'instruments and tools . . . trades and manufactures' is clear throughout.

55. On similarities between Swift and Rabelais and Hall, see Eddy, *Critical Study*, pp. 57 ff.

56. Cf. Vincent Guilloton, 'Autour de la Relation de Samuel Sorbière en Angleterre', in *Smith College Studies in Modern Languages*, XI (1930) no. 4, pp. 1–29.

57. *The London Spy. Compleat in Eighteen Parts*, by Ned Ward, with an Introduction by Ralph Straus (1924) pp. 50 ff, 125 ff.

58. *A Journey to Paris in the Year 1698* (1698) pp. 78 ff and *passim*.

59. *A Journey to London. In the Year 1698. After the Ingenious Method of that made by Dr. Martin L. . . . to Paris, in the same year*, in *Miscellanies in Prose and Verse*, by William King (1705) pp. 224 ff and *passim*. A modern edition may be found in *A Miscellany of the Wits: Select Pieces by William King, D.C.L., John Arbuthnot, M.D., and other Hands*, with an Introduction by K. N. Colville (1920) pp. 15 ff and *passim*.

60. In *Miscellanies in Prose and Verse*, pp. 324–38; *A Miscellany of the Wits*, pp. 69–80.

61. William King, *The Transactioneer, with some of his Philosophical Fancies, in Two Dialogues* (1700).

62. The similarities between Swift, Brown and Holberg have been pointed out by Eddy, *Critical Study*, pp. 160–3.

63. *Journal to Stella*, in *Prose Works*, ed. T. Scott, II 72.

64. Nehemiah Grew, *Musæum Regalis Societatis. Or a Catalogue and Description of the Natural and Artificial Rarities Belonging to the Royal Society and preserved at Gresham Colledge* (1681) pp. 253, 265.

65. From the time that the president, Newton had declared it necessary that they 'have a being of their own' (C. R. Weld, *History of the Royal Society* (1848) I 387), one of the most persistent problems reflected in the records is that of moving to larger quarters. When in 1705 the Council received word from the Mercers' Company that the latter had decided 'not to grant the Society any room at all' (ibid.), purchase of property became imperative. In 1710 two houses in Crane Court in Fleet Street were bought, though the Council was far from unanimous in its decision as a pamphlet of the day indicates (*An Account of the late Proceedings in the Council of the Royal Society, in order to remove from Gresham College into Crane Court in Fleet Street*, 1710). During the next few years the Society came to pride itself upon its increasing importance. On 15 Dec. 1710 the Society was appointed Visitors and Directors of the Royal Observatory at Greenwich (Weld, op. cit. I 400 ff). Its property, received by deed and bequest, was so extensive that a petition to the King in 1724 mentions 'two messuages in Crane Court; certain lands and hereditaments in Mablethorpe, Lincolnshire; two houses in Coleman Street . . . and a fee-farm in Sussex' (ibid. I 431 n).

66. Each of these other groups has, however, its relation to the Royal Society. I have treated elsewhere the 'projectors in speculative learning' and the 'school of languages', since, in spite of their scientific heritage, each of these groups has its part in the literary controversies of the day. I may, however, mention at this point that, although Professor Eddy feels that the division into 'experimental' and 'speculative' scientists follows a similar division in Tom Brown's *Amusements* (Eddy, *Critical Study*, p. 162), my own impres-

sion is that both Brown and Swift were reflecting a common enough division in the minds of men – that between the 'Baconians' and the 'Cartesians' of the Royal Society. It is hardly possible here to go into the evidence for this belief. M.H.N.

67. 'Of the Usefulness of Mathematical Learning' (unpaged).

68. Eddy, *Critical Study*, p. 163.

69. Cf. Eddy, *Critical Study*, p. 162. Swift himself would seem to indicate this source in his phrase, 'the most ancient student of the Academy'. It is possible that there may also be a reflection here of Leeuwenhoek's microscopical observations upon human excrement.

70. Eddy points out (op. cit. p. 163) the similarity between this passage and one in Tom Brown's *Amusements*. There were however certain architectural experiments not entirely dissimilar, which might well have attracted Swift's attention. Wallis had proposed in 1664 'A Geometrick Flat Floor', working on the problem of how to support a floor over an area wider than the length of the timbers available for joists (cf. R. T. Gunther, *Early Science in Oxford*, I 211). Of a similar nature was the roof of the Sheldonian Theatre, designed by Wren. Cf. also 'A Bridge without any Pillar under it', 'Journal of the Philosophical Society of Oxford', in *Phil. Trans.* xIV (1684) 714; I 594. In an earlier passage on the architecture of Balnibarbi ('Voyage to Laputa', p. 210), Gulliver finds that a palace may be built in a week 'of materials so durable as to last for ever without repairing'. Swift at this point may well have remembered a man who discovered, after the event, that he had built his house not of stone but of asbestos (*Phil. Trans.* abridged, Iv ii 285).

71. R. T. Gunther, *Early Science in Oxford*, I 317–19.

72. 'The Invention of making Clocks to keep Time with the Sun's apparent Motion, asserted by Mr. J. Williamson', in *Phil. Trans.* xxx (1719) 1080; Iv i 394.

73. Much the same idea – without the mention of a blind man – is used in *Memoirs of Scriblerus*, p. 135: 'He it was that first found out the Palpability of Colours; and by the delicacy of his Touch, could distinguish the different Vibrations of the heterogeneous Rays of Light.' The fact that Swift does not in this earlier work attribute the technique to a blind man may indicate that in the earlier period he was satirizing Newton, while in 1725, in the collected works of Boyle, he found the perfect story for his purposes.

74. Cf. Sir Isaac Newton, *Opticks: or, A Treatise of the Reflections, Refractions, Inflections, and Colours of Light* (1704; 2nd ed. 1717) book II, query 29.

75. 'Dr. Finch' was evidently Sir John Finch, whose career is described by Archibald Malloch, *Finch and Baines: A Seventeenth Century Friendship* (Cambridge, 1917), and in the *Conway Letters*, ed. M. H. Nicolson (New Haven) 1930), Boyle's original paper was written in 1663 and published in 1664. At that time Boyle was prescribing for Lady Anne Conway, sister of Sir John Finch, who received his medical degree at Padua, spent much of his life in Italy and was in close contact with the Grand Duke of Tuscany.

76. *Philosophical Works*, II 10–12.

77. The experiment, satirized by Shadwell, was reported in Sprat's *History of the Royal Society*, p. 232: 'By means of a Pair of Bellows, and a certain Pipe thrust into the Wind-pipe of the Creature', artificial respiration was established and its effects observed.

78. *Phil. Trans.* xxx (1717) 580; v i 270–2.

79. Emile Pons, *Gulliver's Travels*, p. 254 n.

80. *Phil. Trans.* xxvII (1710) 10; v ii 21–4.

81. *Phil. Trans.* xxvI (1708) 69; Iv ii 275–8.

82. *Phil. Trans.* xxvII (1693) 858; II 145. There are several accounts in the *Transactions* of hail and ice, emphasizing the explosive noise of their bursting.

83. *Philosophical Works*, I 573–730.

84. Ibid. section xv, pp. 626–9.

85. Ibid. p. 627.

86. Ibid. I 568.

87. Ibid. pp. 550–72.

88. *Phil. Trans.* XVII (1693) 468; II 126–9.

89. *Statical Essays: Containing Vegetable Staticks: Or, An Account of some Statical Experiments On the Sap in Vegetables* (1st ed. 1727; 2nd ed. 1731). The book is, of course, too late to have served as Swift's source; but, as the title-page indicates, the two volumes 'incorporate a great Variety of Chymico-Statical Experiments, which were read at several Meetings before the Royal Society'. These experiments concerned 'the quantities imbibed and perspired by Plants and Trees', in which Hales followed and improved upon Boyle and Hooke. Hales had followed Boyle's experiments, performed with his air-pump and exhausted and unexhausted receivers, upon 'Grapes, Plums, Gooseberries, Cherries, Pease' and several other sorts of fruits and grains.

90. *Optics*, queries 30 and 31.

91. *Vegetable Staticks*, experiment LXXXVII.

92. Ibid. pp. 63–6. This was a controversial question in Swift's time, involving as it did questions of the nature of air and of heat. Three years later all these theories of Boyle, Newton and Hales and also that of the Dutch scientist Nieuwentyt were brought together and discussed in a paper in the *Phil. Trans.* by J. T. Desaguliers – 'An Attempt to Solve the Phenomenon of the Rise of Vapours', XXXVI (1729) 6; VI ii p. 61.

93. *The Virtuoso*, in *Dramatic Works of Thomas Shadwell*, 4 vols (1720) I 387. The many parallels between Shadwell's work and Swift's would suggest that the *Virtuoso* was one of the important literary sources of the 'Voyage to Laputa'. In each instance, however, Swift has brought Shadwell up to date by material drawn from contemporary science.

94. *Phil. Trans.* XXVI (1708) 59; IV 298–301.

95. Ibid. XXIII (1702) 1164; IV 312–14. (For other possible sources of this passage cf. Pons, *Gulliver's Travels*, p. 254 n.)

96. Ibid. XXVI (1708) 142; IV 301.

97. Ibid. XXIII (1703) 1474; IV 305–8.

98. *Phil. Trans.* XXX (1718) 748; IV 435–51; XXXII (1722) 179; VI i 341–7. In the second, presented to the Society in 1726, Jurin reviews the history of the subject. In the same year J. T. Desaguliers presented (XXXIV (1726) 77; VI i 347–50) 'An Account of several Experiments concerning the Running of Water in Pipes, as it is retarded by Friction and intermixed Air. . . . With a Description of a new Machine, whereby Pipes may be clear'd of Air, as the Water runs along, without Stand-Pipes, or the Help of any Hand'.

99. *Memoires of Scriblerus*, p. 135.

100. *Gulliver's Travels*, p. 349.

101. *Prose Works*, ed. T. Scott, IX 110. Sir Charles Firth, one of the most acute of the commentators on *Gulliver's Travels*, said (*The Political Significance of Gulliver's Travels*, p. 1): 'A critic who seeks to explain the political significance of *Gulliver's Travels* may be guilty of too much ingenuity, but he cannot fairly be charged with exaggerated curiosity. He is searching for a secret which Swift tells us is hidden there, and endeavouring to solve riddles which were intended to exercise his wits.'

102. *Works of Alexander Pope*, with Introduction and Notes by Rev. Whitwell Elwin (1871) VIII 88.

103. Ibid. VIII 88.

104. *The Correspondence of Jonathan Swift*, ed. F. E. Ball (1910–14) III 357.

105. *Prose Works*, ed. T. Scott, VIII p. xvi.

106. *Works of Pope*, VII 89.

107. Ibid. VII 91–2.

108. Cf. *Remarks on the Life and Writings of Dr. Jonathan Swift . . . In a Series of Letters from John Earl of Orrery To his Son* (1752) p. 99: 'He seems to have finished his voyage to Laputa in a careless hurrying manner, which makes me almost think that sometimes he was tired of his work, and attempted to run through it as fast as he could.'

109. Ibid. p. 97.

KATHLEEN M. WILLIAMS

Gulliver's Voyage to the Houyhnhnms (1951)

IT has long been recognised that the fourth Voyage of *Gulliver's Travels*, far from being the outburst of a misanthrope who delighted in 'degrading human Nature', is the culmination of Swift's lifelong attack on the pride of man, especially the pride which convinces him that he can live by the light of his unaided reason, the pride that Swift himself sums up, in the title of one of his imaginary discourses in *A Tale of A Tub*, as 'An Universal Rule of Reason, or Every Man his own Carver'. In particular he is taking up a position opposed to the doctrines of natural goodness which pervade eighteenth-century thought and which find systematic expression in the writings of 'Toland, Collins, Tindal, and others of the fraternity', who, as Swift remarks, all talk much the same language and whose ideas are dismissed in the *Argument against Abolishing Christianity* as 'Trumpery'. It is clear, both from the satires and the religious writings, that Swift was hostile to all doctrines of the natural self-sufficiency of man, whether they were expressed in Deistic terms or in the related pride of neo-Stoicism; and the Fourth Voyage of *Gulliver's Travels* embodies that hostility. But while the object of attack is established, it is not immediately clear, from the Voyage itself, whether any positive position is implied in the Houyhnhnms or in the other characters. The Yahoos, clearly, embody the negative intention, and are to be condemned. This is what happens to man when he tries to live by reason and nature; he falls, as has been pointed out,[1] into a 'state of nature' nearer to that envisaged by Hobbes than that of Locke's *Two Treatises of Government*. It is significant that, according to one Houyhnhnm theory, the Yahoos were descended from a pair of human beings, driven to the country by sea: 'coming to Land and being forsaken by their Companions, they retired to the Mountains, and degenerating by Degrees, became in Process of Time, much more savage than those of their own Species in the Country from

whence these two Originals came'. Presumably these originals, forced
into self-reliance, had degenerated because their feeble human reason
had been overwhelmed by an irrational 'nature', and more adequate
guides had been forgotten.

The ambiguity of the fourth Voyage lies not in the Yahoos, but in
the positions of Gulliver and, especially, of the Houyhnhnms. The
function of the Houyhnhnms may be to present an ideal of the true life
of reason, to be admired even if unattainable, and to be contrasted with
the Yahoos to chasten the pride of that lump of deformity, man, by
showing him the vanity of his pretensions. But if Swift did intend the
Houyhnhnms to stand as an ideal contrast, he has badly mismanaged
the matter. The Houyhnhnms do not strike the reader as altogether
admirable beings; indeed they are sometimes absurd, and even repellent,
and we are disgusted by Gulliver's exaggerated devotion to them. The
dispassionate arguments of the assembly, for instance, about the nature
and future fate of Gulliver and the Yahoos, show the characteristic and
unpleasant coldness of the Houyhnhnm race; while Gulliver's master
displays their equally characteristic self-satisfaction, carried here to the
point of absurdity, when he criticises Gulliver's physical qualities.
Gulliver tells us how his master interrupted his account of the relations
of the European Yahoos with their horses, to point out the inferiority
for all practical purposes of the Yahoo shape – 'the Flatness of my Face,
the Prominence of my Nose, mine Eyes placed directly in Front, so that
I could not look on either Side without turning my Head; that I was not
able to feed myself without lifting one of my fore Feet to my Mouth;
and therefore Nature had placed those Joints to answer that Necessity'.
Throughout the book there are obvious blunders which cannot be
explained away by the inevitable lack of positive attraction in rational
Utopias. One of Swift's most attractive characters, Don Pedro de
Mendez, is placed in a position at the end of the book where comparison
with the Houyhnhnms is inevitable, and our sympathies are alienated
by the humourless arrogance both of the Houyhnhnms themselves, and
of Gulliver when, absorbed in admiration of his former master, he
avoids his own family to concentrate on 'the neighing of those two
degenerate Houyhnhnms I keep in my Stable'. Clumsiness of this kind
is not usual with Swift, who is well aware, as a rule, of the way to
enlist our sympathy for a character, and shews his awareness in the
drawing of M. B., Drapier, and of Gulliver in the Voyage to Lilliput.
The whole course of his work makes it unlikely that he could be un-

aware of the unpleasantness of such passages as these. Possibly, then, the effect is a deliberate one, and the Houyhnhnms, far from being a model of perfection, are intended to show the inadequacy of the life of reason. This would be in keeping with the usual method of Swift's satire, and with the negative quality which has been observed in it. The characteristic of Swift's satire is precisely his inability, or his refusal, to present us straightforwardly with a positive to aim at. It may be, at bottom, a psychological or a spiritual weakness; he turns it to satiric strength, and produces satire which is comfortless but is also disturbing and courageous. He will leave us with nothing more than a few scattered hints of what is desirable and attainable, or sometimes, when what is desirable is clearly not to be had, with a half-ironic acceptance of the best that is to hand. A full, clear, and wholly unambiguous account of a state of life to aim at would be unusual and unexpected in Swift. It is his habit to look sceptically, not only at the evils of the world, but at those, including himself, who criticise such evils, and at those who present schemes for the betterment of mankind. Gulliver is quaintly indignant and surprised at the evils which still exist six months after the publication of his travels, and in *A Tale of A Tub* the Digression on Madness ends with a confession which undermines the whole: 'Even I myself, the Author of these Momentous Truths, am a person whose Imaginations are hardmouth'd, and exceedingly Disposed to run away with his Reason.' In fact, there is not usually a 'norm' in Swift's satire, positively and unequivocally stated. As far as any positive position can be discovered, it must be by piecing together the hints and implications and indirections typical of Swift's whole method; it is foreign to that method to embody in one person or one race a state of things of which he fully approves. It is, indeed, more than a matter of satiric method for a man 'betwixt two Ages cast', who had little of which he could approve wholeheartedly. The spirit of compromise and common sense, the love of the middle way, affected him sufficiently to undermine any more rigorous standards, while failing to satisfy him as it satisfied his younger contemporaries; and his position was further complicated by a strong feeling for existing forms and a dislike of innovation, which, like Dryden, he regards as dangerous. Any suggestion of radical remedies is distrusted by him even as he presents it and he will withdraw from it into irony, or fall back into compromise as he does in the ambiguous *Argument against Abolishing Christianity*.

In *Gulliver's Travels*, this characteristic method re-appears. In the first two books, no one person or group of persons is put forward for our approval, and neither the Lilliputians, the Brobdingnagians, nor Gulliver himself, can be regarded as a consistent satiric norm against which the moral and political vagaries of eighteenth-century England are to be precisely measured. Swift slips from one side to another according as his isolated satiric points require it, and we are at one moment to admire, at another to dislike, the creatures of his imagination. Even in Laputa, a set of serious political schemes, such as the visionary project of 'persuading Monarchs to chuse Favourites upon the Score of their Wisdom, Capacity, and Virtue', appears among the absurdities of the projectors. Gulliver himself is now honest and kindly, now credulous or pompous, according to the momentary demands of the satire. During his adventures in Brobdingnag he is frequently ridiculous and on one occasion definitely unpleasant; his complacent attitude to warfare, in chapter VI, horrifies the giant King. In none of the first three books are we left with a consistent standard embodied in any creature, and it would seem that if the Houyhnhnms are presented fairly and squarely for our approval a change is involved not only in Swift's normal method but in his whole attitude of mind. He would hardly present the radical primitivism and rationalism of Houyhnhnm-land as desirable, at least without the ironic and sceptical withdrawal which his uncertain temperament demanded.

One would expect to find that Swift uses the Houyhnhnms in the same indirect way as he does the peoples of the earlier books, not as a complete statement of the right kind of man or society, attainable or not, but as a satiric contrast in which good and less good are mixed in a proportion which we must decide for ourselves, with the aid of such hints of the author's as we can piece together. And in fact Swift is just as ready to sacrifice the consistency of the Houyhnhnms to their satiric function of innocent comment on unknown humanity as he is any of his other creatures. The opinion of Gulliver's master on the 'prodigious Abilities of Mind' of English lawyers, which should qualify them to instruct others in wisdom and knowledge, leads to a valid satiric point, but does not show the Houyhnhnm in a very good light when one considers the damning account he has just heard of their moral depravity and lack of intellectual integrity. No doubt one reason why the Houyhnhnms are a race of animals is for satiric distance; but of course Swift's insistence on the animal in Book IV has a significance beyond that of satiric effectiveness. Several of the Houyhnhnms' characteristics seem to be intended to show their remoteness, and their irrelevance to the ordinary life and standards of mankind. Primitivism is used for this effect; they have great difficulty in understanding such humanly simple matters as Gulliver's clothes, his ship, his writing, and the Houyhnhnm in his dealings with Gulliver in chapter III is not only unattractive, but unattractive in a particular way. 'He brought me into all Company,' Gulliver says of him, 'and made them treat me with Civility because as he told them privately, this would put me into good Humour and make me more diverting.' This may be intended to lessen Gulliver's status and lower his pride, but Swift could hardly have missed its effect of displaying the lack of humanity and sympathy, the cold curiosity of the Houyhnhnms. There is, too, the solemn criticism of Gulliver's physical characteristics in chapter IV, part of which has already been quoted. This passage stresses the fact that man is not well endowed, either physically or mentally, to live a 'natural' life; but it also shows the Houyhnhnm's inability to grasp the human point of view, his self-righteousness, and his determination to belittle these creatures who in their own land claim to rule over the Houyhnhnm race. The Houyhn-hnms are alien and unsympathetic creatures, not man at his best, as Godwin suggested, or man as he might be, but a kind of life with which humanity has nothing to do. The word Houyhnhnm, we are told, means 'Perfection of Nature'. These are not human beings, but virtuous animals, perfect but limited natural creatures, of a 'nature' not simply unattainable by man, but irrelevant to him, and incapable not only of the depths, but also of the heights, to which humanity can reach. The Houyhnhnms have no shame, no temptations, no conception of sin: they are totally unable to comprehend the purpose of lying or other common temptations of man. They can live by reason because they have been created passionless. In man, we know, the passions are apt to get astride of the reason, which is not strong enough to restrain them, and the result in its extremest form is seen in the Yahoos, but the Houyhnhnms have no passions to control: 'As these noble Houyhn-hnms are endowed by Nature with a general Disposition to all Virtues, and have no Conceptions or Ideas of what is evil in a rational Creature, so their grand Maxim is, to cultivate Reason, and to be wholly governed by it.' The point of the description lies in 'as' and 'so'. The Houyhn-hnms can live harmlessly by reason because their nature is different from ours.

Swift makes much of the differing natures of the Houyhnhnms, the

Yahoos, and Gulliver himself. In the Houyhnhnms, nature and reason are one and the same. They have no 'natural affections' in our sense; Nature, they say, has taught them to be equally benevolent to everyone, and to make a distinction of persons only on the rational grounds of 'a superior Degree of Virtue'. Marriage is undertaken simply as 'one of the necessary Actions in a reasonable Being'. Nor have they any fear of death, which they greet with the same complete absence of emotion that they show towards every other event, great or small. These attitudes are not those which Nature teaches human beings, as Swift recognises both in *Gulliver's Travels* and elsewhere; man has affections and passions, and Swift seems not to regard them as wholly bad. The painful and universal fear of death in mankind was a subject which particularly interested and affected him, and the curious episode of the immortal Struldbrugs in the third Voyage is an attempt to deal with it. Gulliver wished to take some of the Struldbrugs back with him to England, 'to arm our People against the Fear of Death', that dread which Nature has implanted in us, but not in the Houyhnhnms. In the *Thoughts on Religion* reason is brought to bear on the problem: 'It is impossible that anything so natural, so necessary, and so universal as death, should ever have been designed by providence as an evil to mankind.' But reason is powerless against man's fear of death, and his clinging to life on any terms; and Swift puts forward the idea that although in general reason was intended by Providence to govern our passions, in this God intended our passions to prevail over reason. Man cannot in all respects govern his passions by reason, he suggests, because he has not been equipped by Providence to do so; perhaps both love of life and the propagation of the species are passions exempted by Providence, for particular purposes, from the control of reason. The precise amount of irony in such statements is always difficult to gauge, though the *Thoughts on Religion* are not satirically intended; but at least the passage shows Swift's feeling that such deep-rooted passions as these are part of the nature of man, created by God, and cannot and perhaps should not be ruled by reason. The Houyhnhnms are rational even in those things in which the wisest man's passions inevitably and even perhaps rightly rule him, and the handling of them seems to suggest not only the remoteness but the inadequacy by human standards, of the life of Reason. They have only the negative virtue of blamelessness.

The Houyhnhnms refer repeatedly to Gulliver's fellow-humans in terms which press home the contrast between themselves and mankind.

Men are creatures 'pretending to Reason', the character of a rational
creature was one which mankind 'had no Pretence to challenge'. Again
the Houyhnhnms thought that 'Nature and Reason were sufficient
Guides for a reasonable Animal, as we pretended to be'. Man has no
right to lay claim to the life of Reason, for in him nature and reason are
not, as in the Houyhnhnms, identical, and there is that in his nature
which is outside reason's legitimate control. But this is not necessarily
to say that man's nature is thoroughly evil, and his situation hopeless, as
in the case of the degenerate Yahoos, nor is man treated in these terms.
Gulliver and the other humans of Book IV are clearly distinguished from
the Yahoos as well as from the Houyhnhnms, and the difference in their
mental and physical habits is strongly insisted upon. They stand apart
from the two races of this animal world, separated from both by
characteristics of which neither the naturally virtuous and rational
animals, nor the vicious and irrational ones, have any knowledge – in
fact by the characteristics proper to humanity. Man does indeed share
the Yahoos' propensity to evil, but he has compensating qualities which
the bestial Yahoos have not possessed since their first degeneration; and
with these qualities he may surpass the cold rational virtue of the
Houyhnhnms. The member of that race who is treated with most
sympathy by Swift is the humble sorrel nag, one of the servant breeds
who were 'not born with equal Talents of Mind'. Into the incompletely
rational mind of the nag, some near-human warmth and devotion can
creep, and he is the only creature in Houyhnhnm-land to show any
affection; Gulliver's last link with the country as he sails away is the
voice of the 'Sorrel Nag (who always loved me) crying out . . . Take
Care of thyself, gentle Yahoo'.

   With this partial exception, there is no sign among the Houyhnhnms
of kindness, compassion, or self-sacrifice, yet elsewhere in *Gulliver's
Travels* there is sympathetic treatment of love, pity, and a deliberate
intervention of one man in the life of another, very different from the
Houyhnhnm's equal benevolence, detachment, and rational respect for
virtue. Even in Book I, where moral satire is not at its most serious,
there is an insistence on the importance of gratitude among the Lilliputians, by whom, we are told in chapter VI, ingratitude is regarded as a
capital crime. Gratitude is shown in action in Gulliver's behaviour to
the Lilliputian King, when despite the King's unjust sentence upon him
he cannot bring himself to retaliate, for, he tells us, 'Neither had I so
soon learned the Gratitude of Courtiers, to persuade myself that his

Majesty's present Severities quitted me of all past Obligations'. In Book II there is the forbearance of the giant King and the affection between Gulliver and the protective Glumdalclitch, and in Book IV great prominence is given to the Captain and crew of the ship which rescues Gulliver. Swift makes it plain that the Portuguese sailors are admirable human beings, and emphasises in them the very qualities which the Houyhnhnms neither possess nor would understand. It is Don Pedro who persuades Gulliver to abandon his design of living as a recluse, following as far as he can the life of a rational detached virtue which the Houyhnhnms have taught him to admire, and instead to commit himself once more to the human relationships proper to mankind. Gulliver's duty as Don Pedro sees it is to return to a life of humanity, tolerance, and affection among his own people, and Gulliver, finding he can do no better, reluctantly agrees. But his behaviour towards his own family, set in a place where it contrasts forcibly with the tolerant practical goodwill of Don Pedro, is exaggerated to the point of madness. Only with difficulty can he endure the sight of the wife and children for whom he had shown so charming a fondness in the past. Gulliver, once a normal affectionate human being, concerned with the well-being of his friends, is now a solitary misanthrope, absurd and yet terrible in his self-concentration and his loathing of those he had once loved. He had been, he tells us, a great lover of mankind, and his conduct in the previous voyages shows that he was particularly affectionate to his own family. Now they 'dare not presume to touch my Bread, or drink out of the same Cup'. To this point Gulliver has been led by his pride in the unaided reason. He has become inhuman, losing the specifically human virtues in his attempt to achieve something for which humanity is not fitted. He is ruined as a human being, and the failure of his fellows to attain his own alien standards has made him hate them. We are reminded of Swift's letter (26 November 1725) to Pope: 'I tell you after all, that I do not hate mankind: it is "vous autres" who hate them, because you would have them reasonable animals, and are angry for being disappointed.' Gulliver is one of 'vous autres', for to set for humanity the irrelevant standards of absolute reason is to end as Gulliver ended, in hatred and defeat. Swift was well aware of the process of disillusionment which has been attributed to him, and he exemplifies it in Gulliver, the true misanthrope, who believes man should try to rule himself by 'Reason alone'.

On this interpretation, neither the master Houyhnhnm nor the misanthropic Gulliver who once thought so highly of mankind is presented as an ideal of behaviour. Like all the peoples of the *Travels* the Houyhnhnms have some characteristics, such as honesty and truthfulness, which we might well try to follow, and they are used for particular satiric points, but as a whole they represent an inadequate and inhuman rationalism, and the negativeness of their blameless life is part of Swift's deliberate intention. For us, with our less perfect but also less limited nature, to try to live like them would be to do as the Stoics did, according to Swift's remark in his *Thoughts on Various Subjects*: 'The Stoical Scheme of Supplying our Wants by lopping off our Desires, is like cutting off our Feet when we want Shoes.' It would mean abandoning the purely human possibilities as well as the disadvantages of our own nature. The Houyhnhnms may indeed be compared with the passionless Stoics of the sermon 'Upon the Excellency of Christianity', who are contrasted with the Christian ideal of positive charity. Gulliver, in his turn, shows the loss of hope, proportion, and even common humanity in a man who tries to limit the complex nature of man to 'Reason alone'. Something more than Houyhnhnm harmlessness is needed in a world of human beings, and in so far as there is any positive presentation of right living to be found in *Gulliver's Travels*, it is in the representatives of that humanity which Gulliver rejects. For it is not, after all, a purely destructive view of humanity that Swift shows us. 'Reason and Nature' indeed are set up only to be shown as inadequate. Swift never doubted that man should make use of reason to control his bad instincts where he can, but to live by reason alone is neither possible nor desirable if we are to remain human beings. Yet we have the generous King of Brobdingnag, whose people are the 'least corrupted' of Yahoos or humans, and of whom Swift says, with his habitual indirection, 'it would be hard indeed, if so remote a Prince's Notions of Virtue and Vice were to be offered as a Standard for all Mankind'. And there is Don Pedro de Mendez, who shows to what unselfish goodness man can attain. Don Pedro is guided by 'Honour and Conscience', and for Swift, as we know from the sermons, conscience was not a natural sense of right and wrong or Shaftesbury's 'aesthetic perception of the harmony of the universe', but a faculty which must itself be guided by the divine laws which we can know only from a source outside ourselves, from revelation. 'There is no solid, firm Foundation for Virtue' – he tells us in the sermon 'On the Testimony of Conscience' – 'but on a Conscience which is guided by Religion.' 'There is no other Tie thro' which the Pride, or Lust, or

Avarice, or Ambition of Mankind will not certainly break one time or other.' For him, as for so many Churchmen concerned with the controversies of the period, Reason is an insufficient guide without Revelation. The sermons, with their systematic attack on the supposed sufficiency of the moral sense, the scheme of virtue without religion, are clearly relevant to the theme of the fourth Voyage of *Gulliver's Travels*, and here we find the positive aspect of Swift's intention more explicitly set out. The sermon 'Upon the Excellency of Christianity' shows, in its account of the ideal Christian, a creature who is meek and lowly, 'affable and courteous, gentle and kind, without any morose leaven of pride or vanity, which entered into the composition of most Heathen schemes'. The description applies far more nearly to Don Pedro and the early Gulliver than to the Houyhnhnms, or to Gulliver the misanthrope into whose composition pride certainly enters. While allowing a place to the passions and affections, and their possibility, under guidance, for good, Swift does not fall into the Tillotsonian position that human nature's 'mild and merciful' inclinations and the maternal and other natural affections are more important than revealed religion. An implied disapproval of such a position is expressed in Swift's version of Anthony Collins' *Discourse of Freethinking*, in which Tillotson, naturally, is praised. Both affections and reason have their place in the well-regulated man, but they are to be subjected to the laws of God. Reason and gratitude may both suggest to a man that he should obey his parents, but the surest and most lasting cause of obedience must be the consideration 'that his Reason is the Gift of God; that God commanded him to be obedient to the Laws, and did moreover in a particular manner enjoin him to be Dutiful to his Parents' ('On the Testimony of Conscience'). Swift would no doubt have agreed with that passage from Butler's sermon 'Upon Compassion' (published in the same year as *Gulliver's Travels*) in which passions and affections, carefully guided, are treated as necessary in creatures who are imperfect and interdependent, 'who naturally and, from the condition we are placed in, necessarily depend upon each other. With respect to such creatures, it would be found of as bad consequence to eradicate all natural affections, as to be entirely governed by them. This would almost sink us to the condition of brutes; and that would leave us without a sufficient principle of action.' The passage forms a comment on the contrasting creatures of Houyhnhnm-land, for Swift is as well aware as Butler of the complex nature of man, the possessor not only of evil impulses but of passions and affections which under the guidance of conscience and religion (to which reason must be subject) can issue in virtuous action, especially that compassionate assistance to our fellow men, whether or not our reason judges them worthy of it, which 'the Gentile philosophy' fails to produce. In *Gulliver's Travels* there is not only a traditional Christian pessimism; there may well be a positive Christian ideal suggested in the conduct of the good humans, though it is presented with Swift's habitual obliquity and restraint.

NOTE

1. By T. O. Wedel, 'On the Philosophical Background of *Gulliver's Travels*', in *Studies in Philology*, XXIII (1926).

W. E. YEOMANS

The Houyhnhnm as
Menippean Horse (1966)

BOOK IV of *Gulliver's Travels* has become a battleground for two opposing armies of critics in this century. On one side are the critics who take the traditional view of the Houyhnhnms (a view which flourished almost unquestioned in the nineteenth century), solemnly seeing them as ideal creatures, and on the other side are the critics who see the Houyhnhnms as ironic. Among others, George Sherburn, W. A. Eddy, J. Middleton Murry, A. E. Case, Charles Peake, and Ricardo Quintana have written in terms of, or in direct defense of, the traditional view. The battle line is not always clearly drawn; Martin Price and W. B. Ewald seem to hold the traditional view, but they tend to see some irony in Swift's portrayal of the Houyhnhnms. And Quintana's later discussion of the Houyhnhnms in *Swift: an introduction* (1954) differs in a vital way from his earlier discussion in *The Mind and Art of Jonathan Swift* (1936; reprinted 1953). In the later book Quintana wonders whether he should be quite so solemn about the Houyhnhnms: 'there are moments when we have to ask ourselves whether our imaginary voyage is not becoming a parody of itself – whether, for instance, the Utopian elements are not slyly humorous'.

T. O. Wedel was the first to question the traditional view of the Houyhnhnms in our century, and many critics have followed him. Ernest Tuveson, Kathleen Williams, and Samuel H. Monk see the Houyhnhnms as representing an ironic ideal ill-suited to the emulation of men; John F. Ross believes that Swift intended the Houyhnhnms to appear ridiculous, and Samuel Kliger argues that Swift was demonstrating the absurdity of perfectionism in terms of the Houyhnhnms. Then there are the critics, among them Irvin Ehrenpreis, Martin Kallich, and Calhoun Winton, who see the Houyhnhnms as ironic mainly because they appear to represent a deistic outlook upon life.

There are very strong arguments on both sides, and it is most unlikely that resolution of the conflict will ever come about through the breakdown of one side or the other. Fortunately there is another way to bring about resolution, and the exploration of that way is the purpose of this essay.

Northrop Frye, in *Anatomy of Criticism* makes the very important point that *Gulliver's Travels* should not be judged as a novel but as fiction written within the conventions of Menippean satire. Many of the characteristics of Menippean satire which Frye cites one can easily discover in *Gulliver's Travels*, such characteristics as the free play of intellectual fancy and the practice of dealing with mental attitudes rather than with people as such; the loosejointed, digressing narrative; the ridicule of the *philosophus gloriosus*; and the use of the dialogue for the interplay of ideas or attitudes.

In addition, *Gulliver's Travels* is in that long-standing tradition of fantastic travel tales told by a brilliant liar which have as their progenitor Lucian's *A True Story*. In fact the essential ideas for Gulliver's visit to Glubbdubdrib is probably borrowed from the visit to the Isle of the Blest in Lucian's *A True Story*. Furthermore, the philosophic outlook of the Cynics can often be detected in Menippean satires including those of Lucian, who was heavily influenced by Menippus himself – a student of the Cynic Metrocles. The extreme asceticism of the Cynics, their heavy emphasis upon a simple, virtuous life, and their tendency to be scornful of commonly accepted standards of social behavior are very deeply a part of *Gulliver's Travels*.

All of these things lead to the conviction that *Gulliver's Travels* is written in a tradition which is distinctly different from that of the novel. The characters in a novel tend to be naturalistically portrayed, whereas characters in Menippean satires like *A True Story*, *Gargantua*, *Candide*, and *Gulliver's Travels* are stylized, for they are subservient devices conveying ideas, theories, or general attitudes. When tight laws of character and story plausibility are lifted, the author of a Menippean satire can more effectively carry out his main purpose – the expression of intellectual concepts. As a result we can never expect to be enchanted by 'living' characters in this form of literature; instead, we can anticipate being overwhelmed by amazing erudition, by massive catalogues of social follies, by extravagant elaborations upon professional abuses, by fantastic caricatures of certain people or certain types of people, and by other dazzling displays.

Robert C. Elliott argues very effectively against the tendency of readers to interpret *Gulliver's Travels* from a novel-oriented point of view. He demonstrates that Swift pays little regard to psychological consistency, and that Lemuel Gulliver is now one type of person and now another. 'Gulliver is, in fact, an abstraction manipulated in the service of satire. To say this of the principal character of a novel would be damning, but to say it of a work written according to the conventions of Lucian's *A True Story*, *Gargantua*, *The Satyricon*, is simply to describe.'

Perhaps this battle has been won, for many critics today are willing to accept this view of Gulliver. Not all of them refrain from treating other aspects of *Gulliver's Travels* from a novel-oriented point of view, however – the Houyhnhnms, for example. And if we are to escape dead-end dissension over the Houyhnhnms, we must treat them, and the Yahoos, as Menippean characters.

Not only Gulliver, a single character, but groups of people, in addition to the Houyhnhnms, are adjustable according to satiric needs. The contrast between the original Utopian institutions of Lilliput and their state when Gulliver arrives there is extreme, and the brief paragraph which merely mentions their degeneration is adequate only for a work in which realistic character depiction is far from being a main concern. In Book III the Laputans are first depicted as introverted theoreticians of music and mathematics almost totally incapable of coping with practical affairs. Later they become the opposite – shrewd, tyrannous politicians exploiting their neighbors below with the flying island (itself an incongruous, masterful feat of practical engineering). Swift saw a chance to use the Laputans for two different satirical purposes and he did so, allowing satiric concepts to take full priority over consistent, realistic character depiction. There is no special merit in this in itself; the point is that we should allow the writer of a Menippean satire a kind of 'poetic licence' in this regard as long as it serves his main purpose well.

Like the Laputans, and like Gulliver, the Houyhnhnms are flexible agents or abstractions subservient to intellectual purposes, and, as such, they can be allowed to have two different functions to perform for Swift, functions which, at first sight, might seem to be incompatible. They have a solemn function to perform (which critics holding the traditional view of the Houyhnhnms understand very well), and they also have a burlesque or comic function to perform (which critics who see the Houyhnhnms as ironic creatures understand very well).

If we study the solemn function of the Houyhnhnms in relation to *Gulliver's Travels* as a whole, we find that there is much that coaches us towards acceptance of the Houyhnhnms' ascetic Utopia. The excellence of Houyhnhnm reasoning is based strictly upon a supreme comprehension of virtue and morality and clear perceptions about simple practicality, rather than brilliant ratiocination or any kind of dazzling sophistication. Their kind of reasoning is 'recommended' in each book of *Gulliver's Travels*. In Book I the original and Utopian institutions of Lilliput have many points in common with Houyhnhnm institutions. In Book II the learning of the Brobdingnagians consists 'only in Morality, History, Poetry, and Mathematics, wherein they must be allowed to excel'.[2] Like the Houyhnhnms they are ignorant of abstract theory and lead simple, practical lives.

We find the same practical, unadventurous outlook in Lord Munodi in Book III, and cannot fail to notice how superior the outlook is made to appear when contrasted with the adventurous, experimental chaos of Lagado and the metaphysical void of Laputa. In Book III we learn not only to love the simple, practical view of life, but to despise all abstract thought and all technical innovation which necessity is not the mother of. Book III as a whole represents the extreme pole of rejection (i.e. a way of life most objectionable because it is the worst conceivable) in *Gulliver's Travels*, just as the Houyhnhnms represent the extreme pole of acceptance (i.e. a way of life most acceptable because it is the best conceivable), even though Swift personally might not have gone all the way with these extremes. An author may often find that his fiction, especially satiric fiction, requires extremes of conflict which he himself would not hold to in everyday life.

Thirty years ago it would not have been necessary to affirm that Swift's depiction of the Houyhnhnms contains much that is to be regarded solemnly as Utopian, but so many critics of our day have seen them as anti-Utopian, that counter-arguments are necessary.

The descriptions throughout *Gulliver's Travels* of the corruption and misery brought about by proud, ambitious leaders, unfaithful or luxury-mad wives, doting parents, greedy entrepreneurs, unscrupulous professional men, etc. who are governed by ruling passions, lead the reader towards an acceptance of the ascetic but harmonious world of the Houyhnhnms ruled by reason. The Struldbrugs prompt us to reject a desire for an earthly immortality and prepare us for an acceptance of the Houyhnhnms' serene attitude towards death. Such serenity may be impossible for men, but it is the ideal way – the extreme pole of acceptance – rather than an attainable goal.

Gulliver's description of the delightful, and wise, parlour-conversation of the Houyhnhnms is amusing and, in some ways, suggests burlesque. And yet the situation has its solemn side too. The pleasant harmony of their conversation and the complete absence of all rigid ceremony seems an excellent demonstration of certain principles and suggestions to be found in those essays by Swift entitled *On Good Manners and Good Breeding* and *Hints Towards an Essay on Conversation*.

'Temperance, Industry, Exercise, and Cleanliness' are things that Swift himself respected just as much as the Houyhnhnms do. And Gulliver's Houyhnhnm master thinks it monstrous to give 'the Females a different Kind of Education from the Males, except in some Articles of Domestic Management; whereby, as he truly observed, one Half of our Natives were good for nothing but bringing Children into the World: And to trust the Care of their Children to such useless Animals, he said, was yet a greater Instance of Brutality' (GT p. 253). Behind these solemn lines there is an equally solemn Swift, for we find a similar attitude towards female education, not only in the Utopian section of Book I, but also in Swift's unfinished essay entitled *Of the Education of Ladies*.

In the face of all this can there be any doubt that Swift intended the Houyhnhnms to represent, at least in part, solemn models of behaviour truly worthy of the emulation of men?

The purpose of the solemn function of the Houyhnhnms is the portrayal of the good life towards which all men would tend to move if they consulted reason more and passion less. The Houyhnhnm idea is impossible for men to achieve and rightly so, for ideals give permanent direction to men, not attainable, and therefore temporary, goals.

In using the Menippean satire form to convey Utopian concepts Swift is not really departing from the tradition, for Utopian stories in general owe a big debt to Menippean satire, especially to Lucian's *A True Story*; Sir Thomas More's *Utopia*, for example, adopts the form of the satiric, fantastic travel tale and adapts it to a much more solemn purpose.

Those who agree that positive Utopian ideals are depicted through the Houyhnhnms, but who reject any comic interpretation of the Houyhnhnms, are probably applying principles which are appropriate to the novel. But since *Gulliver's Travels* is a Menippean satire, its characters are subservient to its Utopian and satirical ideas rather than to any rigid principles of consistent character portrayal. Granted this, it should not be difficult to allow a combination of solemn and comic functions in the Houyhnhnms. The satirical purpose of the comic function of the Houyhnhnms, more like burlesque than any other type of comedy, is to assault pride in men by means of shock, humiliation, insult, embarrassment, invective, and, most devasting of all, the laughter which inevitably accompanies good burlesque.

The entire burlesque hinges very delicately upon pure shapes – the man-shape as compared with the horse-shape. In Houyhnhnmland the usual man-horse relationships are inverted satirically, and the satire is further accentuated by making the horse-over-man superiority of Houyhnhnmland far greater than the man-over-horse superiority of Europe. The Houyhnhnm's comments upon Gulliver's 'inferior' man-shape, for example, are burlesque remarks, and should not be read in any sense solemnly; it would be all too easy to demolish this aspect of Houyhnhnm wisdom and superiority.

When Gulliver first meets the Houyhnhnms, the man-shape image is subjected to humiliation as Gulliver is forced to neigh like a horse in order to be understood, instead of using his 'barbarous English'. But the satire goes far beyond humiliation and embarrassment into the realm of shock when we learn that Gulliver makes his shoes and covers his boat with the man-shaped Yahoo hides instead of horse-hide.

Not only are Yahoo skins used in place of horse skins, but the man-shaped creatures take over all the duties assigned to horses in Europe. The sight of several man-shaped Yahoos pulling a sledge while the horse-shaped creatures sit with dignity in carriages and wield a masterful whip, is pure burlesque. The Houyhnhnms are not at all models of behaviour in these scenes, they function here only as agents of burlesque attack upon man's pride.

Burlesque elements and solemn elements are sometimes subtly interlaced in Book IV, and at other times whole sections are given over to one or the other. The latter half of chapter 9 and the latter half of chapter 8 are given over to solemn praise of the noble Houyhnhnm race, and the burlesque side all but disappears. But Gulliver's diatribe-description of Europe in chapters 5 and 6, bitter as it is, is almost exclusively shocking burlesque – an insulting caricature of a whole race. Caricatures of individuals and groups are very much a part of Menippean satire, and they abound in the works of Lucian and Rabelais. The scene, already cited, where Gulliver listens in awe to the wise parlour-conversation of a group of Houyhnhnms sitting on their haunches, is an excellent example of the way the solemn and the burlesque elements can work together. The Houyhnhnms are truly admirable in this scene even though the sight of horses outdoing a man in the parlour is both humorous and humiliating.

The main shock of Book IV is the burlesque equation between man and Yahoo which underlies the last three chapters. We begin to build towards this burlesque equation early in Book IV when Gulliver and a Yahoo are placed side by side and the similarities noted. Then, after Gulliver's diatribe-description of Europe, the Houyhnhnm master describes, almost point for point, similar peculiar practices among the Yahoos. Finally, when Gulliver is sexually attacked by a female Yahoo, the burlesque equation between man and Yahoo is complete, and the burlesque (as opposed to the solemn) superiority of horse-shaped creatures over man-shaped creatures is fixed for ever in Gulliver's mind. Thereafter Gulliver has only contempt for those with man-shaped bodies, no matter how good they are. 'When I thought of my Family, my Friends, my Countrymen, or human Race in general, I considered them as they really were, *Yahoos* in Shape and Disposition, perhaps a little more civilized, and qualified with the Gift of Speech, but making no other Use of Reason than to improve and multiply those Vices, whereof their Brethren in this Country had only the Share that Nature allotted them' (*GT* p. 262). When passages such as this are treated as though they were part of a naturalistic novel instead of a Menippean satire, there tends to be excessive concern about Gulliver's madness and his grossly unfair, oversimplified portrait of the human race. Gulliver here is merely the vehicle for an extravagant burlesque attack which takes up almost all of the three climactic concluding chapters and which is continued in 'A Letter From Capt. Gulliver to His Cousin Sympson'.

When Gulliver sees his own form reflected in a lake or fountain, he turns away in 'horror and detestation', perhaps to practise the 'Gait and Gesture' of a horse, and feels greatly complimented if someone tells him he trots like a horse. Plainly, all solemnity has departed here, and we are being 'needled' by Swift. Sometimes the needle goes very deep; for example, when Gulliver is about to leave Houyhnhnmland, he is overcome with gratitude because his Houyhnhnm master not only allows him to kiss his hoof, but brings it up to Gulliver's mouth.

The frequently repeated judgement of this last episode, that the Houyhnhnm is guilty of pride here, is true as a solemn view of the matter. But this comic episode is one hundred per cent burlesque, and solemn views of it are out of place. It is also often argued that the kind and generous Don Pedro is as good morally as the Houyhnhnms, and many have argued that he is much better. Once again the argument is beside the point, for we are dealing with a burlesque satirical attack. The vital factor is the fact that Don Pedro is man-shaped and not horse-shaped. We are supposed to be shocked, embarrassed, humiliated, and insulted as we realize that even the cleanest and most virtuous of our kind give off bad odors and seem grossly inferior when compared with the magnificence of those who are horse-shaped. Looking at them solemnly, we can see a big difference between Don Pedro and a Yahoo, but we are supposed to go along with a burlesque satire which is based upon the fantasy that any man returning from Houyhnhnmland would find all man-shaped creatures hideous and all horse-shaped creatures beautiful, and to find ourselves properly chastened and pride-purged by the mockery of it all.

The combination of solemn and burlesque elements in Book IV, far from being incompatible, support and reinforce each other. Even in the most laughable Houyhnhnm situation the other side of these creatures, their solemn side, is there to haunt us and accentuate the satire, for we recognize that the superiority of the Houyhnhnms is not always a burlesque superiority. Conversely, the burlesque side of the Houyhnhnms prevents their solemn side from becoming oppressively solemn at any time.

Critics, in this novel-oriented age, tend to think that the Houyhnhnms must fulfil one role or another, but not several roles. Swift, with satiric ideas and Utopian concepts uppermost in his mind, allowed his characters to be altogether subservient to his intellectual purposes – and had much Menippean precedent behind him. Because of this, the Houyhnhnms are sometimes solemn models of the good life, sometimes vehicles for satiric burlesque attack, and sometimes a combination of both.

If Book IV, as well as the other books of *Gulliver's Travels*, is studied for what it is – Menippean satire – we will recognize that its unity and strength are based upon an intellectual vision of morality and technology, and that its characters are idea-spectrums rather than likenesses of flesh and blood. We will also recognize that there is much truth on both sides of the Houyhnhnm debate, and that these truths are not incompatible, even though they sometimes appear to be.

NOTES

1. *The Power of Satire* (Princeton, 1960) p. 200.
2. *The Prose Works of Jonathan Swift*, ed. H. Davis, XI *Gulliver's Travels* (1941) 120.

Select Bibliography

The Introduction to this volume deals in some detail with editions and bibliographical, biographical and critical studies (in both book and article form) of Swift and his writings. This Bibliography, therefore, mainly lists recent work on Swift which is generally available in book form. The reader who wishes more detailed bibliographical information about other Swiftian studies between 1945–65 is referred to Miss Claire Lamont's Checklist in *Fair Liberty was all his Cry*, ed. A. Norman Jeffares (Macmillan, 1967; St Martin's Press, 1967).

BIBLIOGRAPHY

H. Teerink, *Bibliography of the Writings of Jonathan Swift*, 2nd ed. revised and corrected by Dr H. Teerink; ed. Arthur H. Scouten (U. of Pennsylvania Press, 1963).

Louis A. Landa and James Edward Tobin, *Jonathan Swift: a list of critical studies published from 1895 to 1945 to which is added 'Remarks on some Swift manuscripts in the United States' by Herbert Davis* (Cosmopolitan Science and Art Service Co. 1945).

James J. Stathis, *A Bibliography of Swift Studies, 1945–1965* (Vanderbilt U.P., Nashville, Tennessee, 1967).

EDITIONS
(a) *Collections*

Poems of Jonathan Swift, ed. Harold Williams (Clarendon P. 1937; 2nd ed. 1958).

Prose Writings of Jonathan Swift, ed. Herbert Davis, 14 vols (Blackwell, 1939–66).

Correspondence of Jonathan Swift, ed. Harold Williams, 5 vols (Clarendon P. 1963–5).

Jonathan Swift: Poetical Works, ed. H. Davis (Oxford U.P., 1967).

(b) *Individual Works*

Journal to Stella, ed. Harold Williams, 5 vols (Clarendon P. 1963–5).

Swift's Polite Conversation, ed. Eric Partridge (Deutsch, 1963; Oxford U.P. 1963).

A Tale of a Tub, ed. A. C. Guthkelch and D. Nichol Smith, 2 vols (Clarendon P. 1920; 2nd ed. 1958).

Gulliver's Travels, A Tale of a Tub, Battle of the Books, etc. ed. William A. Eddy (Oxford U.P. 1933).

The Drapier's Letters, ed. Herbert Davis, 3 vols (Clarendon P. 1937; 2nd ed. 1958).

(c) *Selections*

Selected Prose Works of Jonathan Swift, ed. John Hayward (Cresset P. 1950).

Selected Prose and Poetry, ed. Edward Rosenheim, Jr (Rinehart, 1959).

Jonathan Swift: Poetry and Prose, ed. Herbert Davis (Clarendon P. 1964).

Jonathan Swift: A Selection of His Works, ed. Philip Pinkus (Macmillan, 1965; St Martin's Press, 1965).

BIOGRAPHY AND CRITICISM

Henry Craik, *Life of Jonathan Swift* (Murray, 1882; 2nd ed. Macmillan, 1894). Still a standard work.

Ricardo Quintana, *The Mind and Art of Jonathan Swift* (Oxford U.P. 1936; Methuen, 1953). A good introduction to Swift.

James Sutherland, 'Dr. Swift in London', in *Background for Queen Anne* (Methuen, 1939). Though this civilised and eminently readable account of a period of Swift's life is out of print it is well worth tracking down in libraries.

Herbert Davis, *Stella: a Gentlewoman of the Eighteenth Century* (Macmillan Co. N.Y., 1942). An elegantly written life of Stella which throws light on Swift also.

John Middleton Murry, *Jonathan Swift: a Critical Biography* (Jonathan Cape, 1954). Superficial, useful as a preliminary introduction only.

Louis A. Landa, *Swift and the Church of Ireland* (Clarendon P. 1954). A detailed study which gives an excellent account of Swift's dedicated, genuine service in the Church of Ireland.

Ricardo Quintana, *Swift: an Introduction* (Oxford U.P. 1955). A modest and excellent guide.

Michael Foot, *The Pen and the Sword* (MacGibbon & Kee, 1957).

Kathleen Williams, *Jonathan Swift and the Age of Compromise* (U. of Kansas Press, 1958). Thoughtful and thorough, though not all its arguments need be accepted.

Bonamy Dobrée, *English Literature in the Early Eighteenth Century*. Volume VII of the *Oxford History of English Literature* (Clarendon P. 1959). His critical accounts of Swift's work (unfortunately placed in various parts of this book so that use of the index is necessary) are original, illuminating and stimulating.

Denis Johnston, *In Search of Swift* (Hodges Figgis, 1959; Macmillan, 1959; Barnes & Noble, 1959). Scholars question certain theories put forward in this book, but it provides lively reading. (Sir Harold Williams, *TLS* 29 Nov. 1941, might be read in conjunction with it and T. de Vere White's 'Jonathan What?' in the supplement to the *Irish Times*, 22 March 1967, questions Professor Johnston's arguments and those of Mrs Le Brocquy's *Cadenus* (Oxford U.P. 1962).

Irvin Ehrenpreis, *Swift: The Man, His Works and the Age*, vol. I *Mr. Swift and his Contemporaries* (Methuen, 1962; Harvard U.P. 1962). The first volume of a new, large biographical study: it contains some new material on Swift as an undergraduate and provides background information. Volume II, *Dr Swift* (1967) covers the years 1699–1714.

Oliver W. Ferguson, *Swift and Ireland* (U. of Illinois P. 1962). A scholarly and skilful account of Swift in Ireland.

Herbert Davis, *Jonathan Swift: Essays on his Satire and other Studies* (Oxford U.P. 1964). A discerning series of studies of Swift's literary abilities and intellectual power, some of which appeared in *The Satire of Jonathan Swift* (Macmillan Co. N.Y., 1947).

Nigel Dennis, *Swift* (Macmillan Co. N.Y., 1964; Weidenfeld & Nicolson, 1965). A short study which emphasises the importance of Swift's English family connections.

Fair Liberty was all his Cry, ed. A. Norman Jeffares (Macmillan, 1967; St Martin's Press, 1967). This collection of essays includes work by Beckett, Marjorie Buckley, Davis, Dobrée, Ehrenpreis, Mackie L. Jarrell, Leavis, Mayhew, Mercier, Marjorie Nicolson and Nora Mohler, Nichol Smith, Orwell, Quintana, Rowse, Kathleen Williams, T. G. Wilson, Virginia Woolf and Yeats.

Jonathan Swift. A Dublin Tercentenary Tribute, ed. Roger McHugh and Philip Edwards (Dolmen Press, Dublin, 1967). Most of the papers in this collection were read at the Swift Tercentenary Symposium, Dublin, in 1967.

Notes on Contributors

HERBERT DAVIS was a Professor of English in the universities of Toronto (1922–37) and Cornell (1938–40), then President of Smith College from 1940 to 1949. At the University of Oxford he was Reader in Textual Criticism (1949–53) and Professor until his retirement in 1960. He was the Editor of the *Prose Works of Jonathan Swift*, 14 vols (1939–66) and also edited *The Drapier's Letters* (1935; reprinted 1965). He has written various essays on Swift, some of which appeared in *Jonathan Swift: Essays on his Satire and other Studies* (1964); he has edited the *Complete Poems of Pope* in the Oxford Standard Authors (1966) and the *Complete Plays of William Congreve* (1966). His last book, *Jonathan Swift: Poetical Works*, was published in 1967, the year of his death.

BONAMY DOBRÉE was educated at the Royal Military Academy, Woolwich, and the University of Cambridge. He was a lecturer at London University before becoming Professor of English at the Egyptian University, Cairo (1926–9); he was Professor of English Literature at the University of Leeds from 1936 to 1955. His publications include *Restoration Comedy* (1924); *Essays in Biography* (1925); the Nonesuch *Vanbrugh* (1927); the World's Classics *Congreve* (1928); *Restoration Tragedy* (1929); *The London Book of English Prose*, with Herbert Read (1931); *The London Book of English Verse*, with Herbert Read (1949); *Alexander Pope* (1951); *The Early Eighteenth Century: The Oxford History of English Literature* (1959). He is at present completing a study of Kipling.

IRVIN EHRENPREIS was educated at the City College of New York (B.A. 1938) and Columbia University (Ph.D. 1944), and received an honorary degree (Docteur Honoris Causa) from the University of Besançon in 1965. Following a long career at Indiana University, he is now Professor of English at the University of Virginia. He has held research fellowships of the Guggenheim Foundation and the American Council of Learned Societies. Among his recent publications are *Fielding: Tom Jones* (1964) and an essay on Robert Lowell in *American Poetry* (1965), a collaborative volume of which he was an associate editor.

WILLIAM B. EWALD, JR is Director of National Studies at the head-
quarters in New York of the International Business Machines
Corporation. During the administration of President Eisenhower,
Dr Ewald served as a Special Assistant on the White House Staff,
and at the end of the administration he assisted the former President
in the preparation of *Mandate for Change* and *Waging Peace*, two
volumes of memoirs of the White House years.

Dr Ewald received his Ph.D. from Harvard University in English
Literature in 1951 and between 1951 and 1954 taught there in
English and the humanities. In addition to *The Masks of Jonathan
Swift*, from which this essay on *The Drapier's Letters* comes, he has
published a book on the beginnings of English journalism *Rogues,
Royalty, and Reporters: the Age of Queen Anne through its Newspapers*.

J. J. HOGAN was Professor of English at University College, Dublin,
1934–64, and has been President of the College since 1964.

A. NORMAN JEFFARES, who was educated in the universities of Dublin
and Oxford, was Jury Professor of English in the University of
Adelaide before becoming Professor of English Literature in the
University of Leeds in 1957. He has lectured in various African,
American, Canadian, European and Indian Universities, edits the
quarterly *A Review of English Literature*, is Chief Editor of the
Writers and Critics series, Co-Editor of the Biography and
Criticism series and General Editor of the New Oxford English
Series. He has written biographical and critical studies of Yeats as
well as editing his plays, poems, prose, and criticism in Pocket
Papermacs and his poetry in the Scholar's Library. He has written
on American and Commonwealth Literature as well as Anglo-
Irish, his main field of critical and editorial interest.

J. W. JOHNSON became Professor of English at the University of
Rochester in 1955. His publications include *Logic and Rhetoric*
(1962) and *The Formation of English Neo-Classical Thought* (1967).

LOUIS A. LANDA is a Professor of English at Princeton University. He
is the author of *Swift and The Church of Ireland* (1954) and has
edited *Gulliver's Travels and Other Writings* (1960). He was also
Co-Editor with Herbert Davis of the Shakespeare Head edition of

volumes IV and IX of Swift's *Works* and Co-Editor of *English Literature 1660–1800: A Bibliography of Modern Studies* 2 vols (1950–2).

F. R. LEAVIS, visiting Professor of English in the University of York since 1965, and Honorary Fellow of Downing College, Cambridge since 1962, was educated at the Perse School and Emmanuel College, Cambridge. He was a Fellow of Downing College, Cambridge (1936–62) and University Reader in English (1959–62). He was one of the founders and the Editor of *Scrutiny* (1932–53). His publications include *D. H. Lawrence* (1930); *New Bearings in English Poetry* (1932;) *Revaluation: Tradition and Development in English Poetry* (1936); *Education and the University* (1943); *The Great Tradition: George Eliot, James and Conrad* (1948); *The Common Pursuit* (1952); and *D. H. Lawrence: Novelist* (1955).

NORA M. MOHLER, D.Sc., Ph.D., Professor Emeritus of Smith College, has – except for three years at the Radar Division of the National Research Commission (1944–6) – held academic positions in physics at Smith College from 1927 until 1962. She is the author of journal articles on ultraviolet spectroscopy, photography, nuclear physics, and the history of physics. She is a Fellow of the American Physical Society and the American Association for the Advancement of Science.

MARJORIE NICOLSON, Ph.D., D.Litt., L.H.D., has held distinguished academic posts, including professorships of English at Smith College (1929–41) and Columbia (1941–62) and the professorship of Renaissance Studies at Claremont Graduate School (1962–3). She is a member of the Institute for Advanced Study, Princeton. Her books include *The Art of Description, Newton Demands the Muse, Voyages to the Moon, The Breaking of the Circle, Mountain Gloom and Mountain Glory,* and *A Reader's Guide to Milton.*

GEORGE ORWELL (1903–50) was born in Bengal. He was educated at Eton, and served in the Indian Imperial Police from 1922 to 1927 before becoming a writer. His novels include *Burmese Days* (1934); *A Clergyman's Daughter* (1935); *Keep the Aspidistra Flying* (1936); *Coming up for Air* (1939); *Animal Farm* (1946); *Nineteen Eighty-*

Four (1949). He also wrote *Down and Out in Paris and London* (1933); *The Road to Wigan Pier* (1937); *Homage to Catalonia* (1938); *Socialism and the English Genius* (1941); *Critical Essays* (1946); *Shooting an Elephant* (1950); *England, Your England* (1953); *Collected Essays* (1961).

A. L. ROWSE was a Scholar in English Literature at Christ Church, Oxford, but took the History school and was elected a Fellow of All Souls College, in History. His work exemplifies his beliefs in the value of the historical approach to literature, and in history as equally a branch of literature. Major works: *The England of Elizabeth, The Expansion of Elizabethan England, William Shakespeare: A Biography*, a family history, *The Churchills*, studies of Sir Richard Grenville, Sir Walter Ralegh, Marlowe, and Southampton. Two volumes of autobiography and five volumes of verse attest his dual interest in literature and history. A Fellow of the British Academy. Work in progress: *The Cornish in America* and *Poems of Cornwall and America*.

KATHLEEN WILLIAMS was educated at Somerville College, Oxford, and was for some years in the English Department at the University College of South Wales and Monmouthshire as Lecturer and Senior Lecturer. She joined the University of California at Riverside in 1964, and is now a Professor of English at the Rice University, Houston, Texas. Her book *Jonathan Swift and the Age of Compromise* was published in America in 1958 and in England in 1959, and *Spenser's World of Glass*, a study of *The Faerie Queene*, appeared in 1966. She is currently working on contemporary criticism of Swift and on Renaissance poetry.

VIRGINIA WOOLF (1882–1941) was a daughter of Sir Leslie Stephen, the scholar and critic who edited the English Men of Letters series. She was privately educated. In 1912 she married Leonard Woolf, with whom she founded the Hogarth Press in 1917. Her novels include *The Voyage Out* (1915); *Night and Day* (1919); *Jacob's Room* (1922); *Mrs. Dalloway* (1925); *To the Lighthouse* (1927); *Orlando* (1928); *The Years* (1937). Some of her critical work is included in *Mr. Bennett and Mrs. Brown* (1924); *The Common Reader* (1925); *A Room of One's Own* (1929); and *The Second Common Reader* (1932).

W. EDWARD YEOMANS is an associate Professor at the University of British Columbia, Vancouver, where he teaches contemporary literature. He has written articles on W. B. Yeats and Dylan Thomas, and his poems have appeared in various magazines.

Index